Enigma Books

Also published by Enigma Books

James P. Duffy and Vincent L. Ricci

Target Hitler

The Plots to Kill Adolf Hitler

Enigma Books

Published by
Enigma Books
New York

Target Hitler: The Plots to Kill Adolf Hitler by James P. Duffy and Vincent L. Ricci
was originally published in hard cover by Praeger Publishers.
http//www.greenwood.com/praeger, an imprint of Greenwood Publishing
Group, Inc., Westport, CT. Copyright © 1992 by James P. Duffy and Vincent L.
Ricci. This paperback edition by arrangement with Greenwood Publishing
Group, Inc. All rights reserved.

First Paperback Edition 2011

Printed in the United States of America

ISBN: 978-1-936274-02-4
eISBN: 978-1-936274-03-1

To the men and women who lost their lives in the
struggle against Adolf Hitler

The worth of a man is certain only if he is prepared to sacrifice his life for his convictions.

—General Henning von Tresckow[1]

I beg the world to take our martyr's deaths as penance for the German people.

—Dr. Carl Goerdeler[2]

Fate was against us.

—General Karl-Heinrich von Stulpnagel[3]

We have accepted the necessity to do our deed in order to save Germany from untold misery. I expect to be hanged for this, but I do not regret my action and I hope that someone else in luckier circumstances will succeed.

—Fritz-Dietlof Count von der Schulenburg[4]

A little encouragement to those Germans ready to risk their lives to free Germany of Hitler could have brought peace before the Russians had crossed the Vistula and before the Western Allies had advanced beyond Normandy.

—William Casey[5]

Table of Contents

Acknowledgements

So many people have helped us in many ways to research the material in this book that it is impossible for us to list them without accidentally leaving some out. Therefore we have decided once again to simply express our appreciation to each of you as we did at the time you gave us your assistance.

Having said that, we would like to recognize the work of two men whose scholarly studies of the German resistance have contributed greatly to our ability to write this book: Peter Hoffman, Professor of German History at McGill University, and Harold C. Deutsch, Professor of History Emeritus at the University of Minnesota.

James P. Duffy and Vincent L. Ricci

Introduction

During his infamous regime, Adolf Hitler had many enemies among the German people. These included persons of high position in the military and the government as well as among the general population. From 1933 through 1945, thousands of Germans performed innumerable actions to attempt to stop the Nazi regime from committing the crimes it did, some in large ways and many others in small, personal ways. It is regrettable that the courage of many of these individuals, who in the course of their lives under such a ruthless tyranny took grave risks to commit small acts of defiance, will never be acknowledged properly. Most of them simply vanished into the oblivion that claimed millions of others during Hitler's reign.

Many people in Germany wished to see an end to the rule of terror that represented the Nazi regime. Few of them had the resources to commit the supreme act, the murder of Adolf Hitler. This book is about those who had the resources and acted on them, what motivated them to attempt to assassinate the Führer, and why they failed.

Those living in open societies typified by the Western democracies may find it difficult to understand how people of high rank, including the Chief of the General Staff of the German army, would be unable to successfully move against a regime soaked in the blood of its own people. There are some critical elements of society under the Nazis that the reader should keep in mind while reading this book.

The first is that no one in Germany escaped scrutiny by the Gestapo or other secret police forces created by the Nazis. Not even generals and field marshals were immune. They were followed and their actions were reported just as were citizens. Gestapo agents were charged with ferreting out any act of opposition or disloyalty to the regime, from an incautious remark made at a cocktail party to a plot to kill a ranking Nazi official. The regime knew it had many enemies among the German people, and it employed agents to find them. Their performance rating depended on the number of subversives they exposed and arrested. Not infrequently their evidence was fabricated to lend credibility to their charges and increase the stature of the security forces.

Hitler's enormous popularity was a second factor that worked against those who plotted his death. It must be remembered that the German people of the 1930s and into the war years had no history of democracy other than the time of chaos and economic deprivation they had experienced during the short-lived Weimar Republic of the 1920s. Historically, Germanic people were more in tune with an orderly, militaristic society than one in which they participated in elections to choose their leaders.

Just as the Italians overlooked the evils of Benito Mussolini's regime with the simplistic rationalization "He made the trains run on time," the Germans endured the Nazis largely because they succeeded where no earlier government had in stabilizing the economy and ending the violence in German cities provoked by clashes between paramilitary forces representing opposing ideologies. Hitler abrogated the oppressive Treaty of Versailles, won back the Rhineland, brought Austria into union with Germany, annexed the Sudetenland to the Reich, and deposed the despised government of Czechoslovakia, all without committing a single German soldier to battle. These accomplishments earned him hero status in the eyes of many, if not most, Germans. There is no avoiding the fact that he was extremely popular. This popularity was a factor that lay heavily on the minds of the men who would depose Hitler. They knew their actions would not be viewed favorably by a large share of the population, civilian or military.

In order for a generals' coup to be successful it requires the support and obedience of a large number of lower-ranking officers and the troops who would be called on to arrest or shoot government officials. The enlisted ranks of the German army, as with most modern armies, were more typical of the general populace than were the higher ranks, so Hitler's popularity with them was about equal to that of the general population. The possibility that troops would refuse to obey orders to arrest government officials, including the Führer himself, or to engage in combat against the Nazi regime was a specter that haunted the men who plotted against Hitler. There was also the possibility that a coup, or even an attempted coup, could result in a prolonged conflict between pro- and anti-Nazi forces, throwing Germany into a bloody civil war that might lay the country open to attack from other European states. Plotting a coup against Hitler was a complex matter that involved much more than choosing the method by which to arrest or kill him.

From the time Hitler came to power in January 1933 until his death in April 1945, countless attempts were planned on his life. Some small number of these plans were actually executed or came close to execution. Those that bore the best possibility of success, both in terms of killing Hitler and replacing his regime, involved generals and other high ranks of the German army.

To document all the accounts of the many individuals and groups who actively opposed the Nazi regime would take several volumes. This chronicle of the attempts to take Hitler's life and replace his regime acknowledges the perseverance of two dedicated men, General Ludwig Beck and Lieutenant Colonel Hans Oster. Their ceaseless activity in the resistance against Hitler and the Nazis is the thread that runs through this book beginning with Chapter 4, when the resistance of military officers first took the form of a planned coup.

Many of the individuals who appear in this book will be unknown to most readers, but it is important that their actions and motives are known and understood so that we may all know that even in the darkest and most tyrannical states, there will always exist men and women who are willing to risk their lives, their fortunes, and their honor to oppose evil.

Target Hitler

The Plots to Kill Adolf Hitler

1.

A Question of Loyalty

I swear by God this holy oath, that I will render to Adolf Hitler, Führer of the German Reich and people, Supreme Commander of the Armed forces, unconditional obedience, and that I am ready, as a brave soldier, to risk my life at any time for this oath.

When Adolf Hitler imposed this oath on all German military personnel he bonded the fate of the armed forces irrevocably to his own. It was August 2, 1934, just hours after President Paul von Hindenburg's death. Hitler had already determined to abolish the presidency and declare himself Führer. Every German soldier, sailor, and airman would swear personal allegiance to Hitler, as would every subsequent member of the armed forces of the Third Reich, from privates to field marshals.

At the start of the twenty first century, it seems almost ludicrous that so many intelligent, educated, and powerful senior officers acceded to such an oath and allowed its implications to cause the death of millions of people and the devastation of their own nation. However, history has recorded that most of them did exactly that.

Many German military leaders entered into a pact with one of the most evil men in history because they believed that collectively they could control him, and because most considered themselves above politics and therefore safe from the machinations of politicians. Years later at the Nuremberg Tribunals they learned differently.

The significance of an oath sworn to Hitler personally is enormous. It is best understood in the context of the Prussian-German officer class, men born to a heritage of unconditional obedience to the head of state. Traditionally, each officer had a personal identification and a personal bond with his ruler. This code of unquestioned obedience and fidelity extended to every soldier of every rank.

The practice of swearing a personal oath to the leader did not originate with Hitler. More than sixty years earlier, Article 64 of the Prusso-German Constitution of 1871 demanded similar loyalty from the armed forces to the person of the Kaiser: "All German troops are obliged to obey unconditionally the commands of the Emperor. This obligation is to be incorporated in the military oath."

Americans in particular find it difficult to understand the subtle difference between the oath sworn by German soldiers and their own. American soldiers pledge their allegiance to the nation, the ideals on which America was founded and on which it has flourished, not to an individual political leader. It is an oath of loyalty freely given by the individual to the nation. German soldiers, on the other hand, swore their allegiance not to a principle or a belief but to an individual, whether he was the Kaiser or the Führer. They pledged to obey the leader's commands, even if it meant personal or national suicide, as it ultimately did.

Before World War I the German army played no role in the political life of the nation. In fact, it was a court martial offense for an officer to express a political opinion differing from that of the Kaiser, who was acknowledged to be the state. To reinforce the army's isolation from public policy, Wilhelm II issued a decree in 1907 prohibiting members of the armed forces from discussing political issues.

The urgency for decisive action in the conduct of the war caused this situation to change slightly when Generals von Hindenburg and Erich Ludendorf were required to step into the vacuum created by the Kaiser's inability to provide strong political leadership. From 1916 until the collapse of the monarchy in 1918, these two men functioned as surrogate despots, operating behind the throne, governing the country as a virtual military dictatorship.

The war's end caused the collapse of the monarchy and brought about the disintegration of social order in Germany. What remained of the army became hopelessly politicized. Coup was followed by counter-coup, and groups of soldiers known as Freikorps (Free Corps) roamed the country engaging in sundry activities, ranging from repelling a Polish invasion to waging pitched battles with private political armies. In several regions localized revolts against the new democratic authorities spawned fledgling communist soviet states, most of which were promptly put down by Freikorps forces.

The situation came to a head on March 13, 1920, when the capital, Berlin, was occupied by a mostly Freikorps coup under the right-wing leader Dr. Wolfgang Kapp. Most of the government leaders, having been forewarned of the impending coup, escaped to Stuttgart. From this sanctuary they issued a call for a general strike in the capital. The strike was eminently successful, and on March 17 Kapp was forced to withdraw from Berlin.

While a scattering of the army joined the Kapp coup, most remained neutral, especially those who were trying to hold together the remnants of the old general staff. In many ways the Kapp coup was the turning point for the army's relations with politics. As a result of what he saw as the potential disintegration of the army through political upheaval, army Commander General Hans von Seeckt initiated a process designed to re-establish the army as an apolitical body. His plan was to use the 100,000-man German army sanctioned by the Versailles treaty as the nucleus for a revival of a grand army on the order of the old Imperial Army. To accomplish this, the army had to be isolated from the chaos of the current German political scene.

Under von Seeckt's leadership soldiers were commanded to ignore politics and concentrate on "the old spirit of silent, self-effacing devotion in the service of the Army."[1] Many willingly followed the general's dictates.

In 1930 General Wilhelm Gröner re-emphasized the importance of a soldier remaining aloof from politics when he said, "The soundness of any armed force rests upon unreserved, unlimited obedience." He went on to point out the dangers of officers allowing personal political views to dictate whether certain orders would be obeyed.[2]

When Hitler came to power, military discipline was firmly re-established in the German army. While this obedience had its virtues, its greatest weakness was that German army leaders were insulated from political decisions, especially decisions that could lead to war. For the most part the generals were innocents in the arena of power politics. Hitler would take full advantage of their political naiveté.

Why would the imperious members of the German officer class reduce themselves to swearing unconditional obedience to a criminal who headed a gangster organization that happened to momentarily control the central government? Many simply conformed to secure their positions of power and privilege. For others, the oath merely represented a routine requirement in their customary tradition of virtually blind obedience to the state and whoever happened to be in command.

On January 30, 1933, Adolf Hitler became chancellor of a Germany torn by internal strife and teetering on the brink of economic disaster. Although in later years he liked to claim he had been swept into power through a popular mandate, he was actually appointed to the post by the old, sick, and semi-senile Reich President and Supreme Commander, Field Marshal Paul von Hindenburg, who would have appointed as Chancellor practically anyone who offered even a glimmer of hope of bringing peace to the nation. Adolf Hitler was the last in a long line of Hindenburg's appointments. He was destined to serve the longest term.

Before Hitler's appointment the army had a brief attempt at running the country with Hindenburg's selection of General Kurt von Schleicher as Chancellor. Von Schleicher actually held three positions simultaneously: Defense Minister, Commissioner for

Prussia, and Reich Chancellor. Although he enjoyed the complete support of the two most influential men in the military, Army Commander-in-Chief General Curt von Hammerstein-Equord, and Chief of the General Staff General Wilhelm Adam, his tenure as Chancellor survived only fifty-seven days. He was a master manipulator whose personal duplicity prevented him from creating an effective government capable of restructuring the country.

In an ironic twist of fate, Schleicher, the man who had plotted against so many earlier Chancellors, was himself undone by the malicious intrigues of Werner von Alvensleben, a notorious rumor monger. Alvensleben disseminated vicious rumors that Schleicher was scheming to place President Hindenburg under house arrest and assume dictatorial powers over the country.

Shocked by this fabrication, which he believed, Hindenburg dismissed Schleicher and handed the reins of government to Adolf Hitler, who had garnered 36.8 percent of the popular vote to come in second in a three-way race for the presidency against Hindenburg and a communist candidate in 1932. Once firmly settled in the Chancellory, Hitler swore that no power on earth would "ever get me out of here alive."

Loyal to their Prussian tradition, most military officers continued to remain aloof from politics, except when their personal stations of power and privilege were threatened. One real danger was the rise of the National Socialist Party's paramilitary organization, the SA, Sturm Abteilung or Storm Detachment.

In 1933 the German army numbered 100,000 men. The SA membership exceeded one million men, many of them hardened criminals who respected no moral code. From the time Hindenburg appointed Hitler Chancellor until the old field marshal's death, two armies existed in Germany: the constitutionally sanctioned Reichswehr, referred to by many people as "the President's Army," and the SA, "the Chancellor's Army." Outnumbered more than ten to one, without considering the other private armies across the country that would likely support the SA in a civil war, the regular army, with no tanks or artillery, had little chance of defeating the SA in a direct confrontation.

Adolf Hitler realized he needed the unequivocal support of the army to hold power and expand the German Reich. He also recognized that the Prussian tradition of loyalty and obedience could work for him once he won the generals over to his side. On the other hand, the SA had outlived its usefulness. With its membership consisting predominantly of street fighters and assassins, Hitler recognized it would be no match for a well-trained and professionally led army of an enemy nation. The SA was incapable of fighting the wars that were required to fulfill Hitler's dream of a vast German empire.

A long-simmering dispute between Hitler and SA head Ernst Röhm over the role of the storm troopers had persisted for some time. Hitler continued to view the SA as a political force useful for inflicting terror and death on the Führer's opponents. A member of the "radical" wing of the Party, Röhm wanted his force to sweep away the regular army along with its officer class. The SA would then become the nucleus for a people's army. The generals were aware of Röhm's plans but were helpless to do anything about them.

Early in his rule, Hitler successfully wooed the army. Less than twenty-four hours after his appointment as Chancellor, he addressed the Berlin garrison without waiting for an invitation to do so. He told the troops of the new spirit he intended to infuse in the future Germany. Two days later, on February 2, 1933, Hitler met with a group of generals and admirals at the home of General von Hammerstein. In a two-hour session he promised them there would be no need to fight a civil war against the SA, and he further assured them that they could begin a full-blown rearmament program even though the Versailles treaty forbad it.

June 30, 1934, became known as the Night of the Long Knives, as Adolf Hitler made good on his promise by initiating a bloody purge of the SA. More than two thousand people, mostly SA leaders, were killed by Heinrich Himmler's Schutztaffel (SS), which was in fact a subsidiary of the SA and therefore technically under Röhm's control. Röhm's murder, along with many of his closest associates, ended forever the possibility of the SA posing a genuine challenge to the army.

Although some generals were repulsed by the blood lust of the Nazi purge, Hitler effectively blunted any hostility from the military by giving them anything they wanted, including money and estates that were provided as gifts to selected senior officers. Less than a month later the generals reciprocated and gave Hitler what he wanted, their pledge of unconditional loyalty.

Several generals objected to the personal oath of allegiance to Hitler—especially General Ludwig Beck, who called it the blackest day of his life. Beck was prepared to resign rather than take the oath but was dissuaded from doing so by his friend, Army Commander-in-Chief General Werner von Fritsch. Beck later became chief of the rejuvenated General Staff. However, he never wavered in his opposition to Hitler. If anything it grew stronger, finally culminating in his resignation on August 27, 1938, over the planned invasion of Czechoslovakia. He promptly became the central figure in the military opposition to the Nazis.

General Beck was everything a good Nazi was not. Born to an upper-middle-class family near Wiesbaden in the Rhineland in1880, he was the son of a metallurgical engineer. In 1898 he entered the Fifteenth Prussian Field Artillery, completed General Staff training in 1911, and served as a staff officer at various headquarters during World War I.

It was at these staff postings that Beck acquired the habit of working long hours, often arriving before dawn and remaining until the early hours of the following day. During the war Beck had enjoyed a brief encounter with private life, something he never had again. On May 12, 1916, he married Amalie Pagenstecher, a merchant's daughter. The following year they had a daughter, Gertrud, but shortly after the baby's birth this happy occasion was marred by Amalie's death on November 16, 1917. Beck apparently never considered remarrying.

A man of high moral character, charming but austere, Beck earned a reputation as a great military planner largely because of two outstanding accomplishments. The first was his planning of the withdrawal, under exceedingly difficult conditions, of ninety divisions of the German army at the close of World War I. The second was a book on military tactics that he wrote between 1931 and

1933. *Die Truppenführung* is one of the best-known German military publications. This volume of tactics was widely read and earned its author great respect both for its contents and for the elegance and clarity of its prose.

If Beck had a weakness, it was that he was more a man of thought than a man of action. He took a long time to make decisions because he carefully weighed all sides of an issue and considered all the possibilities. However, unlike many other great thinkers, once he had deliberated on his course of action, Beck was prepared to take daring risks. This was clearly demonstrated by his unswerving leadership of the anti-Nazi conspirators in the army for almost six years.

Ludwig Beck became the center of resistance to Hitler and the Nazis not because he was a dynamic leader and man of action but because he stood well above Hitler: He occupied the high moral ground that attracted the loyalty of men with moral character.

The history of the military opposition to Hitler's regime has been scarred by charges of opportunism, largely because the most widely publicized attempt to overthrow Hitler occurred in the summer of 1944, when most German military leaders recognized that the war was lost. Had that been the only attempted coup, the charges might carry the weight of truth, but the famous bombing of the map room at Hitler's headquarters near Rastenburg in East Prussia on July 20, 1944, was actually the last in a series of attempts on the Führer's life. Most of them were carried out by military officers working in close contact with Beck.

Even now, almost a half-century after the war, many people are only vaguely aware of the fact that anti-Nazi groups operated in Germany throughout Hitler's regime. The roster of anti-Nazis includes civilians, government officials, and military officers. Their views ran the gamut of political philosophies, from rightwing monarchists through democratic republicans to socialists and, finally, to communists.

The dissidents engaged in a myriad of activities, including sabotaging manufacturing plants that produced gas for the concentration camps and printing and distributing anti-Nazi propaganda. However, in a totalitarian society under the vigilant control of the secret police forces, these efforts ultimately accomplished little except the deaths of most of the conspirators. In reality only one opposing faction could bring about change, the anti-Nazi group in the German army.

Hitler's only serious opposition in the armed forces came from the army. The air force was headed by Hitler's close confidant and ardent Nazi supporter, Hermann Göring. The navy, grateful to Hitler for its escape from the constraints of the Versailles treaty, was loyal to him, although considerably less committed to Nazism than the air force. The army alone remained to stop Hitler, and only a small number of its officers took part in attempts to do so.

Resistance to Hitler was swiftly punished by the Gestapo and the SS security forces. It is therefore remarkable that many of the men who first formed the core of army opposition in 1938 were still alive to advance their cause when the July 20, 1944, plot was planned.

Many of these men struggled with their consciences because of the oath they had sworn to Hitler, balancing inborn Teutonic fealty against the devastation they saw him bringing to Germany and the world. But let it be said that these men, whose actions we will examine in the coming chapters, made a moral decision to risk their lives and oppose evil.

Some German army generals were ardent supporters of Hitler, including Hans Krebs, Walter von Reichenau, Alfred Jodl, Wilhelm Keitel, Walther Model, Eduard Dietl, and Schörner. Generals who were anti-Nazi and active conspirators for the overthrow of the regime included Ludwig Beck, Hans Oster, Erwin von Witzleben, Karl Heinrich von Stulpnagel, Henning von Tresckow, Thomas, and Alexander von Falkenhausen. Only a small fraction of staff and field officers felt strongly on either side of the issue of Hitler and the Nazis. The overwhelming majority of German officers took no side in the conflict between the Nazis and the anti-Nazis. Like most people everywhere, they quietly followed orders.

Conspicuously absent from the roster of anti-Nazi generals is the name of Field Marshal Erwin Rommel. Although historians and novelists have speculated about Rommel's alleged role in the conspiracy against Hitler, in truth there is no hard evidence that Field

Marshall Rommel participated to any degree in the July 1944 attempt to kill Hitler.

Part of the difficulty in determining whether Rommel was actually involved is that most of the plotters died as a result of the bomb's failure to kill Hitler. Since few conspirators keep diaries that could fall into the hands of the government, it is not even possible to ascertain with any degree of certainty that Rommel was taken into their confidence. We do know that Rommel was considered "Hitler's General" by many of his contemporaries. Hitler clearly liked Rommel; the field marshal was one of only a handful of people, civilian or military, who could speak openly with the Führer, even when they disagreed with him.

Two days after the attempt on Hitler's life, one officer, under severe interrogation, is alleged to have confessed to the Gestapo that Rommel was among the conspirators. On the other hand, there are indications that not only the leaders of the plot, Beck and Stauffenberg, but most of the others involved regarded Rommel with suspicion. He was felt to be at best a questionable ally.

Lieutenant General Dr. Hans Speidel was the one member of the conspirators who survived the war to claim that Rommel was a co-conspirator. Six years Rommel's junior, Speidel was born in the same German province of Württemburg. He became Rommel's close friend during World War I when they served together in the same Brigade. In April 1944 Speidel was appointed Rommel's Chief of Staff in France, as the Desert Fox anticipated the Allied invasion.

Although Speidel flagrantly used Rommel's headquarters to further the cause of the anti-Nazi conspirators, he was never able to recruit Rommel in any plot against Hitler. Although evidence exists that Rommel may have favored coming to terms with Eisenhower after the Allied forces had secured a solid position in France, Rommel, the quintessential German soldier, would never break the oath he had taken to the Führer. Speidel so cleverly covered his tracks and camouflaged his part in the plot that the Nazi court that tried him for treason following the July 1944 attempt on Hitler's life returned a verdict of not guilty. He was released despite Hitler's personal message to the court claiming that he believed Speidel to be guilty.

In the postwar years anyone associated with the plot to kill Hitler was considered a "good German" by the Allies and therefore trustworthy. Speidel later served in the postwar German army and as Allied Commander of Land Forces, Central Europe, under the North Atlantic Treaty Organization (NATO).

Two factors fomented the myth that Rommel was an active participant in the July 1944 attempt to kill Hitler. The first was the revelation, made public in April 1945 by Rommel's son, Manfred, that the field marshal was pressured to commit suicide by Hitler's emissaries. That revelation, coupled with the fact that many officers involved in the attempted coup took their own lives when it failed, made it easy for Rommel's supporters to conclude that he too was a member of the conspiratorial circle.

The second factor involved reports circulated after the war ostensibly by Hans Speidel, implying that he had discussed the plot against Hitler with Rommel. Speidel never directly claimed that Rommel was actually involved, simply that he had talked to Rommel about the fact that there was an anti-Nazi coup plan at work involving several generals. This in itself is evidence of nothing, since it was widely known among a great many generals who were not involved that a plot to kill Hitler existed. In fact, some were later executed simply because they knew about the conspiracy but failed to warn Hitler.

Based on these two factors, stories were fabricated about secret meetings between Rommel and Count von Stauffenberg, the driving force behind the July 20 assassination attempt and the man who carried the bomb into Hitler's conference. There is no evidence to confirm that such meetings ever took place, nor is there any reason they should have. There is no evidence Rommel ever took part in any meeting of conspirators. The extent of Rommel's involvement was to listen quietly to the circumspect conversations of Speidel and Lieutenant Colonel Caesar von Hofacker as the two tried unsuccessfully to enlist him in their cause.

Why the Rommel myth? Perhaps the answer lies with those Americans who romanticize some of our military opponents whose feats have become legendary. Mention of the civil War calls to most Americans' minds the name of Robert E. Lee, the aristocratic con-

federate commander who came close to winning the war and
destroying the nation. Myth has made Lee appear larger than life, a
romantic leader who fought gallantly for a lost cause. Myth had
dealt with the evil of Lee's cause by saying, "Lee was such an
effective military opponent, surely he didn't believe in slavery." We
now know this was not the case.

Another enemy commander on his way to being whitewashed
by American historians is Japanese Admiral Yamamoto, the man
who led the sneak attack on Pearl Harbor. We are now asked to
believe he was the "reluctant admiral," a man of honor who was
merely following orders. A man of honor would not launch a sneak
attack against a country with which his nation was not at war. The
Yamamoto myth deals with that evil by saying, "Yamamoto was
such an effective military opponent, surely he didn't believe in
starting a war against the United States." Although there may be
some truth in the statement, the fact is that he did plan the attack
and did command the forces that carried out the deed.

Field Marshal Rommel was a formidable commander in North
Africa against the British and American forces. At Kasserine his
forces devastated the U.S. army in its first major encounter with the
Axis, killing hundreds and taking thousands prisoner, His tactics in
desert warfare earned him the respect and grudging admiration of
many Allied commanders. The result of these feelings led in-
escapably to the myth that said, "Rommel was such an effective
military opponent, surely he couldn't have been a Nazi. Rommel
was such an effective military opponent, surely he must have been
part of the plot to kill Hitler."

It was false. For Rommel it was a matter of remaining loyal to
his oath to Hitler. It was simply a question of loyalty.

Perhaps the last word on the myth that has developed around
Rommel and the plot to kill Hitler should come from his wife,
Lucie. On September 9, 1945, while many Germans were desperately trying to prove they were neither Nazis nor Nazi
supporters, she issued a statement that said in part, "I want it made
quite clear that my husband had no part whatever in the preparations for, or execution of, the July 20th plot."[3]

2.

The Early Assassins

Long before he attained power in Germany and well before dissident officers in his own army plotted his death, Adolf Hitler had political enemies who were trying to kill him. Most of the initial attempts on Hitler's life were made by what could be termed the "usual suspects." That is, for the most part, Hitler's political opponents, including but not limited to communists, socialists, right-wing extremists, Jews, Christians, and even disaffected National Socialists.

Society in Germany of the 1920s was a nightmare far worse than an untamed American frontier town of the late nineteenth century. Lawlessness was the order of the decade. Private armies and militias proliferated, many of them created to serve as bullyboys for political parties, which themselves multiplied rapidly. No matter how extreme or ridiculous one's views, there was bound to be a political party that embraced them.

Many of these parties habitually resorted to violence to curb their opponents. Private political armies not only provided protection at party rallies and demonstrations but also frequently disrupted rallies staged by opposition parties. Countless pitched battles were waged by these armed gangs in towns and cities throughout Germany. When Hitler began his climb to power, political assassination had become a fact of life in Germany.

Assassination attempts on Hitler's life began long before he ascended to political power. The first recorded attempt occurred in Munich in 1921. In November of that year Hitler spoke at a beer hall rally that was attended by a large audience, which included some three hundred people who were either members of opposition groups or merely violently hostile to him. The crowd included members of the Independent Socialist Party, the Majority Socialist Party, and the Communist Party.

Hitler's speech, "Who Are the Murderers?", was a vitriolic denunciation of the assassination on October 25, 1921, of Majority Socialist Reichstag Deputy Erhard Auer.

It was routine at such gatherings for the audience, both pro- and anti-speaker, to consume beer in inordinate quantities and to cache the empty steins under the tables to use as ammunition in the inevitable melee. During Hitler's speech sharp remarks were exchanged between members of the gathering: this triggered first an avalanche of steins, then the throwing of chairs, and finally a brawl that erupted throughout the hall. In the midst of the ensuing battle, the twenty-five Nazi Storm Troopers on hand for just such an eventuality managed to shepherd most of the three hundred opponents out of the building before the police appeared in sufficient strength to secure the hall.

Before the police arrived several unknown assailants fired shots at Hitler, none of which hit the target. The gunfire was returned, possibly by Hitler himself, who always carried a pistol. These shots also failed to find a target. By the time the SA men cleared the hall of opponents many people had been injured, however, none seriously.

Incredibly, Hitler persisted with his tirade for fully twenty minutes more, until police reinforcements finally closed the hall and dispersed the crowd into the street. Police reports show that some 150 steins were smashed, together with a number of chairs and tables, and the hall was strewn with lengths of brass pipe, brass knuckles, and similar weapons commonly used in civilian riots.

In 1923 Hitler again narrowly escaped death. Two attempts were made on his life by unknown assassins. The first occurred in Thuringia; a second, in which shots were fired at his car, in Leipzig.

In 1929 an SS soldier on guard duty at the Sportpalast reportedly secreted a bomb under the speaker's platform minutes before Hitler was scheduled to appear. After the usual introductions, Hitler began a speech anticipated to last several hours. The SS guard felt a sudden need to use the men's room; confident that there was ample time in which to set off the bomb, he left his position for what he expected would be only a brief absence. Unfortunately for him and the rest of the world, he was accidentally locked in the toilet. Unable to free himself from the locked room in time, he failed to trigger the bomb. Hitler escaped injury or death because of an odd twist of fate. A friend later called it the joke of the century. "The history of the world might have been changed if he hadn't had to go to the bathroom."[1]

Three more failed attempts on Hitler's life occurred in 1932, all by unknown persons. The first took place on March 15 when a fusillade fired at him while he rode a train from Munich to Weimar missed the mark. The following June his car barely escaped attack by a group of armed men who waited in a blind on a roadside near the town of Straslund. A month following this ambush, another ineffective assault failed to kill Hitler when his car was stoned, although one rock did graze his head.

After Hitler became Chancellor, the assassination attempts not only persisted but in fact increased. On March 3, 1933, one day before the newly appointed Chancellor was to address a political rally in Königsberg to campaign for his slate of candidates in the March 5 Reichstag elections, police moved against a communist group whose leader, a ship's carpenter named Kurt Lutter, had organized a plot to blow up the speaker's platform while Hitler spoke. The plan took form during two clandestine meetings held in February that were infiltrated by a police informer who leaked the information to the authorities. An investigation failed to uncover the explosives, and since none of the conspirators would confess to the crime of attempted political assassination, which carried the death penalty, Lutter and his group were ultimately released after being detained for several months.

Lutter was not the only conspirator against Hitler that year. Hardly a week passed without an assassination plot being unearthed, or at least a report of one filed with the police authorities. In February a schoolteacher reported a plot to poison Hitler, and the Bavarian Legation in Berlin revealed that Ludwig Assner, a former Nazi turned communist, claimed that Hitler was a madman who would plunge Germany into misery and that he, Assner, would kill him to prevent this from happening. Although police were on alert for the would-be assassin, his threats against Hitler were dismissed as trivial when he demanded a large sum of money in exchange for abandoning his plans.

Again in 1933, Hitler's life was threatened by a would-be killer at Hitler's country house not far from Berchtesgaden. The hilly countryside surrounding the house was crisscrossed with numerous walking paths along which Hitler liked to stroll, usually accompanied by a small entourage of security people and political followers. The Führer generally led the column while his disciples alternated walking alongside him to exchange a few words of intimate conversation. The security men maintained a discreet distance and performed their duties as unobtrusively as possible.

However, since the grounds which Hitler's party strolled were public property, it was not unusual for them to meet other strollers, sometimes even exchanging pleasantries. Repeated observances of a man in an SA uniform who was acting in a suspicious manner and was watching Hitler's group carefully did not escape the attention of the security forces. During a routine security check, a personal search revealed that he was carrying a loaded handgun, a serious violation of law, and he was immediately arrested.

Throughout 1933 and 1934, reports of planned attempts on Hitler's life were received almost weekly by police. They included bizarre stories of exploding fountain pens, tunnels crammed with explosives dug under buildings in which he was to appear, poison squirted in his face, and dozens of others including one claiming his plane would be shot down over East Prussia. Many of these rumors were not taken seriously, largely because of the sources; however, at least fourteen were deemed sufficiently valid to merit earnest investigation by criminal police officials.

An alleged coup attempt against the Führer in 1934 by the leaders of the SA, which is perhaps the next best known plot against Hitler after the famous bombing of July 1944, remains an enigma to this day. The SA leader, Ernst Röhm, had long advocated replacing the German army with his own organization. Unproven rumors persisted that Röhm coveted the position of Führer for himself. Whether the rumors were valid or Hitler simply decided to appease his army generals and rid them of a nuisance, the alleged plot was Hitler's pretext for the arrest and murder of several hundred SA leaders from June 30, 1934, through July 2, 1934.

Hitler himself participated in Röhm's arrest while the latter was vacationing in Bad Wiesse, south of Munich. With the arrests accomplished and the prisoners en route to Stadelheim prison near Munich, Hitler and his entourage, including an SS security contingent, prepared to drive to Munich. Minutes before they were to leave, a truck carrying heavily armed SA bodyguards known as the Stabswache drove up. Learning that their leaders had been arrested, the SA men assumed combative positions against Hitler's cadre, creating a highly charged and dangerous situation for the Führer.

Hitler somehow persuaded the SA team to retire. Reluctantly they returned to their truck and started out on the road to Munich. Minutes after leaving Bad Wiesse, the men had a change of heart and resolved to kill Hitler, disarm his security force, and rescue the SA leaders. Concealing their truck well off the highway, they established a deadly ambush. Machine guns set up on both sides of the road created a lethal field of fire that could not fail to annihilate Hitler's party. However, Hitler distrusted the SA group and decided to take an alternate route to Munich as a precaution against just such a contingency. Had Hitler traveled the main road, it is likely the SA unit would have killed him.

Lacking documented hard evidence that the SA leaders planned to murder Hitler, and since Röhm and his closest confederates were executed, it will never be known whether the plot actually existed.

Hitler's brutal action against the SA caused former Nazis to join a growing list of those who wanted him dead.

In 1935, a right-wing group hatched an elaborate scheme to kill Hitler. The group's leader, Dr. Helmuth Mylius, was head of the Radical Middle Class Party, an industrial entrepreneur, and editor of a right-wing newspaper. Mylius and retired Navy Captain Hermann Ehrhardt developed a plan to infiltrate Hitler's SS bodyguard units with their own supporters. So successful were they that 160 men penetrated SS security and began accumulating data on Hitler's movements. The coup never came about because the Gestapo, having been informed of the plan, infiltrated the group and arrested most of the participants.

During 1936, David Frankfurter, a Jewish medical student living in Berne, killed Wilhelm Gustloff, Hitler's deputy in Switzerland. Gustloff became Frankfurter's substitute target when the assassin realized his primary target, Adolf Hitler, was beyond his reach. A year later it was learned through SS contacts with the Haganah, the Jewish intelligence service in Palestine, that Gustoff's murder was part of a failed assassination plan against Hitler by a Paris-based group known as the Alliance Israélite Universelle.

In December 1936, a young German Jew who had been living in Prague infiltrated into Germany as part of a plot to kill Hitler by blowing up a building in the Nuremberg Stadium. Helmut Hirsch, acting under the influence of Otto Strasser, one of Hitler's most virulent opponents, agreed to plant the bomb built by another of Strasser's followers.

Hirsch arrived in Stuttgart on December 20, three days before the scheduled meeting with his contact, a Strasser disciple who was to deliver the bomb. Hirsch did not know his contact had been arrested crossing the German-Polish border with the bomb, and under questioning by the Gestapo he revealed the bombing plan and identified the would-be bomber. Since Hirsch had used his own name at the hotel when he completed the forms required of all guests, it was a simple matter to track him down and arrest him.

On March 8, 1937, Helmut Hirsch was tried, convicted, and sentenced to death by beheading. The execution was carried out on June 4 in Plötzensee.

Otto Strasser had long been an irritant to Adolf Hitler, and he probably instigated more than a few death plots against him. Otto and his brother, Gregor, were socialists before joining Hitler's National Socialist Party. Gregor entered into an unqualified allegiance to Hitler, but Otto held some serious reservations. He openly disagreed with Hitler on important issues such as a major strike by metalworkers in Saxony. Otto Strasser championed the workers; Hitler, who was being subsidized by wealthy industrialists, was ordered by them to disclaim Strasser and condemn his support for the strikers. Hitler and Strasser met twice in Berlin's Hotel Sanssouci on May 21 and 22, 1930, to reconcile their differences. Neither man budged from his position and they parted enemies. Expelled from the Party, Otto Strasser formed his own socialist organization, which he called the Black Front.

When Gregor Strasser died in Hitler's attack on the SA, Otto realized that he had lost the protection his brother's position in the Nazi Party had afforded him and that his own life was now in danger. He fled Germany and continued to scheme against Hitler from asylum in Poland, Czechoslovakia, and later Paris. Throughout 1937 and 1938, German intelligence uncovered a steady flow of information revealing plots to kill Hitler by the Black Front, as well as other opponents of the Führer, many of whom were German émigrés.

The year 1938 was a busy time for another would-be assassin, Maurice Bavaud. Through a strangely twisted logical reasoning, Bavaud concluded he must kill Hitler because the German dictator had reneged on his promise to squash the communists. Bavaud was a Swiss citizen attending a French Catholic seminary in Brittany when he came under the influence of another seminarian, Marcel Gerbohay. Gerbohay founded a small secret society of seminarians who called themselves the Compagnie du Mystère. This group was pledged to fight communism wherever it appeared, especially in Russia.

Gerbohay portrayed himself as a descendant of the Romanov dynasty that had ruled Russia for over three hundred years. He prophesied they would rule again when the communists were overthrown. Hitler, whom many thought would be the instrument for the destruction of the Russian communists, was now showing every indication that he intended to co-exist peacefully with the Soviet Communist regime.

At Gerbohay's bidding, Bavaud set off from the seminary on a mission to assassinate Hitler because of his outward tolerance of the communists. He returned to his family's home in the west Switzerland town of Neuchâtel and lived briefly with his parents and his five brothers and sisters. While he earned his keep helping his mother in a small grocery she ran to supplement her husband's postal worker's salary, Bavaud studied German and read the French translation of *Mein Kampf*.

On October 9 he bid his family farewell and set off on an odyssey that would crisscross Germany in pursuit of Adolf Hitler. He told his family he was going to Germany to find work as a draftsman, a trade he had learned before joining the seminary. He spent a fortnight visiting relatives in the German resort town of Baden-Baden. Telling these relatives he was going to Mannheim to seek work, he instead left Baden-Baden and proceeded south to the Swiss border town of Basel, where he purchased a 6.35-millimeter Schmeisser automatic pistol. He then traveled four hundred miles by rail to Berlin, where he expected to find Hitler.

In Berlin Bavaud learned that the Führer was at his mountain retreat near Berchtesgaden. Determined to kill his quarry, Bavaud immediately entrained for the resort three hundred miles to the south. Arriving in Berchtesgaden on October 25, he checked into an inexpensive hotel, the Stiftskeller, and found a source where he purchased extra ammunition for his pistol. To improve his non-existent shooting skills he went deep into the woods and used trees for target practice. He decided that he would be able to shoot Hitler if he could get within twenty-five feet of him. It apparently did not occur to Bavaud that there was no guarantee that if he was success-ful in shooting Hitler the Führer would necessarily die.

Unfortunately, Bavaud again missed connections when Hitler left Berchtesgaden shortly after he arrived. Dejected over this second failure to find his target, Bavaud decided to plan more carefully by learning as much as possible about Hitler's movements before taking further action. However, his German was only rudimentary, and he was severely handicapped in these inquiries.

One afternoon while eating lunch he met two French instructors with whom he carried on a lively conversation, claiming to be an ardent admirer of Hitler who wanted to meet the Führer. Although his companions could not be of any help, the conversation was overheard by a police captain sitting at the next table who spoke French. Captain Karl Derkert told Bavaud that he was connected with Hitler's security and assured the young Swiss that to arrange a personal audience with Hitler would require a letter of introduction from a high-ranking foreign official. But if he only wanted to see Hitler up close, Derkert advised, he should go to Munich in time for the anniversary of the November 9, 1923, putsch. Hitler traditionally led a parade through the city's streets that retraced the route he and his band had taken in 1923.

On October 31 Bavaud once again boarded a train, this time for Munich, where he rented a furnished room. Using a tourist map, Bavaud plotted the route of the march during the days preceding the celebration, looking for a vantage point from which to shoot Hitler. A series of grandstands had been constructed along the route, and for one of them he was able to obtain a ticket by impersonating a reporter for a Swiss newspaper.

Not entirely confident with his marksmanship, he located a suitable site about twenty-five miles from the city where he could safely practice his shooting skills.

The morning of November 9 was cold and clear. Dressed in a heavy overcoat, with his pistol inside the coat pocket, Bavaud made his way through the thousands who thronged the streets of Munich and arrived at the grandstands near the Marienplatz with time to spare. He found a front-row seat and sat quietly, hoping to remain inconspicuous while he waited for Hitler. The street in front of him, as well as along the entire march route, was flanked on both sides with two rows of burly SA men who stood shoulder to shoulder to keep the crowd from rushing into the streets. The intended assassin knew he would have to shoot Hitler from the grandstand because it would be impossible for him to push his way through the brownshirted guards. Suddenly the cry went up, "The Führer is coming!"

Rising as one, the people in the grandstand, Bavaud included, stood to view the approaching parade. Inside his pocket his hand gripped the pistol tightly, ready to remove it quickly when Hitler came within range. With his heart pounding, the young man stood poised to act as the line of marchers approached. When the parade drew abreast of Bavaud, disappointment gripped him as he realized that Hitler was marching on the opposite side of the street, not in the center as he had expected. This placed his target more than fifty feet away, twice his confidence range with his weapon. Bavaud released his hold on the Schmeisser and could do nothing except watch Hitler and his entourage turn a corner and disappear from view.

Bavaud was disappointed but far from discouraged. He purchased some tastefully expensive stationery and envelopes and returned to his room, where he proceeded to forge a letter of introduction to Hitler from French Foreign Minister Pierre Flandin. The letter stated that Bavaud carried a second letter that was to be read by Adolf Hitler only. It was a poorly conceived ruse born of desperation. That Bavaud even imagined such a letter would gain him admittance to Hitler's presence is incredible. To believe that the foreign minister of France would use this young Swiss citizen to carry important correspondence to the Führer of Germany instead of his own ambassador was the height of foolishness.

Hearing erroneously that Hitler had returned to his retreat, Bavaud again boarded a train for Berchtesgaden. At the station he hired a taxi to take him to the Berghof, but he was prevented from entering the grounds by the armed guards who told him Hitler was not there, but still in Munich. Bavaud rushed back to the railroad station and took the next train to Munich, arriving about the same time Hitler's private train left on its way to Berchtesgaden.

Frustrated and nearly out of money, Bavaud gave up his quest to kill Hitler and decided to leave the country. He did not have enough money to travel to Switzerland, so he hid aboard a train bound for Paris where he hoped to obtain from the Swiss embassy sufficient funds to return to his parents' home. When he was discovered by a railroad conductor he was turned over to the police at Augsburg, who handed him to the Gestapo because he was a foreigner and because he was carrying a gun and letter addressed to Hitler. For some insane reason Bavaud had failed to dispose of the incriminating letters and the weapon he intended to use against Hitler.

Under arduous interrogation Bavaud eventually confessed his plan to the Gestapo. He was put on trial, found guilty, and on May 14, 1941, was beheaded.

Having traveled hundreds of miles pursuing his fantasy to kill Hitler, Marcel Bavaud succeeded only in bringing about his own demise. Perhaps he would have accomplished his mission had he been a bit more imaginative and more resourceful, but he was doomed from the beginning because of a grievous lack of planning. Even when certain failure became apparent, the poor fellow was not smart enough to rid himself of the evidence that ultimately incriminated him.

Also active in 1938 was a group of would-be assassins gathered together by Dr. Wilhelm Abegg, a former Prussian state secretary. Abegg's plan was to build a compact bomb small enough to be concealed inside the clothing of an assassin yet powerful enough to cause widespread damage when it exploded. Abegg sought to eliminate as many Nazi leaders as possible along with Hitler.

Abegg devised an imaginative scheme to accost Hitler and the other Nazis with a deception that just might have worked. He formed a team of ten assassins, all former Prussian police officers who had served time in Nazi concentration camps and who had been ransomed by Abegg. The Prussians were to be dressed in stolen uniforms of Italian army courier officers. Each man was assigned a target whom he would approach, presumably with an important message from the Italian government. The man assigned to Hitler was to blow himself up along with his target, while the others were to shoot their assigned targets at the same time.

Abegg's plan was never activated because he had difficulty constructing a suitable bomb. After learning through contacts in the military that high-ranking officers were planning a coup against Hitler, he decided to step aside and leave Hitler's assassination to the generals. He believed they could carry it out much more effectively than he could.

There were countless other plans by civilians to kill Hitler, but none of them ever came as close to achieving their goal as those described here—except for the determined attempt by Georg Elser, which is related in the following chapter.

3.

Himmler's Bomb Plot

Heinrich Himmler was undeniably Adolf Hitler's most sadistic henchman, an epitaph befitting the abominable crimes he committed against humanity. When this unimposing, pudgy little man wearing pince-nez spectacles bit open a cyanide capsule lodged between two teeth on the right side of his mouth during an examination by a British army doctor on May 23, 1945, he took many secrets with him. The most ominous was his role in a bombing that barely missed killing Hitler in 1939.

Hitler customarily participated at the annual meeting in Munich commemorating the failed putsch of November 8–9, 1923. The meeting, held in a large hall of the Burgerbraukeller, was always well attended by the "Old Fighters" who had participated in Hitler's first attempt to seize power.

The SS routinely began guarding closely any facility in which the Führer was scheduled to appear at least several days before his arrival. This tight advance security was calculated to preclude the possibility of a political antagonist placing a bomb in the building set to explode during Hitler's visit. The "Old Fighters" convention was no exception to this practice. Several days before the meeting, crack SS guards placed the hall under maximum security.

Despite stringent security precautions, a thirty-six-year-old artisan named Georg Elser who was both a trained carpenter and master electrician unaccountably managed to slip undetected into the vast beer hall over a span of several nights just before the meeting. Elser had only recently been discharged from the concentration camp at Dachau where he was serving an indeterminate sentence for his activities as a member of a communist organization, the Red Front Fighters League.

Each night Elser worked quietly at his deadly task alone in the darkened hall. A diminutive man with a pale complexion and long dark hair offset by bright darting eyes, Elser bent to his work preparing the instrument for Adolf Hitler's demise with a special dedication.

Directly behind the platform from which Hitler traditionally delivered his speech was a pillar that was a main support for the roof. Dark wood paneling encased the support column. Elser cut an opening into the paneling allowing him entrée to a narrow space between the panel and the support. The opening was sufficiently wide to permit him access to the space, yet small enough to escape notice by a casual observer. He fashioned a tiny door from a matching piece of paneling to disguise the opening. Elser's only fear was that a close examination of the pillar would expose his miniature door.

Incredibly, Elser managed to conceal himself inside the hall, undetected, on thirty-five separate occasions. As the date for Hitler's speech drew near, Elser worked feverishly to complete the preparations for his bomb.

As part of his death plot he had taken a job at a quarry specifically to enable him to steal donarit, an explosive with the properties he required. He added to the donarit some black powder and the explosive removed from a stolen 75-millimeter shell. The final touch was two Westminster clocks synchronized to pinpoint the timing of the explosion.

Because the Führer was in the midst of the invasion of Poland, and because Germany was technically at war with both France and Britain, the meeting organizers planned a scaled-down program for the 1939 ceremonies. At first Hitler decided to forego his customary speech and delegate his second in command, Rudolf Hess, to broadcast a nationwide radio address commemorating the anniversary. At the eleventh hour Hitler changed his mind. He would attend the ceremonies and deliver the speech in person.

On November 8 Hitler flew to Munich, but in deference to the foggy November weather he ordered that his personal train meet him there for the return trip. To avoid disrupting the normal train traffic, Hitler's train was scheduled to leave the Munich station at 9:31 p.m. that evening. To meet this departure time he would have to leave the beer hall no later than 9:10 p.m. Hitler's previous habit at these gatherings was to begin his speech at 8:30 p.m., speak for about one hour, and then spend approximately thirty minutes sipping weak beer and chatting with the rank and file members who had supported him from the early years.

When the Führer arrived, the large hall, gaily decorated with flags and banners, was packed with three thousand celebrants. The Blood Banner, the Nazi flag that had been used on the day of the putsch, was in its place of honor, and the party luminaries who were attending had taken their seats. Most prominent among them were Heinrich Himmler, Joseph Goebbels, Hans Frank, and Alfred Rosenberg.

The crowd rose to its feet and cheered when Hitler strode in at 8:00 p.m. He waved and smiled broadly. Hitler stepped to the platform and waited the better part of ten minutes, allowing the ovation to die down before beginning his speech. When the room was finally quiet he launched into a diatribe against Great Britain that lasted nearly one hour.

Predictably, Hitler accused Britain of fighting in World War I and then, just a month earlier, declaring war on Germany again purely for her own imperialist motives. He denounced the British claim that they were fighting for liberty and justice, and he mockingly shouted that God had rewarded Britain's good deeds with 480 million people around the world to dominate. Again and again his speech was interrupted by wild cheering.

Seated in the front row was a nervous Max Wunsche, the Führer's young military aide, who kept checking his watch. He feared Hitler's speech would run too long and he would miss the train. Wunsche had given the train crew strict orders to leave the station precisely at 9:31 p.m., as Hitler had instructed. While a backup train would arrive a short time later as a security precaution, the young officer did not relish the prospect of waiting around the empty station for the alternate train while the Führer's temper rose.

As Hitler continued his attack on Great Britain, only a few feet behind him Georg Elser's two Westminster clocks quietly ticked away the minutes.

Hitler laughed at the British claim that they were fighting for civilization, and he questioned whether the civilization for which they fought was to be found in the mining districts of Newcastle or the urban slums of London. Meanwhile, the Westminster clocks ticked off their inexorable countdown to destruction.

At seven minutes after nine Hitler ended his speech. Joined by Himmler, Goebbels, and his personal bodyguard, he promptly left the hall amid the deafening cheers of his supporters. Hitler's party boarded a fleet of waiting automobiles and sped directly to the railroad station. Wunsche was enormously relieved; the convoy would arrive in time to depart on the first train.

Thirteen minutes after leaving the hall, as the entourage proceeded through the city toward the station, a loud explosion was heard coming from the direction of the hall. Everyone turned instinctively to the rear window of their cars, but they were too far from the explosion to see what had caused the blast. By the time they arrived at the station the night was filled with the sounds of police and ambulance sirens and the ringing of fire bells.

Minutes before Hitler's train left the station, Eva Braun and her close friend, Herta Schneider, were welcomed aboard. As the train gathered speed through the darkness, the privileged passengers partied, with Hitler the only teetotaler aboard. When the train arrived in Nuremberg, Goebbels got off and entered the stationmaster's office to send several messages and receive the latest dispatches.

The propaganda chief returned pale and obviously shaken. In a trembling voice he told Hitler of the bombing of the Burgerbraukeller. At first Hitler thought Goebbels was joking, but when he realized it was true he too turned pale and sat quietly for a few minutes to regain his composure. As the color returned to his face he spoke with controlled emotion. He attributed his timely exit from the hall only minutes before the explosion to a benevolent Providence and insisted it was a sure sign he was destined to reach his goal. Hitler then commanded his personal adjutant, Julius Schaub, to ensure that everything possible would be done for the victims of the explosion.

Georg Elser's bomb caused a section of the Burgerbraukeller's roof to collapse on the Nazi Party gathering. Eight people died and sixty-three were injured. Eva Braun's father was among the injured. The ensuing peculiar series of events defies logic.

Ever wary of the omnipresent British intelligence, Hitler quickly concluded that two British agents operating in Holland were responsible for the bombing. The two agents, Major R. H. Stevens and Captain S. Payne-Best, were negotiating with a man they believed to be a member of an anti-Nazi conspiracy in the German High Command. The man was actually an SS double agent.

Late that night Himmler telephoned the agent, SS Major Walter Schellenberg, in Venlo, a hamlet just across the Dutch border. He instructed Schellenberg to break off negotiations with the two British officers, kidnap them, and bring them into Germany. Schellenberg was hesitant at first, but Himmler made it clear the order came directly from Hitler.

The following day Schellenberg waited at a café in Venlo for his scheduled meeting with Stevens, Payne-Best, and a Dutch military intelligence officer, Lieutenant Klop. When the Buick carrying the three arrived at the café at precisely 4:00 p.m., the man known to them as Major Schaemmel was seated on the café terrace casually sipping an aperitif. Suspecting nothing, the trio stepped from the car and immediately came under deadly fire from a crack squad of SS Security Service men commanded by the notorious Alfred Helmut Naujocks.

Naujocks had been responsible for the staged attack on a German radio station in Gleiwitz, using prison camp inmates dressed in stolen Polish army uniforms. The incident had provided Hitler with an excuse for attacking Poland. A man of useful SS talents, Naujocks later disguised German soldiers as Dutch and

Belgian border guards to prepare for the German invasion of those countries in May 1940.

In the gunfight that erupted behind the Venlo café, Lieutenant Klop was mortally wounded and both British officers taken prisoner. The SS squad then towed the disabled Buick across the frontier, less than two hundred feet away.

On the same day, Georg Elser was arrested near the town of Constance as he attempted, along with thousands of others, to flee into Switzerland. A search uncovered a large amount of incriminating evidence, including an unused postcard from the Burgerbraukeller, drawings of detonators and shells, parts of a detonator, his old membership card in the Red Front Fighters League, and a substantial sum of money in Swiss and German currency.

The kidnapping of Stevens and Payne-Best proved futile. Intense questioning of the two men failed to produce the slightest shred of evidence that they were even remotely connected to the Munich bombing. Elser, however, confessed to setting the bomb but refused to implicate anyone else. He told his interrogators that he had acted alone and had told no one of his scheme to kill Hitler. When they demanded to know why he wanted to kill the Führer, Elser said he thought it was the only way to prevent Germany from going to war.

Despite repeated beatings and torture by Gestapo agents, Georg Elser insisted he had acted alone. Meanwhile, Hitler publicized the bombing as an "English plot." He wisely recognized the propaganda value of the assassination attempt, and he shrewdly used it to incite German public resentment against Great Britain. On November 21, Hitler declared he had incontrovertible proof that the British Secret Service was behind the bombing and that two British agents had been arrested near the Dutch border.

Finally, in the official explanation of the conspiracy to kill him, Hitler strung together every faction or individual that had ever opposed him. Elser was labeled a communist activist (to which there was some truth) who had been persuaded to become a British agent by Hitler's old National Socialist nemesis, Otto Strasser. The British were accused of supplying Elser with the materials to construct the bomb and promising him safe passage to sanctuary in Switzerland after the assassination.

In a Gestapo-produced film, Georg Elser actually demonstrated how he had manufactured the bomb that devastated the Burgerbraukeller meeting hall, and he explained how he had planted it behind the wood paneling covering the support pillar. When Himmler brought the film and the Gestapo report to the Führer, he refused to view the movie. Hitler categorically denounced the conclusion, which Himmler supported, that Elser had acted alone. Hitler rejected the report and attacked Himmler personally for failing to expose the conspiracy.

Himmler's advocacy of the conclusion that Elser acted alone in spite of his knowledge that Hitler believed the bomber was part of a conspiracy—and wanted the Gestapo investigation to indicate so— is out of character for a man whose reputation was one of total subservience to the Führer's wishes. The logical position was for him to agree with Hitler and place the blame on the two British intelligence officers whom Schellenberg had kidnapped. It was completely unlike Himmler, and without explanation, to take the position he did, unless he was withholding information about the bombing from Hitler.

Major Stevens and Captain Payne-Best spent five years in various concentration camps but managed to survive the war. Shuttled from camp to camp, the two were eventually confined at Niederdorf in South Tyrol. There American forces liberated them on April 28, 1945. Several survivors of plots to kill Hitler on July 20, 1944, were rescued at the same time.

Himmler rewarded Schellenberg for his kidnapping of the two British officers by promoting him to major-general in the SS. He soon became a specialist in foreign espionage, and in early 1940 he furnished Hitler with a report that claimed to prove the existence of close ties between British military intelligence and Dutch military intelligence agencies. Hitler cited that report as part of his justification for invading Holland, which was a neutral country.

Georg Elser's punishment for attempting to kill Hitler was most unusual. It raises provocative questions about exactly who was actually behind the Burgerbraukeller bombing.

Dictators such as Hitler and Stalin relish a prominent, well-publicized trial of their enemies, real or imagined. It allows them to convince the public that evil men and women exist who plot against their authority, thereby justifying the need for draconian security measures. Holding these show trial victims up as examples, even if the evidence is fabricated by the prosecution, serves as a powerful deterrent to other potential opponents. There was ample precedence to expect that the Nazis would parade the Munich bomber before the public in a show trial, presenting all manner of evidence to implicate Hitler's personal and public enemies, especially the British. Incredibly, no such trial ever took place. Not until after the war was lost did Elser pay with his life for the attempted assassination.

Instead of a trial and public execution, Georg Elser was interned as a prisoner with special privileges by Himmler's SS. In a succession of concentration camps he was treated decidedly better than other inmates. He was referred to as a "special prisoner" known under the code name "Eller." In his biography of Adolf Hitler, Robert Payne described Elser as a prisoner who was to be feared or at least respected because he possessed important state secrets.

Ironically, although Elser did not know Stevens and Payne-Best, who were both alleged by the Nazis to be his accomplices, he met them in prison. At Sachsenhausen Elser met Payne-Best whom he learned the Nazis wanted to implicate in the bombing. Elser told the Briton a fascinating story about how he had come to plant the bomb.

According to Elser, he was arrested as a communist activist in Munich during the summer of 1939 and sent to Dachau for reeducation training. One day during his stay at Dachau he was summoned to the commandant's office, where he was questioned about his carpentry and electrical skills. His interrogators confided to him that several high-ranking Party officials were suspected of plotting to kill Hitler, but despite sufficient evidence the Gestapo was reluctant to arrest them because of the chaos it would cause in the upper echelons of government while the country was at war. Elser was asked if he would build and plant a bomb timed to explode shortly after Hitler completed his speech at the annual Munich celebration. In return for his cooperation he would be released from the camp, given a large sum of money, and allowed to escape to Switzerland.

Elser accepted the offer. After he fulfilled his part, he was arrested in a gross breach of agreement. Following his arrest he was told it was a mistake because several overzealous border guards had not been informed of the plan. While he was held in custody, Gestapo agents coached him in testimony he was to deliver implicating both Stevens and Payne-Best in the bombing. Unaccountably, the expected trial never took place.

Later, after he was transferred from Sachsenhausen to Dachau, Elser related essentially the same story he had told Payne-Best to a noted Dachau inmate, the prominent anti-Nazi pastor, Reverend Martin Niemöller.

Georg Elser finally paid for his crime four and one-half years later, just weeks before the end of the war. In the declining months of the Third Reich, many opponents of the regime being held in concentration camps and prisons were slaughtered by the Nazis. Elser's death was made to look as if it happened during an Allied bombing raid.

Among the documents uncovered after the war was a letter from Gestapo chief Heinrich Müller to the commandant of Dachau, SS-Obersturmbannführer Eduard Weiter, instructing him to kill Elser during the next air raid. Müller even told Weiter the exact words to use when announcing Elser's death. On April 16, 1945, Weiter announced that Georg Elser had been mortally wounded during an Allied bombing raid.

Unfortunately for historical accuracy, the elusive answer to the question of who was actually behind the bombing of the Munich beer hall will probably never be resolved. Three viable possibilities exist; (1) Himmler arranged the bombing with Hitler's approval to stir up anti-British hatred among the German population; (2) Himmler arranged the bombing, without Hitler's knowledge, for whatever personal reason he may have had; and (3) Elser accomplished the entire task himself.

Taking the last first, practically no one with any understanding of the workings of Nazi Germany could conclude that Georg Elser, a man of limited intelligence, could possibly have succeeded in placing the bomb undetected by security agents. Most historians agree that Himmler, for some unclear motive, planned the entire incident. At the time of the bombing, William L. Shirer wrote in his diary the phrase, "smells of another Reichstag fire." Robert Payne concluded that Elser had been Himmler's tool.

If in fact Shirer and Payne are correct and Himmler actually did arrange the bombing, an important new question requires an answer. Was the bomb planted with Adolf Hitler's knowledge and approval? This question may be easy to answer by looking at the political result of the explosion. Hitler used the attempt on his life to arouse German resentment against Britain. He accused the British of trying to win the war by killing him. His strategy worked. Hitler's wild, unsupported accusations radically increased anti-British feelings among the German population.

It is difficult, though, to imagine Adolf Hitler allowing Himmler or anyone else to plant a time bomb just a few feet away from where he stood. It is even more difficult to imagine Hitler per-mitting a known communist and enemy to plant the bomb. Without question, if the bomb had exploded while Hitler was speaking, he would have died. It is hard to believe that even Hitler would take such a chance with his life merely for propaganda reasons. Surely the same thing could have been accomplished by the arrest of known British agents, such as Stevens and Payne-Best, and by prosecuting them before a Nazi court on fabricated charges using bribed or coerced witnesses to testify that the two had planned to kill Hitler. The effect might have been less spectacular than a bomb that killed seven people, but the result would have probably been no less effective in its impact on the public's perception. It is un-likely that Hitler would actually risk his life to achieve such a ques-tionable propaganda advantage.

When all the facts are assembled, it seems reasonable to assume that Heinrich Himmler plotted the bombing. If, as is likely, Hitler knew nothing of the plan in advance, it is clearly possible that Himmler, an ambitious schemer who longed for great military power (as evidenced by his ultimately building the SS into a private army of thirty-five divisions), could have contrived to kill Hitler so he could replace him as Germany's triumphant head of state just as the Third Reich stood on the verge of military conquest.

4.

The Resistance Is Born

During 1938 latent anti-Nazi and anti-war sentiment among individual officers in the German army gradually coalesced into a hardcore group determined to depose Hitler. Early in the year the first tentative beginnings of an organized coup took form. By year's end a solid nucleus of ranking officers was plotting to kill the Führer. However, many of the generals who recognized that Hitler's plans for conquering Europe harbored the seeds of Germany's destruction rejected assassination, opting instead for arrest and imprisonment.

The year began in grim fashion for the old-line officer corps. Two of their respected comrades were forced into retirement in disgrace, victims of scandals instigated by Nazi leaders who were determined to seize control of the army. The first was fifty-nine-year-old War Minister Field Marshal Werner von Blomberg. Blomberg an unabashed admirer of the Führer, had become one of his favorite generals. Only a year before he had represented Hitler at the coronation of Britain's King George VI.

A widower with three grown children, the field marshal made the foolish mistake of marrying a young woman he met during one of his secret forays into the decadent netherworld of Berlin night-life. When Blomberg married Erna Gruen in a civil ceremony conducted in the War Ministry Building on January 12, 1938, Hitler and Luftwaffe Chief Hermann Göring were their witnesses. Blomberg had invited their participation, hoping they would protect him if his young bride's questionable background became a problem.

Blomberg misjudged his Nazi friends. Not only after the wedding, allegations (almost surely raised by Göring, who coveted Blomberg's post of war minister) were leveled against the field marshal's new wife, exposing her as a woman who posed for and sold pornographic photographs. On January 27, 1938, under pressure from Hitler, who felt betrayed by this old aristocrat, Blomberg resigned "for reasons of health." He never again served in a military capacity.

Despite his ouster, Blomberg demonstrated his loyalty by recommending that instead of replacing him with one of the senior generals in line for promotion, all known or suspected to be anti-Nazi, Hitler should assume the war minister's post himself. Blomberg may have been motivated to make this recommendation in order to keep the War Ministry out of Göring's hands once he recognized the latter's role in his downfall. Hitler thought it an excellent idea and promptly appointed himself to the position, giving himself direct control of the armed forces. He rewarded Blomberg for providing the opportunity by financing a world tour for the field marshal and his wife.

Following swiftly on the heels of Blomberg's removal was the dismissal of Army Commander-in-Chief General Baron Werner Freiherr von Fritsch. Once described by a French general as having all the character faults of a Prussian general staff officer, Fritsch was extremely popular and highly respected in the German army. Fritsch disliked the Nazis and had little use for the Führer, which made him an obvious target for Hitler.

Because he was more a soldier than a diplomat, Fritsch was too honest to conceal his low regard for the Nazis and Adolf Hitler. On numerous occasions Fritsch voiced this contempt, which was surely documented by hidden Gestapo microphones and duly reported to Himmler and the Führer. Two such incidents graphically reveal

Fritsch's feelings toward the Nazis and his total disregard for caution. He once asked an aide, Colonel Gotthard Heinrici, why the streets were crowded with people obviously celebrating a joyous event. When Heinrici informed him that it was Hitler's birthday, he boomed sarcastically, "Why celebrate that?"

In his book *Berlin Diary*, William L. Shirer relates another incident that demonstrates clearly Fritsch's lack of discretion. Shirer was standing next to the army Commander-in-Chief on a reviewing stand prior to a parade of army and SS troops on March 1, 1935. Although Fritsch knew Shirer only as one of many American correspondents covering the event, the general fired off a string of contemptuous and sarcastic comments about the SS, the Nazi Party, and the Nazi leaders, including Hitler himself. When it was time for Fritsch to take his place behind Hitler on the platform, he did so with a grunt of displeasure.

In Hitler's view Fritsch was a colossal nuisance, particularly for his ceaseless opposition to the Nazification of the army. In 1936, as part of his tireless efforts to humiliate the army leadership and destroy its independence from the Party, Himmler had presented Hitler with what he claimed was evidence the general was a homosexual. Despite his pique with Fritsch, Hitler dismissed the obviously fabricated evidence and in fact told Himmler to destroy it. It was a strange accusation to present to Hitler. If the charge was proven Fritsch would lose the respect of his fellow officers, but Hitler already had several well-known homosexuals in high positions and would appoint others. It was doubtful he would fire the general just because he was a homosexual.

However, by late 1937 and early 1938 Fritsch had become so vociferous in his opposition to Hitler's plans and presented such differing views that Hitler decided Fritsch must go. The old evidence was resurrected, and on January 26, 1938, Hitler appointed Göring president of a special court assigned to investigate the charges. Four days later Fritsch resigned his post, despite urgings from fellow officers to stand and fight. They wanted him to go to trial and receive what they expected would be total exoneration.

So adamant was Hitler about removing the general that the Führer personally took part in the shameful farce aimed at destroying Fritsch. Before he appointed the court to investigate the charges against Fritsch, Hitler called the Commander-in-chief into his study. Fritsch, who until that moment was unaware there were charges against him, was stunned to find Hitler, accompanied by Göring, in a foul mood. The Führer waved a thick dossier in the air and confronted the general with the charges. Fritsch vehemently denied any homosexual activities and did what every honorable officer would do, giving Hitler his word as a German officer that there was not a shred of truth to the accusations.

Fritsch's denials failed to sway Hitler, who had convinced himself his evidence was incontrovertible and now was the time to use it. Rising from his chair, Hitler stalked across the room and threw open an anteroom door. Behind the door stood twenty-eight-year-old Otto Schmidt, who without any prompting from Hitler pointed at the Commander-in-Chief and uttered the incriminating words, "That's the man."

Hitler closed the door and turned to Fritsch, whose face flushed red with rage. The general regained control of himself and, expecting Hitler to listen to reason, calmly explained that the man behind the door was obviously mistaken. Hitler remained unmoved. A man of honor who would not dream of making a false accusation, Fritsch failed to understand that Hitler was not above doing so. The general searched his mind for something, however insignificant, that might have led to the accusation. All he could think of was that he had recently evicted from his home a Hitler Youth member, to whom he had given shelter, after the boy was found to be a petty thief. Perhaps, he told Hitler, this boy's desire for revenge was the motive behind the charges.

Choked with anger and still not comprehending Hitler's duplicity, Fritsch was struck inarticulate by his own rage. He blurted out this information as the only explanation he could offer. He accomplished nothing except to convince Hitler that the youth was probably another party to Fritsch's homosexual activities. Hitler pounced on the opening, demanding Fritsch's immediate resignation. In return, Hitler would squelch the charges. Fritsch refused, insisting on a full investigation. A disappointed Hitler told the general he would consider his request and dismissed him.

The next day Hitler instructed Fritsch to report to Gestapo headquarters on Prinz Albrechtstrasse to clear up the charges. Incredibly, Fritsch did as ordered, subjecting himself to hours of abusive and humiliating interrogation by an SS lieutenant who showed no respect for Fritsch's uniform or position. When Hitler requested his "temporary" resignation, Fritsch obliged.

On February 4 Hitler formally announced replacements for both officers. He took over Blomberg's former post himself, making himself commander of all military forces, and he promoted Colonel-General Walter von Brauchitsch to Commander-in-Chief of the army. On March 18 the special court found Fritsch innocent of the charges despite Göring's ill-concealed efforts to influence a verdict of guilty. Otto Schmidt was unmasked as a pimp and blackmailer who was well known to the Berlin police. His primary source of income was blackmailing homosexuals, one of whom was a retired army captain named von Fritsch. Capitalizing on the similarity in names, Göring and Himmler had the Gestapo investigate the theory that the blackmail victim was actually the army Commander-in-Chief. When the investigation confirmed the victim's real identity, it was suppressed and Schmidt was induced to charge Fritsch in Hitler's presence.

Vindication came too late; Fritsch was out of office and remained on the army's inactive list until September 1939, when he was recalled to active duty. The former army commander was killed by a Polish sniper on September 22 during the fighting around Warsaw. Many of General Fritsch's friends believed his death in battle had all the earmarks of a virtual suicide by a man disgraced.

The Fritsch affair led to the first tentative efforts to involve the army in an action against the regime, but the early rumblings, mostly by civilians and police officials, failed to gain sufficient support in the senior ranks. It was also a critical juncture in Hitler's relationship with the army. In one brilliant stroke Hitler had managed to take personal control of the armed forces and replace an antagonist, Fritsch, with Brauchitsch–who, although opposed to Hitler's military ambitions, was more inclined to follow orders and less likely to speak his mind and act on his beliefs.

While the Fritsch affair was playing out to its shameful conclusion, a group of civilians tried to raise support for a coup against the SS and Gestapo. This group included such prominent citizens as the former Lord Mayor of Leipzig Carl Goerdeler, Criminal Police Inspector Arthur Nebe, former Reich Minister of Economics and one-time and future President of the Reichsbank Hjalmar Horace Greely Schacht, Police President of Berlin Wolf Heinrich Count von Helldorf, and German diplomat Dr. Hans Gisevius.

Unfortunately, civilians, even police officials, lacked both the manpower and wherewithal to challenge the powerful Nazi organizations. It became obvious to the conspirators that it was a job for the armed forces. At first these civilians expected that the Nazis wrongful treatment of Blomberg and Fritsch would awaken the military to what they saw as an SS coup against the army. Regrettably, it was not so obvious to many key officers. Several factors mitigated against the military taking preventive retaliatory action against the Nazis. Because under Hitler's direct orders the Blomberg and Fritsch dismissals were closely kept secrets until they were publicly announced, except for a handful of the highest ranking officers, few military men knew of the intrigues. General Heinz Guderian said later that the facts about the Blomberg and Fritsch affairs "remained obscure" for the majority of ranking army officers.

The second deterrent to a concerted action by the military was inter-service rivalry. Two of the three armed service branches, the navy and air force, could not be depended on to impeach their Nazi sponsors. The air force owed its very existence to Hermann Göring and was at the time under his complete control. The navy was in the early stages of recovery from virtual extinction during World War I, owing that recovery to Hitler's resolve to build a powerful fleet. Even the army, a hotbed of monarchists and conservative traditionalists, benefited from Hitler's plan to expand the German military.

In 1932 the German army had forty-four officers with the rank of major-general or higher. By 1938 that number had ballooned to almost three hundred. The brotherhood of generals was no longer an elite, close-knit order that could act swiftly and cohesively. It had been injected with an infusion of Nazis and pro-Nazi sympathizers having no military legacy and small concern for the army's traditional independence from politics.

Desperate to enlist support for a crusade against the Nazis, a tall, thin, long-time civil servant, Dr. Hans Gisevius,- turned to his friend Hans Oster, Chief of Staff of the Abwehr, the counterintelligence section of the military High Command. Lieutenant Colonel Hans Oster was a much-decorated veteran of World War I. He was a deeply religious parson's son, a highly charged and temperamental man who appreciated beautiful women and fine horses. A man without personal ambitions, Oster viewed Nazism as anti-Christian and persisted in his efforts to depose Hitler until his own execution in 1945.

Gisevius produced information given him by Nebe, who as head of the Criminal Police had access to the confidential files on Blomberg's wife and the charges against Fritsch. When Oster learned that Fritsch had consented to interrogation by the Gestapo, he flew into a rage. For years German soldiers had been assured they were immune from Gestapo authority and could not be arrested or questioned by them. With the Commander-in-Chief having been subjected to Gestapo power, Oster saw the entire affair as a conspiracy to bring the army under SS control.

Incensed, Oster brought the information to his boss, Abwehr chief Admiral Wilhelm Canaris. A former U-boat commander and master of espionage, Canaris had until this time supported most of Hitler's policies, especially military reconstruction and expansion. Under the expansion program the admiral built the Abwehr from 150 employees in 1933 to 956 officers and civilians by 1937. Fritsch's humiliation by the Gestapo and SS was the catalyst that enabled Oster to prod Canaris into accepting a role in the resistance against the Nazis.

Canaris had little success trying to mobilize army officers with whom he was acquainted to rally against the Nazis for their unconscionable treatment of their Commander-in-Chief. He ran head-on into General Ludwig Beck, who as Chief of the General Staff counseled against openly opposing opposing the government. A loyal officer, Beck believed that Hitler had been duped into acting against Fritsch by the Gestapo. He hoped that the Führer could be made to see the injustice through reasonable means. Beck put a gag order on discussing the Fritsch affair, fearing an open debate among the officers could trigger a full-blown rebellion. He stood behind his commitment that "mutiny and revolution" are words not permitted in a German officer's vocabulary. Ironically, the man who aborted the fledgling coup was destined to become the central figure in several later attempts to unseat the Nazi regime.

Although he was not unfeeling about Fritsch's disgraceful treatment, Beck was far more concerned with the outcome of the Blomberg scandal. He saw the small measure of independence the army enjoyed with the War Ministry jeopardized when Hitler took control of the ministry, and he sought to preserve it by enlisting support for a separate Army Ministry.

Despite Beck's reluctance to participate, pressure for a military response to the Fritsch affair persisted. Goerdeler and Schacht traveled to Dresden to see General Wilhelm List, IV Military District Commandant. List was sympathetic but unwilling to act on his own. He told Goerdeler and Schacht that it was virtually impossible to move his troops from Dresden to Berlin to attack Gestapo headquarters. Permission was required from the High Command in Berlin. He also needed railroad transports, which he did not have, to accomplish the move. In any case, it would take three days just to transfer a full division to Berlin, ample time for the SS and Gestapo to take countermeasures within the government.

List's Chief of Staff, Major General Friedrich Olbricht, told Schacht and Goerdeler that it was impossible for troops stationed so far from Berlin to undertake such an ambitious action. Olbricht advised that because their proximity to the capital would afford them the advantage of a surprise strike, the troops of the III Military District, which included Berlin, were far better suited for such a mission. Unfortunately, III Military District Commanding Officer Erwin von Witzleben was ill and away from his post. Both Olbricht and Witzleben would soon become important players in schemes to overthrow the Nazis.

At the heart of the army's failure to respond to the censure of its senior generals was a widespread ignorance of Hitler's culpability in the affairs. Even Fritsch, who could easily have rallied most of the army, failed to understand that Hitler, who had supported the army against the Party's own army, the SA, could now turn on them so quickly and treacherously. It was beyond their understanding that Hitler was scheming to rid himself of military advisors and leaders who would disagree with his plans to conquer Europe. Fritsch as much as anyone deserves a lion's share of the blame for the army's lethargy. Had he not been so blinded by his faith in the Führer's integrity, he might have thwarted Göring and Himmler and prevented Hitler's personal takeover of the German armed forces.

Although this effort to organize resistance against the SS and Gestapo by both civilians and military dissidents fizzled, it served as a rallying point for the growing number of anti-Nazis. Hans Oster, who seldom missed an opportunity to voice his contempt for Hitler, emerged as a central figure in the anti-Hitlerite movement, frequently acting as liaison between the military and civilian sectors.

Dr. Johannes von Dohnanyi became a welcome new addition to Oster's circle of anti-Nazis based in the Abwehr. He was personal advisor to Reich Minister of Justice Franz Gurtner, and he had disapproved of Hitler and his Nazi Party almost from the beginning when, through his post in the attorney general's office, in Hamburg, he was exposed firsthand to Nazi brutality. As early as 1937 Dohnanyi tried to recruit Hitler's adjutant, Hans Wiedemann, in a plot to shoot the Führer. Now he joined an inner circle of Nazi detractors who resolved to undertake any means within their power to remove the Nazis from power.

During the Fritsch scandal Hitler sent German army troops into Austria, ostensibly to support the newly constituted Nazi government. Two years earlier German troops had crossed the Rhine bridges and occupied the former demilitarized zone established by the Treaty of Versailles. In both instances Hitler ignored his generals' advice and warnings of potential danger, and both were total victories for Hitler. Austria soon lost its independence and became part of the Greater Reich under Hitler.

Hitler gained enormous popularity for these stunning victories that had cost no German lives, forcing his opponents to suspend any plans that were in the development stage. The general public would never understand (much less support) a coup against a leader who had done so much for Germany at so little cost.

Hitler's next target was the Sudetenland of Czechoslovakia. It had been obvious to knowledgeable Hitler watchers that his plans included incorporating the Sudetenland into the Reich. Hitler believed its 3.5 million German-speaking inhabitants should rightfully be part of his emerging new super-state, and he was determined to annex them. Unfortunately for the world, British and French political leaders failed to perceive Hitler with the same clear insight as the dictator's internal enemies.

The 1919 Treaty of Saint-Germain-en-Laye between the Allies and what remained of the Austro-Hungarian Empire ceded the Sudetenland, a section of Bohemia, to the newly formed Czechoslovak nation. The population was primarily ethnic German, although the Sudetenland had been part of Austria and had not actually been part of Germany. For two decades following the treaty an uneasy hostility smoldered between these Germans and the majority population of the country who were Czechs and Slovaks. Hitler decreed that all Germans must live inside the Reich and that the Sudeten Germans were no exception.

The Nazi Party of the Sudetenland, under the leadership of a gymnastics teacher named Konrad Henlein, waged a relentless and often bloody campaign for Sudetenland autonomy. As Hitler's power base grew stronger, Henlein's party treasury was heavily subsidized by the German Foreign Office specifically to persuade the Sudeten Germans to join the Reich. By 1938 the Party had won the support of most Sudeten Germans. Henlein's years of blaming the Czechs and Slovaks for discrimination against the German minority reached a sympathetic audience within the German-speaking population.

Bringing the German population into the Reich was not Hitler's only reason for wanting the Sudetenland. The area was rich in mineral resources, and an important munitions factory in the Sudeten city of Pilsen could contribute significantly to Nazi

Germany's expanding war machine and Hitler's future military might.

Emboldened by Hitler's bloodless annexation of Austria, Henlein and his followers increased their agitation, engaging in pitched battles with police in towns across the Sudetenland. On March 28, 1938, Henlein met with Hitler in Berlin. The Führer directed him to make a series of totally unacceptable demands on the Czech government, including complete autonomy for the Sudetenland and reparations for real or imagined economic losses suffered by the German-speaking population since it was incorporated into Czechoslovakia.

Within weeks of the meeting, plans for a surprise attack on Czechoslovakia were being drawn under the direction of General Wilhelm Keitel, who would serve as Hitler's personal military flunky until the end of the war. The attack was designed Operation Green and would begin at "a suitable moment," as Hitler put it. Toward the end of May Hitler personally informed the chiefs of the army, navy, and air force that it was his "unalterable decision to destroy Czechoslovakia by military action within a foreseeable time."

In the opinion of many ranking German officers, an attack on Czechoslovakia could bring grievous consequences for Germany. Czechoslovakia was the child of the Allied victory in World War I and had reciprocal military treaties with France and the Soviet Union. Many German army officers feared that an attack on Czechoslovakia could bring on another two-front war, with France attacking Germany from the west while Germany was occupied in the east. Despite his generals' misgivings, Adolf Hitler was determined to possess the Sudetenland. He did not want it to be given to him; he wanted to take it by force.

Fearing German and Hungarian designs on its territory, Czechoslovakia had earlier sought to protect its sovereignty by entering into treaties with larger nations. Czechoslovakia believed that its treaty with the French guaranteed France would attack Germany if the Germans violated Czech territory. In 1935 a treaty also had been concluded with the Soviet Union that required the

Soviets to come to the assistance of Czechoslovakia if it was invaded.

However, the Czech treaty with the Soviet Union called for the Red Army to help only if France upheld its treaty obligations. The result was that the only democratic state in central Europe depended for its safety on the French taking action against the Germans should Hitler invade Czechoslovakia. For their part the French felt they were too weak militarily and too disunited politically to act without active support from Great Britain. Britain, through ineffective and hopelessly outmaneuvered Prime Minister Neville Chamberlain and his appeasement policies, had little stomach to stand up to the Nazi dictator and support the democracy it had helped create. Czechoslovakia's fate was sealed long before Hitler informed his military commanders he intended to crush it.

In the spring and summer of 1938 Adolf Hitler was likely the only leading German who foresaw that the Allies would not go to war to defend Czechoslovakia. Most of his generals were convinced otherwise, as they were the following year when the Führer erroneously made the same assumption about Poland.

The Czech government was intent on retaining the Sudetenland. The munitions plant and natural resources aside, the topography of the territory provided a natural defense against Germany, and Czechoslovakia was also plagued with territorial claims by its other neighbors, Hungary and Poland. If Czechoslovakia acceded to German demands, it might be forced to acknowledge those of Poland and Hungary as well. The Czechs relied on their treaties with France and the Soviet Union to guarantee their independence. They would be badly disappointed.

As for the Sudeten Germans, while their claims carried some validity, on the whole they had little cause to complain. They were in effect a minority in a nation of minorities, and if anything, their lot was better than most in Czechoslovakia. Their unrest was fomented by Joseph Goebbels's propaganda machine in Berlin. Goebbels generated stories aimed at enflaming the passions of all Germans against the government of Czechoslovakia. German newspapers regularly published accounts of atrocities committed against the Sudeten Germans, such as mass arrests and wholesale executions of the civilian populations. The execution sites were usually cloaked in vague references to unnamed villages, making it impossible to corroborate the truth of the accounts.

At first the Czech government denied the stories, but it soon abandoned all attempts to disprove the accusations as futile. Goebbels's persistence won out. Meanwhile, excellent Czech intelligence sources inside the Reich forewarned the Czech government of Hitler's impending military invasion. What they could not learn was when it was scheduled.

As German troops occupied threatening positions near the border, President Eduard Beneš feared the moment was at hand and on May 20, 1938, ordered a partial mobilization of the Czech army. That same day General Keitel handed Hitler copies of the invasion orders drafted as part of Operation Green. The outside world, either unaware of or deliberately blind to Hitler's menacing actions, condemned Czechoslovakia for provocation. Hitler, enraged by the Czech's affront of daring to stand up to him, insisted that Beneš had treated him with contempt. He assembled his military chiefs and reiterated his determination to destroy Czechoslovakia.

The Czechs mobilized in response to the threat posed by twelve German divisions poised at their border, prepared, according to German staff records, "to march within twelve hours." The German force consisted of ten infantry divisions, one mountain division, and one armored division. Rumors and newspaper accounts of German troop movements preceded the Czech mobilization order and forced British, French, and Soviet spokesmen to issue strong warning statements intended to stem Hitler's plans.

In a black mood, provoked by the warnings from Paris, London, and Moscow, Hitler reluctantly issued assurances to the Czech government that reports of German troop movements on the border were unfounded and that he had no plans to invade Czechoslovakia. The leaders of all four countries genuinely believed they had successfully faced down the German dictator. They thought the crisis and possibly another war had been averted. They badly underestimated Hitler's resolve.

Throughout the following week Hitler seethed with fury, his personal animosity toward Czech President Beneš growing into a fierce determination for revenge. On May 28 he called his top generals to a meeting in the Chancellery and ordered them to prepare to invade Czechoslovakia no later than October 2. He also issued orders to hasten construction of Germany's defenses on the western border with France, and he gave another directive to create plans to mobilize ninety-six divisions. Hitler then announced his "unshakeable will" to wipe Czechoslovakia off the map.

Objectives for Operation Green were reviewed and updated. The opening statement of the directive for the invasion of Czechoslovakia was changed from a disclaimer denying that Hitler intended to destroy that nation to forthright admission that it was unalterable decision "to smash Czechoslovakia by military action."

The summer of 1938 saw a whirlwind of activity on three fronts. The Nazi propaganda apparatus worked overtime inciting the German population against Czech "atrocities" allegedly committed against the Sudeten Germans. Henlein's Sudetenland Nazi Party conducted demonstrations and other violent provocations aimed at disrupting the central government's relations with its own citizens. In Germany, Hitler stepped up preparations for the coming attack. In June he personally attended maneuvers in Franconia, near the Czech border. Flaunting before his generals what he considered his superior strategic and tactical abilities, Hitler ordered special training in storming fixed fortifications. The targeted fortifications were the Czechs frontier forts known as Czech Maginot Line.

On June 9 Hitler demanded more detailed information on Czech military strength and armaments, especially the strength of forces manning the frontier forts. Then, on June 18, he issued a "General Guiding Directive" for Operation Green in which he claimed there was no danger of Allied intervention against Germany. He explained further that he would issue the final order for the attack only when he was "firmly convinced" that France and Britain would not intervene. On June 22, the German government initiated compulsory civil defense measures.

In the midst of these hectic preparations for war, some army leaders remained skeptical. The first to speak out was General Beck, Chief of the General Staff. As early as April, Beck first began to criticize Hitler's plan to invade Czechoslovakia. In a memorandum to General Walter von Brauchitsch (who replaced Fritsch as Commander-in-Chief of the army) Beck predicted that France and Britain would fight to protect Czechoslovakia. He feared that such intervention could lead to a prolonged war that might ultimately bring the United States into the conflict. In this he only saw defeat for Germany. In his lengthy analysis of the dangers of fighting a two-front or prolonged war and Germany's fragile defense economy, Beck said flatly, "Germany is not fit for a long war."

Beck's memorandum never reached Hitler and his advice was ignored by Brauchitsch. Beck was furious at Brauchitsch's snub and his refusal to discuss with Hitler the opinions of the Chief of the General Staff.

Finally, on July 16 Beck confronted Brauchitsch with another memorandum and demanded that the Commander-in-Chief call a secret meeting of senior generals. This time Beck was adamant and forced his commander to honor his request. The meeting was convened on August 4. Beck read his memorandum of July 16, which met with general agreement from those present. In it he called on Hitler to undertake drastic reforms, which included scrapping plans to invade Czechoslovakia, ending SS and Gestapo terror, and the "restoration of justice" in Germany. Beck had now broadened his demands to include basic changes in the way the Nazis governed as well as the avoidance of a war.

Contrary to the defense theories commonly advanced by German generals at the war crimes trials that it was an officer's duty to simply follow orders, Beck assigned them a higher moral responsibility in his memorandum of July 16 when he told them:

> Vital decisions for the future of the nation are at stake. History will indict these commanders [who blindly follow Hitler's orders] of blood guilt if, in the light of their professsional and political knowledge, they do not obey the dictates of their conscience. A

soldier's duty to obey ends when his knowledge, his conscience, and his sense of responsibility forbid him to carry out a certain order.[1]

Beck called on his peers to unite in protest against Hitler's war plans. If all else failed, he said, the generals must go on strike to prevent war, and if necessary resign their commissions. While a large majority agreed with Beck's views that war would lead to Germany's destruction, few of them were prepared to resign, even as part of a protest to save Germany.

As they listened to Beck's impassioned plea for unity, many of the generals were torn by grave inner conflicts. Few if any of them could separate themselves from their tradition of blind obedience to orders, as Beck had, and examined those orders in light of their moral and political consequences.

Although Beck was encouraged by the favorable response to his ideals, he was disappointed that the meeting ended with no decision for positive action. Perhaps Beck himself had intimidated his fellow generals into noncommittal inaction because of the deeper implications behind his words. Beck was calling for a confrontation between the army and the forces backing Hitler. Although he still believed Hitler could be persuaded to change his course, Beck was convinced that before that could happen the dangerous influence of the SS and Nazi Party leaders must be eliminated. He ended his speech with a strong appeal for an organized protest by the generals, to be followed immediately by a direct confrontation between the army and the SS. Since the SS and the Party were pillars of Hitler's power base, implicit in Beck's remarks were the seeds of a coup d'état.

Beck again approached Brauchitsch with the urgency for a collective protest by the ranking generals. He emphasized that their actions would rescue both Germany and Hitler from SS and Nazi Party corruption. How much of Beck's motivation was a sincere desire to benefit the Führer is questionable. He undoubtedly realized he had little chance of convincing these career officers that their greater duty was to unseat the leader to whom they had sworn personal loyalty. He cleverly couched his words to mask what were likely his true intentions, making it appear he advocated a strategy aimed at shielding Hitler from his own henchmen rather than delivering Germany from Hitler's madness.

Throughout the summer Beck maintained constant pressure on Brauchitsch to take some action to avert the calamity that he fully expected would ensue if Germany invaded Czechoslovakia. A personal rift developed between Brauchitsch and Beck over Beck's persistent carping on this issue. Despite their differences, Brauchitsch declined several times to accept Beck's resignation as Chief of the General Staff.

Walter von Brauchitsch was not a forceful personality. He lacked the dominant traits indispensable to successful command. Elegant and dignified in appearance and bearing, he was never accused of being pro-Nazi. In fact, he was in the habit of telling younger officers who greeted him with the raised-arm Nazi salute that he feared they would poke out his eyes. The son of a Prussian cavalry general, he had served in his youth as personal page to the Empress Augusta Victoria, wife of Kaiser Wilhelm II.

Field Marshal Erich von Manstein described Brauchitsch as "correct, courteous and even charming," although, he added, the charm left one feeling there was no genuine warmth behind it. Brauchitsch's appointment as Commander-in-Chief was as near perfect a choice as Hitler could hope for. Although the general was a well-regarded member of the Prussian aristocracy, he was also pliable and focused on his own career to the exclusion of virtually everything else, including what was best for his country. He was above all else a compromiser, and so terrified of Hitler that he practically quaked in his presence. A fellow officer once described Brauchitsch as standing at attention before Hitler "like a little cadet before his commandant."

Brauchitsch was not the Führer's first choice for Commander-in-Chief. Hitler favored General von Reichenau, a known pro-Nazi, but was told by General von Rundstedt, the oldest and most respected general in the German army, that Reichenau was unacceptable to the army. Von Rundstedt, too old to assume the post himself, enthusiastically recommended Beck. The Führer declined to consider Beck because of his anti-Nazi sympathies and asked whether Brauchitsch was an acceptable candidate. Rundstedt acknowledged that he was.

Rundstedt could not have known that Brauchitsch was a less trustworthy candidate for the post of army commander than a pro-Nazi general such as Reichenau. A pro-Nazi might have united the generals, while Brauchitsch could be made to do Hitler's bidding without his fellow officers' knowledge.

Hitler offered Brauchitsch the two prizes he wanted most: promotion to the highest post in the army, and the opportunity to marry a woman with whom he had been having an affair for over a dozen years. In return he traded away the army's independence and his own authority as a true Commander-in-Chief.

Brauchitsch had tried for years to persuade his estranged wife to grant him a divorce. She agreed but insisted on a large cash settlement, refusing Brauchitsch's offer of monthly payments. Brauchitsch could not meet his wife's demand, and he feared a scandal if she contested a divorce action. His relationship with Charlotte Rueffer remained clandestine. Hitler knew of Brauchitsch's personal problems and was reluctant to make the appointment for fear of creating another Blomberg episode.

Hermann Göring, who learned that Brauchitsch's lady friend was an ardent Nazi, suggested a solution. Hitler gave Brauchitsch a large sum of money, enabling him to purchase his wife's agreement to an uncontested divorce. The amount is variously reported as between 80,000 and 250,000 Reichmarks. In return Brauchitsch agreed to a series of demands that gave Hitler total control over the army and the opportunity to make sweeping personnel changes by replacing many older anti-Nazi officers. Concurrent with Brauchitsch's appointment as Commander-in-Chief of the army, Hitler replaced the War Ministry with a new department called the Supreme Command of the Armed Forces (OKW), naming himself as its Commander-in-Chief and General Keitel as his Chief of Staff. Hitler's new post anchored him firmly in command of all armed forces of the Third Reich.

As the new Commander-in-Chief of the army, Brauchitsch had no authority to act freely. He had sold himself to Hitler, and regardless of his personal feelings toward the Nazis he was now Hitler's paid vassal and would do his bidding. Hitler intimidated Brauchitsch to such an extent that he once confessed to a colleague that when confronted by Hitler, "I feel as if someone were choking me and I cannot find another word."[2]

Walter von Brauchitsch was hardly suited to lead the army in revolt against the Nazis, nor was he capable of confronting Hitler with the growing dissent among his leading generals. Beck finally forced him to do what must have been the most difficult and uncomfortable thing he ever did: he showed Hitler Beck's memorandum of July 16. Brauchitsch stood paralyzed with fear as Hitler read Beck's memorandum with increasing anger.

Determined to clear out the diffident senior generals whom he labeled "disloyal" and anti-Nazi, Hitler called together a group of second-echelon field and staff officers from army and air force units. After an impressive meal Hitler delivered an impassioned three-hour speech calculated to win the officers' support for his military programs. He failed.

Hitler's listeners were not naïve. They knew of their senior generals' disdain for Hitler and knew also of the army's lack of readiness. The highlight of the meeting was "a most serious and unpleasant clash" between Hitler and General Gustav von Wietersheim. As designated Chief of Staff of the Army West under General Wilhelm Adam, Wietersheim objected to Hitler's plans based on his personal knowledge of the military situation on Germany's western frontier. With Germany's forces shifted eastward for the invasion of Czechoslovakia, Wietersheim told the Führer that the western defenses could not hold out more than three weeks against the expected attack from France.

Angered, Hitler shouted at Wietersheim that the position "will be held not only for three weeks but for three years." So incensed was Hitler by the hostility to his plans from these younger officers that this was the last meeting at which any officer would be permitted to discuss or question the Führer's plans. Five days later, Hitler told the senior military commanders that the Czech question would be settled by force. No one was permitted to voice a dissenting opinion.

Before this final decisive meeting, Beck remained hopeful he could convince his fellow officers to resign en masse as a protest against Hitler's plans. He now knew this was a futile hope. On August 18, 1938, Army Chief of Staff General Ludwig Beck took what he saw as the only step open to him. Beck told Brauchitsch that he must accept his resignation because Beck refused to carry out the duties of his office. Three days later, Brauchitsch informed Beck that Hitler had approved the resignation with the proviso that Beck keep it secret. Reluctantly, Beck acquiesced. No other general followed Beck's lead. Adolf Hitler privately savored this unexpected personal victory. He was free of Beck, about whom he once said, "The only man I fear is Beck. That man would be capable of acting against me."[3]

Beck was transferred to command the First Army, which was deployed to defend Germany's western frontier against a possible French attack. On October 19 he asked to retire from active duty, and he officially retired on October 31. No longer bound by the restraints of his active military command or his personal oath, Beck soon became the central figure in plans to overthrow the Nazi dictatorship.

Negative reaction to the forthcoming invasion of Czechoslovakia and the prospects of intervention by France and Britain was growing in other quarters. Anxiety over the implications inherent in Hitler's territorial ambitions spawned resistance in such diverse organizations as the Reich Foreign Ministry and the Abwehr. The growing controversy brought the Abwehr chief, Admiral Wilhelm Canaris, to what his biographer described as a turning point in his attitude toward Hitler.

Until war became inevitable, Canaris shared with his friend General Beck the belief that if Hitler could be persuaded to divorce himself from the Nazi movement he might become a reasonable and worthy German leader. Ironically, Canaris and his agents had covertly fueled anti-Czech feelings among the Sudeten Germans for years. Now his intelligence organization was assigned the task of placing agents inside the Sudetenland to organized pro-Nazi support in preparation for the invasions.

Finally realizing that Hitler's threat to crush Czechoslovakia was genuine and not a bluff to force concessions from the Czech government, Canaris lost all hope of dissuading Hitler. He now believed war could be averted only by convincing the Führer that attacking Czechoslovakia would result in a major conflict possibly greater in magnitude than the world war.

Canaris consulted his aide, longtime anti-Nazi, Lieutenant Colonel Hans Oster, who conceived the idea of sending an envoy to Britain's Prime Minister Neville Chamberlain with the desperate message that the only way to prevent war was to impress Hitler that Britain would fight against Germany over the sovereignty of Czechoslovakia. Such a declaration would also lend backbone to the French, who were afraid to act without British support.

The man chosen for the job was nominated by Oster, who seemed to know intimately the strongest and most dedicated anti-Nazis in Germany. Ewald von Kleist-Schmenzin (not to be confused with General, later Field Marshal, Ewald von Kleist) was a lawyer and a member of a respected family of landowners in Pomerania. As early as 1932, Kleist-Schmenzin had denounced National Socialism as "lunacy." It was, he stated time and again, "the deadly enemy" of the German way of life.

A dedicated anti-Nazi, Kleist-Schmenzin was a lawyer and had been a member of the provincial synod. A supporter of the National Party, he broke all connections with it in 1932 when the Party's leader, Alfred Hugenberg, backed Hitler for Chancellor. Nazi authorities twice arrested Kleist-Schmenzin in 1933. He subsequently retired from active public life rather than have anything to do with the Nazis.

Canaris provided Kleist-Schmenzin with a false passport and other documents to enable him to leave Germany and return safely. General Beck, just days before his own resignation, told Kleist-Schmenzin to bring back assurances that the British would fight to protect Czechoslovakia, "and I will bring about an end to this regime."

5.

Chamberlain and the September Coup

Kleist-Schmenzin's mission to Britain was a failure. He had gone to warn Prime Minister Neville Chamberlain and the British Cabinet that any concessions made to Hitler in the Sudetenland would surely encourage further aggression. Post-World War II survivors of the anti-Hitler resistance place much of the blame for the mission's failure on Nevile Henderson, the British ambassador to Berlin. Many of those who conspired against Hitler believed Henderson was "captivated" by Hitler and National socialism.

Before Kleist-Schmenzin left Germany, Henderson cabled the British Foreign Office that moderate elements of the German General Staff were sending a representative to London "to obtain material with which to convince the Chancellor of the strong probability of Great Britain intervening should Germany take violent action against Czechoslovakia." Henderson then advised his government that "it would be unwise for him to be received in official quarters."[1]

Responding favorably to this urging, British Foreign Secretary Lord Halifax issued instructions that while Kleist-Schmenzin "should not be rebuffed," no government official should take any initiative to see him. The fateful British policy of appeasing Hitler in the hope of buying peace in Europe was now firmly seated in London.

Kleist-Schmenzin did arrange a meeting with Robert Vansittart, the Permanent Undersecretary of State for Foreign Affairs, and opposition leader Winston Churchill. According to Vansittart's account of the meeting, Kleist-Schmenzin confirmed earlier intelligence reports the Undersecretary had passed on to Halifax. These reports contained convincing evidence that war between Germany and Czechoslovakia was imminent unless Britain took immediate preventive measures. When Vansittart asked Kleist-Schmenzin if Hitler was influenced by extremist elements, the German responded, "There is only one extremist and that is Hitler himself."[2]

Kleist-Schmenzin revealed that Hitler and Reich Minister for Foreign Affairs Joachim von Ribbentrop believed that neither France nor Britain would challenge Germany in a show down over Czechoslovakia. He then described for Vansittart the deep concern of many German citizens, politicians, and army generals who had no stomach for a senseless war. He pleaded for "one of your leading statesmen" to make a major speech emphasizing the consequences of the war that would follow a German invasion of Czechoslovakia.

Kleist-Schmenzin made clear to Vansittart that war with Czechoslovakia was inevitable. He said that Hitler was determined to use his military might to gain his ends and that only Britain's promise of intervention could prevent war. Kleist-Schmenzin's description of Hitler's fanatical determination to annex the Sudetenland was not unfamiliar to Vansittart, who in March 1936 had written a memorandum in which he warned that behind the German rearmament program was Hitler's plan to annex Austria, the Sudetenland, the Baltic states, and the Polish corridor separating Germany from East Prussia.

Vansittart sent Prime Minister Neville Chamberlain a detailed report of his meeting with Kleist-Schmenzin. The following day Chamberlain penned a note to Foreign Secretary Lord Halifax comparing the anti-Nazi emissary with "the Jacobites at the court of France in King William's time and I think we must discount a good deal of what he says."[3]

Chamberlain was determined to placate Hitler and preserve peace in Europe. Yet some of Kleist-Schmenzin's message impressed the Prime Minister, because he admitted to Halifax his feeling of uneasiness and confided that we "should do something." What Halifax did was to summon British Ambassador Nevile Henderson from Berlin to discuss the situation. Henderson, who shared Chamberlain's views on appeasement, refused to even consider issuing a public warning to Hitler. After the war Henderson wrote that the idea of such a warning was "dropped at my insistence" because he believed such a message would have "driven him [Hitler] right off the deep end," resulting in an immediate attack against Czechoslovakia.[4]

The day after his meeting with Vansittart, Kleist-Schmenzin met with Winston Churchill, who was at that time an ardent spokesman for anti-Nazi and anti-appeasement factions in Britain. The conversation with Churchill proved more fruitful. At Kleist-Schmenzin's request, Churchill wrote him a letter addressed simply, "My dear Sir," to protect the recipient's identity. In his letter Churchill stated, "I am sure that the crossing of the frontier of Czechoslovakia by German armies or aviation in force will bring about a renewal of the world war."[5]

Churchill went on to say that he was as certain as he had been in 1914 that England and France would march against Germany, and he hinted that the United States would lend its support to the democracies because it was "strongly anti-Nazi."

As a government outsider and a widely known critic of Chamberlain's foreign policies, Churchill had little influence on official thinking. His letter failed to have the impact Canaris and Beck had desired. Another blow to the German resistance leaders who saw strong British opposition to Nazi aggression as vital to their success was Henderson's declaration on August 6 that Britain would not risk "one sailor or airman for Czechoslovakia."

Traveling on his false passport, a dejected Kleist-Schmenzin returned to Germany and reported on his failed mission to Canaris and Oster. Two days earlier, in an attempt to gain support for Kleist-Schmenzin's appeal, Oster had dispatched a trusted emissary to petition the British military attaché in Berlin with the urgent message that Hitler could not survive the blow to his prestige if "firm action abroad" forced him to withdraw his claim in the Sudetenland. Ambassador Henderson dutifully forwarded the message to London, adding the damaging disclaimer that it was "clearly biased and largely propaganda."

While Kleist-Schmenzin pressed for British support, Canaris was busy trying to deter potential European allies from backing Hitler. With the connivance of State Secretary Baron Ernst von Weizsäcker of the Reich Foreign Ministry, Canaris and an outspoken anti-Nazi Abwehr officer, Major Helmuth Groscurth, met with Admiral Horthy, the Regent of Hungary. According to Groscurth's notes, Horthy was "firmly resolved to raise objections to the war" with Hitler. In Italy, Canaris met with the Chief of Staff of the Italian Army, General Alberto Pariani, who "strongly advised against war and will not take part."

During this period General Beck's resignation became effective and he was replaced by his deputy, General Franz Halder. A deeply religious and sensitive man, Halder came from a background steeped in military tradition. His family had a three-hundred-year history of producing ranking officers. Although Halder despised the Nazis and deplored their tyrannical rule over Germany, he also believed strongly in his personal oath of loyalty to Hitler.

Before Beck left the General Staff he confided to Halder about his relations with groups plotting against Hitler. He specifically stressed his liaison with Canaris and Oster, and he urged Halder to trust Oster's appraisal of the political situation. Oster had been a staff officer at Halder's headquarters in Munster when the latter was Chief of Staff of the IV Military District, and they held for each other a mutual trust and respect.

Halder, who shared Oster's resolve to prevent war with Czechoslovakia, was dismayed when he learned Kleist-Schmenzin's mission had failed. One of his first official acts as Army Chief of Staff was to send his personal emissary to London in the person of Hans Bohm-Tettelbach, a retired lieutenant colonel. Bohm-Tettelbach did not know about Kleist-Schmenzin's mission because of the tight security that surrounded it, but his efforts enjoyed even less success. Unable to penetrate the power structure in London, he turned to an old friend, English businessman Julian Piggot. A former Allied high commissioner in Cologne after World War I, Piggot still had some important contacts. One of these was a major in British military intelligence with whom he arranged a meeting for Bohm-Tettelbach. The substance of that meeting, which was relayed to Vansittart, reiterated the ominous warnings voiced by Kleist-Schmenzin. Again they fell on deaf ears.

Still another attempt to arouse British support for curbing Hitler was made by Ernst von Weizsäcker at the Foreign Ministry. Weizsäcker enlisted Theodor Kordt, a counselor in the German embassy in London, to appeal to his highest contacts in London.

Fearing exposure, Weizsäcker employed an intricate charade to communicate with Kordt. Kordt's brother Erich, who held a high post in the Foreign Ministry, sent a female cousin as the courier, helping her memorize the critical message for his brother, which she delivered flawlessly when she arrived in Britain.

When Theodor received the instructions, he called on Neville Chamberlain's close advisor, sir Horace Wilson, and requested a secret meeting with Foreign Secretary Lord Halifax. Halifax agreed, and on the evening of September 7, Kordt was admitted to 10 Downing Street through a rear garden entrance. Kordt prefaced his remarks with assurances that he was delivering a message from concerned political and military circles in Berlin who "desire by all means to prevent war."

The message he brought was yet another desperate appeal to the British government to stand firm against Hitler's planned aggression into Czechoslovakia. While earlier emissaries had merely hinted at a coup against Hitler, Weizsäcker's communiqué made the point unmistakably clear. It concluded with a promise of action by German army leaders opposed to the Nazis.

Lord Halifax received Kordt's message with close attention but less honesty than the German counselor would have liked. Halifax did not tell Kordt that the die of appeasement had already been cast and the decision to send the Prime Minister to Germany to meet with Hitler was already being made.

Some historians have questioned why German resistance leaders were so intent on winning support against Hitler from other nations, especially Great Britain. Some insight into this feeling of urgency for support is given by the memoirs of Fabian von Schlabrendorff, one of the few members of the resistance to survive the war. He wrote, "A tough stand against Hitler by the Western Powers would have strengthened our position immeasurably, and would have brought many still undecided or wavering generals and other key figures into our camp."[6]

These men were essentially a small minority in a totalitarian state that engaged freely in terror, imprisonment, and murder against its enemies, real or imagined. Members of the resistance were scattered throughout the army, the Foreign Ministry, the police, and nongovernmental circles. They could not meet in large numbers to engender support for their struggle against the Nazis without arousing Gestapo interest in them. Nor could many of them risk being seen with each other because of government restrictions. In a few cases, individuals were explicitly forbidden to communicate with one another, notably Generals Halder and Beck after Beck resigned his post and was transferred. Contact between different government agencies was strictly limited and in some cases forbidden, such as between officials of the Foreign Ministry and the General Staff, unless the individual involved was a liaison officer. Gestapo and SS secret police units worked ceaselessly to uncover opponents of the regime. Considering the overwhelming resources against them, it is miraculous that practically everyone who joined the 1938 resistance movement survived long enough to be executed by the Nazis in 1944 and 1945.

As efforts to court British favor continued abroad, in Germany plans went forward for a coup d'état against Hitler. The first formal discussions about a military coup probably took place in late August and most likely were initiated by Hans Oster. Because there could be no central organizational meeting of all the conspirators, planning the coup required a series of discussions involving a divergent group of people, each having his own theories about how and when a coup should take place and what kind of government should replace the Nazis.

General Halder met with Oster, communicated with Beck, and kept in close touch with Weizsäcker at the Foreign Ministry. Oster conferred with civilian supporters, including Dr. Hjalmar Schacht and Dr. Hans Gisevius. Other army officers involved in the anti-government movement pressured Halder to coordinate the planning.

Among the most ardent army officers calling for a coup were General Erwin von Witzleben, who commanded III Military District, which included Berlin, General Erich Hoepner, who commanded an armored division stationed in Thuringia, and Major General Walter Count von Brockdorff-Ahlefeldt, commander of the Twenty-third Infantry Division stationed in the Berlin suburb of Potsdam. These generals were supported by others who commanded troops at various locations throughout the Reich.

Some leading civilian advocates had tried and failed to organize a coup after the Fritsch affair earlier in the year, including Carl Goerdeler, Hjalmar Schacht, Hans Gisevius, Wolf Helldorf, and Fritz-Dietlof Count von der Schulenburg. The last two controlled police units that could lend support to the army. Absent from the planning of this coup was Carl Goerdeler, who was traveling abroad and trying to arouse other nations to the menace of Adolf Hitler.

Halder, Witzleben, and others attempted to win Brauchitsch's support, but the Commander-in-Chief appeared only lukewarm, possibly waiting to see which faction gained an advantage before supporting either one.

Hans Oster struggled diligently to bring the conspirators together. He arranged for General Halder to meet Schacht at the latter's home on Sunday, September 4. During that meeting Halder expressed concern that the coup must not lead to civil war between Nazi and anti-Nazi forces and that stable political conditions must be established quickly. Although he did not specifically voice his fear, it is likely that he felt a failed coup would spread chaos throughout the country, inviting intervention by France or even Czechoslovakia, whose 800,000-man army was massed near the border. In a surprisingly frank and open move, Halder asked Schacht if he was prepared to assume a key role in a new government. Schacht said he was.

The following morning, Halder pressed Oster about the availability of police forces to bolster the army troops supporting the plotters. Oster referred him to Hans Gisevius, an Oster confidant who had served in various police posts, including the Gestapo, and had strong influence with important police officials. A few days later, Gisevius visited Halder's apartment in Berlin-Zehlendorf. Gisevius was surprised at Halder's frank appraisal of the need to overthrow the government. He expected a more cautious Halder to use elusive or ambiguous language, but this forthright anti-Nazi rhetoric from the Chief of staff of the German army shocked Gisevius.

Before the meeting Gisevius determined not to defile Hitler directly because he knew many generals were fiercely committed to their personal oath of allegiance to Hitler and he was not sure of Halder's position on this. When he sought to soften Hitler's ruthlessness as simply flowing along with the current of events, Halder admonished him, calling Hitler a "madman" and referring to him as "this criminal." Citing the reported murders of concentration camp inmates, the General labeled Hitler "a bloodsucker" who was probably driven by a "sexually pathological constitution" to see blood flow.[7]

Gisevius promptly assured Halder that the majority of police forces, both criminal and security, held contempt for the practices of the Gestapo, and that the SS could be stopped and destroyed if the generals stood their ground against them.

Still mindful of the inner conflict created in many officers by their loyalty oath, Gisevius cautioned against a political justification for the coup. He maintained that a better approach would be to emphasize the criminal activities of Nazi government agencies such as the Gestapo. He told Halder that if the general's forces seized Gestapo headquarters he would need only a few hours to find all the evidence any court would require of the crimes of murder, extortion, deprivation of liberty, and corruption.

The two men settled on the concept of a coup and on basic strategy, but they disagreed on the timing. Gisevius was eager to depose Hitler as soon as possible, while Halder favored waiting until a specific incident damaged Hitler's credibility. Halder pointed out that Hitler was not without support among the lower ranking officers and troops, who would be expected to arrest and imprison him and other prominent Nazis. To his credit, Hitler had abrogated the hated Treaty of Versailles, occupied the Rhineland, and annexed Austria without the loss of a single German soldier in combat. Halder argued that a catalyst was needed to change the public reception of Hitler as a national redeemer, a major setback that Goebbels's propaganda machine could not whitewash. This setback might be a declaration of war by the Western powers against Germany or the actual outbreak of hostilities.

There was also a problem about what to do with Hitler. Halder was reluctant to order his execution, yet he would not have minded if someone killed him by planting a bomb, perhaps on his train once war started. It would be a simple matter to claim Hitler died in air raid. Halder did not want Hitler's blood on his hands.

Halter and Gisevius parted amicably, leaving unresolved the question of timing. The next morning Oster told Gisevius that Halder had instructed him to work with Gisevius to prepare a plan for police participation in the event the coup d'état was carried out.

A week or so later another meeting took place in Halder's apartment. Present were Oster, Gisevius, and Schacht. The three found the general's attitude toward the coup somewhat cooled. Although still supportive of a coup, Halder now questioned whether it would actually be necessary. Halder's motivation was not as intensely anti-Nazi as his guests expected. His main concern was to prevent a war that would destroy Germany. It was possible, he told them, that the Western powers would not interfere with Hitler's plans for Czechoslovakia, thereby reducing the risk of war and the necessity for a coup. If, however, a war was unavoidable, there would be ample time to execute the coup between the time Hitler ordered the army to prepare an invasion of Czechoslovakia and the order could be carried out.

All present recognized that once the army moved against Czechoslovakia it would be virtually impossible to reroute troops into Berlin for the coup. Moreover, some generals who supported the coup might have had second thoughts had the country been at war. To participate in a coup in those circumstances would be committing a treasonous act. Halder assured his guests that arrangements had already been made with Hitler's Military High Command that the Chief of Staff would receive notice at least forty-eight hours before the order was to be executed. This would provide leaders of the coup two days in which to forestall the war.

The meeting ended gloomily for Oster, Schacht, and Gisevius. To them Halder, although still ostensibly committed to the coup, was vacillating far too much. His passive "wait and see" attitude, not only about Hitler's plans, but also about the reactions of the Western nations, was unnerving. They decided to seek help from other generals to put pressure on Halder to push him forward.

One man they turned to was General Erwin von Witzleben, commander of the III Military District. There was a further vital need to censure the active participation of other generals. As Chief of Staff, Halder commanded no troops, he could not even issue orders to field commanders to move their troops. All orders involving troop movement had to come from Commander-in-chief Brauchitsch, who could not be counted on for support. Halder had hinted that when it was time to act he would either win over Brauchitsch or have him arrested and issue the orders in his name.

General Witzleben, aware that Halder might lack the resolve to give the order that would trigger the coup, was prepared to act independently of Halder, in which case the Chief of Staff would also be placed under arrest. Quickly the web of conspiracy reached out to envelop other generals around the country who agreed to participate in the coup or, at the least, to remain neutral.

Witzleben assigned Major General von Brockdorff-Ahlefeldt the responsibility of preparing a plan of action for the coup. Gisevius accepted the task of pinpointing critical installations from which a counter-coup could be launched, such as Gestapo facilities and SS garrisons throughout the Reich. These would be high-priority targets if a civil war was to be averted. He received invaluable help in this assignment from Arthur Nebe, Director of the Criminal Police Office of the Gestapo, who worked tirelessly to identify secret SS facilities and passed the information to Gisevius.

Witzleben took the bold and dangerous step of providing Gisevius with an office in his Military District Headquarters at 144 Hohenzollerndamm in Berlin. Gisevius was assigned a room that could only be entered through Witrzleben's office. Inside this sanctuary Gisevius reviewed in complete safety the secret maps and plans brought to him by Oster.

Major General Brockdorff-Ahlefeldt began work on the plan for the strategic dispersement of reliable troops in and around Berlin. For the coup to succeed, it was vital to take all important locations in the city, including the War ministry, the main radio transmitter, Gestapo headquarters, and the Chancellory, simultaneously, to prevent effective countermeasures by SS units. Gisevius helped to coordinate a comprehensive set of orders to be implemented to time with the coup. Every military district commander would receive instructions naming the facilities his troops were to occupy and which people to arrest or detain.

When the details were worked out and the facilities that needed to be occupied or neutralized were identified, the next step was to survey each location so Brockdorff-Ahlefeldt could estimate the number of troops each would require. Because the conspirators had only a limited number of troops, their proper deployment was extremely critical. Neither man could openly visit every location without creating suspicion. They avoided unwelcome attention by arranging to be driven around Berlin by Elisabeth Struenck, a sympathizer whose home would later become a central meeting place for the resistance. The tour proved of immeasurable value because it revealed that without support from the police there would not be enough soldiers to assure a successful coup.

Plans were solidified with certain commanders who were committed to initiate or support the actions in Berlin. General Erich Hoepner pledged to throw his armored division across the road between Munich and Berlin to prevent the SS Leibstandarte Adolf Hitler regiment from attacking the Berlin troops taking up positions in the capital.

In Berlin, Brockdorff-Ahlefeldt's own Twenty-third Division from Potsdam would carry the main thrust of the coup, occupying the primary targets and arresting a long list of key Nazi officials. His division was to be supported by troops from the Fiftieth Infantry Regiment under the command of Major-General Paul von Hase, who had been expressing a desire to take action against Hitler since the Fritsch affair.

As plans for the coup were finalized, Gisevius met secretly with Wolf von Helldorf, President of the Berlin Police, and his assistant, Police Vice President Fritz-Dietlof Count von Schulenburg. He extracted a promise that the police forces under their command would not act against the army and in fact might even be persuaded to support the troops.

At the hub of the action was General Witzleben. Once the coup was under way, Witzleben was to proceed directly to the Reich Chancellory, accompanied by several staff officers. Also with him were to be an escort squad of younger officers commanded by Major Friedrich Wilhelm Heinz, variously referred to as the "assault squad" and the "raiding party." If necessary, Chancellory gates were to be blown off by artillery. Inside, the plotters anticipated trouble with the SS guards employed to protect Hitler. The young escorts were charged with gaining access to Hitler's chambers using fire power if necessary.

Witzleben would confront Hitler, demanding his resignation. If the Führer refused, the escort would arrest him and take him out of the city to a predetermined covert location where he would be held until the coup succeeded. His ultimate fate had not yet been decided, but most senior believed he should be tried on charges of treason for committing Germany to a senseless war, or declared insane and committed to an asylum.

Major Heinz's force was the key to success. It consisted of elite young army officers, disillusioned Abwehr agents, idealistic students, and disgruntled workers. Admiral Canaris, who until now had relegated himself to the role of protector of Oster's activities and supplier of secret diplomatic information about the possibility of French and British resolve to declare war on Germany if Czechoslovakia was invaded, now took a more active role. He commandeered weapons and explosives from the Abwehr's arsenal and ordered them cached in secret "safe houses" around the city, available to Heinz's squad.

Little more is known about the detailed military plans for the coup. Except for General Halder, none of the ranking army officers who were involved survived the war. General Halder confessed that he left the details to Witzleben, keeping for himself only the final authority to issue the order that would begin the coup. Based on the training and background of the men involved, we can assume the strategy was sufficiently coordinated to allow a fair chance for success.

Everyone now waited for the order to come from General Halder, who in turn waited for Hitler's orders to prepare to attack Czechoslovakia before he would commit the coup's forces to action.

During this slack period the conspirators debated Hitler's fate. Halder opposed outright assassination, which might besmirch the army's reputation. If Hitler had to die, Halder preferred it to happen in some way not directly connected with the army or the army's actions in conducting the coup. Other senior officers, including Beck, Witzleben, and Canaris, wanted Hitler brought to trial for the crimes committed by his regime. They wanted the public to clearly understand what these crimes were, so the army could never be accused of stabbing Germany in the back, a reference to the "stab-in-the-back" theory expounded at the end of World War I and which Hitler used to great advantage in his rise to power. The theory, invented by Hindenburg and Ludendorf, held that democratic-minded politicians had stabbed the German army in the back, by calling for armistice, just when it was poised to win its greatest victory in the war.

Hans Oster and others, including Dr. Hans von Dohnanyi, wanted to have Hitler declared insane by a panel of doctors. Dohnanyi had been collecting evidence to submit to such a panel for over five years, and his psychiatrist father-in-law, Professor Karl Bonhoeffer, had already agreed to chair the panel.

Major Heinz and his well-armed escort team (which was to fight its way into the Chancellory) thought otherwise. In Heinz's words, "Hitler alive has more weight than all the troops at our disposal." His plan was to entice Hitler into some action that would provoke a gun battle in which the Führer would be killed.[8] At first Oster refused to go along with murdering Hitler, but Heinz's premise that a live Hitler was too dangerous a force to permit the establishment of a stable government in Germany was persuasive enough to win him over. They agreed, however, that no senior officer, not even Witzleben, was to know of their decision to kill Hitler.

By September 15, Heinz's assault squad was poised for action. They were secreted at the Berlin safe houses maintained by the Abwehr. Throughout Berlin and the surrounding suburbs military officers, police officials, and civilians, all members of the conspiracy to overthrow the Nazi regime, waited tensely for the word to begin. They all felt certain of three facts. First, that Hitler would issue the order to attack Czechoslovakia; second that Britain and France would declare war on Germany, or at least rattle enough sabers to make it clear that they were about to declare war; and third, that the coup would succeed in deposing the Nazis and the war would be prevented. What they did not expect was the willingness of Neville Chamberlain to throw Czech independence to the wolves and allow Hitler to do as he pleased.

The conspirators were certain that war was inevitable unless they removed Hitler from power. Then the unthinkable happened. British Prime Minister Neville Chamberlain decided to confer with Hitler personally. On September 14, Chamberlain announced in the House of Commons that he would meet with the Reich Chancellor the following day. The news stunned the world.

The British rejoiced that their Prime Minister was making this unprecedented move in a bid for peace. In the Czech capital Prague, newspapers headlines cried out that the British Prime Minister was "going begging to Hitler." In Paris, French Premier Edouard Daladier, who had not been told of Chamberlain's plans, called London to find out if the news was true. He was told that the trip was about to take place, and when he asked if he should also go to Germany, he was told to stay in Paris, that the matter was now in British hands. In Washington, President Roosevelt told Secretary of the Interior Harold Ickes that Chamberlain was for "peace at any price." He predicted that France and Britain would turn their backs on Czechoslovakia and "wash the blood from their Judas Iscariot hands."[9]

Germans, both members of the resistance and the general population, held their breath to see what Chamberlain was going to do. To many Germans it looked as if Hitler was about to win another bloodless victory. The conspirators held out hope that perhaps Chamberlain was coming to give Hitler a last warning to abandon his designs for war. Many thought it was a diplomatic mission on Chamberlain's part intended to show Hitler that he badly misjudged Britain's resolved to defend Czechoslovakia. How wrong they were.

Hans Gisevius wrote at the time that his greatest concern was that Chamberlain would push Hitler too far, causing one of the Führer's nervous breakdowns (these were known to occur before Hitler made important decisions). Gisevius wanted Hitler to issue the order to invade Czechoslovakia, giving the conspirators an excuse to strike him down. He did not want Chamberlain to force Hitler to back down, thus nullifying the necessity for the coup in the view of General Halder, on whom everything depended. The members of the resistance knew that if Hitler retreated on this issue now, it would only be temporary. He would strike at Czechoslovakia sometime in the future when he was even better prepared.

In the early hours of September 15, two planes took off from Heston Airport in England and flew a course toward Germany. The lead plane carried Neville Chamberlain and his party which included Sir Horace Wilson and sir William Strang.

Three hours later the planes landed at Munich, where they were welcomed by German Foreign Minister von Ribbentrop and British Ambassador Nevile Henderson. After inspecting an honor guard of SS Totenkopf troops ("Death's Head" concentration camp guards) at the airport, Chamberlain and his party embarked on the second leg of the trip, a train ride to Berchtesgaden. The road to the Munich train station was thronged with Germans who gave the motorcade the Nazi salute and shouted "heil" at "the tops of their voices." Transferring to the train, the party breakfasted in a dining car they were told was Hitler's private car. Throughout the entire trip they passed loaded troop trains ostensibly moving well-equipped German army troops around the country.

At Berchtesgaden Chamberlain again reviewed an SS honor guard before going to the Grand Hotel, where he and his party were given twenty minutes to freshen up before meeting Hitler. With incredible naiveté Chamberlain failed to realize that the entire trip, including the troop trains, was choreographed by the Nazis to impress him with the unity of the German people and the strength of the German army.

The drive from Berchtesgaden to the Berghof where Hitler waited was up a long mountain road lined with black-uniformed SS troops standing at stiff attention giving the Nazi salute.

Hitler greeted Chamberlain on the steps to his headquarters and invited the entire party to lunch in the building's great hall. After lunch Hitler and Chamberlain retired to an upstairs study accompanied only by Hitler's interpreter. The three hours of private conversation between Hitler and Chamberlain ended in a complete capitulation by Chamberlain concerning the Sudetenland, contingent on ratification by the British government and the French. In his account of the meeting Chamberlain wrote, "I had nothing to say against the separation of the Sudeten Germans from the rest of Czechoslovakia, provided that the practical difficulties could be overcome."[10]

The leaders of the coup knew nothing of what was happening at the meeting. It disturbed them that Hitler chose to receive Chamberlain at the Berghof instead of in Berlin because it placed him out of reach, well protected by the SS troops stationed in the area to impress the British. Nevertheless, they remained on alert for Hitler's next move and were ready to receive the order to begin the coup.

Chamberlain left Germany and returned to England with Hitler's demands for an autonomous Sudetenland. It had been easy for the British Prime Minister to see things Hitler's way. He had a low opinion of the Czechs, whom he considered "not out of the top drawer." He also had a low opinion of the French, so it was of little importance that the Czechs were allies of the French. They were all unimportant in the scheme of things, especially when the scheme of things was to avoid another war.

On September 17 Chamberlain met with the British Cabinet. He described the meeting with Hitler, recounting the experience "with some satisfaction," as Admiralty Lord Alfred Duff Cooper later recalled. The stage was now set to submit to Hitler's demand that the Sudetenland be separated from Czechoslovakia and annexed to Germany. Regrettably, Chamberlain failed to understand that Hitler was a bargainer who liked making deals. Instead of caving in to Hitler's demand, Chamberlain should have insisted that the Führer give something in return. When the Prime Minister left the Berghof, Hitler was in a jubilant mood at the result yet disappointed because he believed the victory had been won too easily. He realized he could have demanded more from the British and probably would have gotten it.

The coup conspirators observed the British Prime Minister's actions over the next few days with shock and disbelief. They had expected Britain to take a firm stand, but now it was apparent Hitler was going to get what he wanted simply for the asking. The tensions of anticipating the order to move against Hitler evaporated as despair and gloom settled over the conspirators, who saw their opportunity to drive Hitler from power and destroy the Nazi Party slipping from their grasp. Without a clear-cut act of war, General Halder would not order a coup, and despite General Witzleben's determination to act anyway, the conspirators were not certain they could rely on the commanders of army units beyond the garrisons in Berlin under these circumstances. Another bloodless victory would only increase Hitler's popularity, especially one made at the expense of the prestige of Great Britain, a nation that had never been popular with the German masses anyway.

In Britain the forces for appeasement mobilized to gather public support for Chamberlain's peace plan of giving Hitler what he wanted. Chamberlain's Air Minister, Sir Kingsley Wood, doctored a report from the Air Staff estimating that Germany's entire bomber force was under fifteen hundred planes, with less than one-third of them capable of being a threat to Britain in case of war. The altered report, which was leaked to the press, said that Germany was capable of sending fifteen hundred bombers against Britain, causing a half a million casualties in three weeks. Other Chamberlain supporters claimed there were barely enough firefighting equipment and hoses in London to fight peacetime fires, and certainly not enough to fight the conflagration that would result from the massive German bomber raids. The British public was painted a picture of skies darkened by masses of German bombers turning London and other major cities into infernos.

Chamberlain summoned Daladier, the French Premier, and Georges Bonnet, the French Foreign Minister, to London the day following his cabinet meeting. Since neither had a desire to plunge France into a war over Czechoslovakia, they quickly agreed with everything Chamberlain proposed. They reached agreement without consulting their respective cabinets, and they authorized a joint Anglo-French communiqué to Czechoslovakia warning the Czechs that if they stood up to Hitler they were going to have to do it alone.

> We are both convinced that, after recent events, the point has now been reached where the further maintenance within the boundaries of the Czechoslovak State of the districts mainly inhabited by the Sudeten-Deutsch cannot in fact continue any longer…and the safety of Czechoslovakia's vital interests cannot effectively be assured unless these areas are now transferred to the Reich.[11]

Members of the British and French cabinets who objected to this appeasement of Hitler's demands were assured that the Czechs would not be forced to accept the proposal, although it was clear that by their refusal they would forfeit any chance that France and Britain would come to their aid if the Germans invaded.

When the British and French ambassadors in Prague presented the proposal, Czech President Beneš was disgusted. Bitter at this abandonment by his allies, he refused to be mollified by new guarantees of Czech sovereignty by the British and French. He told his visitors that their previous guarantees had proved valueless and that there was no reason to expect new ones would be any better.

Beneš met with his cabinet the following day and presented the members with the Anglo-French proposal. To a man the cabinet denounced the proposal. The Inspector General of the Czech army and the Chief of the General Staff were asked to attend and give their evaluation of the army's ability to withstand a German attack. Both officers said it would be dangerous to risk a war with Germany without French support.

The Czech President was now caught on the horns of a dilemma. He and his cabinet pondered the options, exploring what they could possibly do next to assure their national survival. By now they understood that Hitler's ultimate goal was the destruction of their country. Trying to escape between the horns, President Beneš played for time as he and his cabinet sought a flat yes-or-no answer, searching for something that might prolong negotiations in the hope of finding another solution. Beneš knew there was opposition to the proposal in both the French and British cabinets; given time, such opposition might improve the situation. Also, his representative in Washington petitioned the State Department to issue a statement supporting Czechoslovakia.

On September 20 the Czech government declined to accept the Anglo-French proposal because it had been drawn without consultation with the Czech government and would mutilate Czechoslovakia both militarily and economically. Further, "the question of peace would in no way be settled." In this decision the Czechs demonstrated far more foresight than their erstwhile allies in London and Paris. The Czechs invoked the arbitration treaty that existed between Czechoslovakia and Germany.

Chamberlain flew into a rage when he received the Czech reply, and with the approval of his French allies he wrote a response that was delivered to Beneš's home at 2:00 a.m. in the morning of September 21 by the French and British ambassadors. Known as the "Dawn Demarche," the message stated that the Anglo-French proposal was the only way to avoid war and that the Czech reply placed full responsibility for war on the Czechs. It made clear that Britain would not fight for Czechoslovakia and that France would not honor its treaty commitment to come to the defense of Czechoslovakia if the British refused to help. It was cruelly explicit. Beneš's government now knew with certainty that it stood alone against Nazi Germany. There was no alternative except to capitulate and accept the proposal, or face a bloody war, Czechoslovakia capitulated.

A jubilant Chamberlain prepared for his next meeting with Hitler, and the German conspirators began to lose faith that their coup would actually have a chance to take place. But then the situation changed abruptly, and the coup attempt once again appeared a viable possibility.

When Chamberlain met Hitler on September 22 at Godesberg in the Rhineland, the Führer put on a display of temper that shook the British Prime Minister. Hitler refused to accept the Anglo-French proposal to which the Czechs had reluctantly acquiesced. In preliminary meetings with representatives of Hungary and Poland, Hitler exacted assurances that they were prepared to press their claims on Czech territory with military force. Hitler told Chamberlain that the claims of Hungary and Poland must be settled along with the Sudeten German question. Czechoslovakia was to be carved up by all her neighbors.

At the meeting, which was attended by Hitler, Chamberlain, and two interpreters, one German and one British, Chamberlain explained the proposal at great length. When he finished, Hitler asked if the Czechs had agreed to the proposal, although he already knew the answer. Chamberlain happily said they had. Hitler's terse response jolted the Englishman, "I am sorry but all that is no longer any use."[12]

Chamberlain was shocked and dismayed that all his efforts appeared to be for naught. Hitler called Czechoslovakia an "artificial structure" to which Germany, Hungary, and Poland had claims that must be resolved before there could be peace in Europe. Still determined to find a way to appease Hitler, Chamberlain asked him what he now wanted.

Hitler's new demands called for a new Czech boundaries based on the language of the local inhabitants. All Czech military, police, and other government agencies were to be pulled back beyond these borders and the territory occupied by German forces; a vote would be taken in the Sudeten area in which Germans who had migrated to the Reich would be permitted to vote, but Czechs living in the areas would be refused a vote. In addition, there would be no guarantees of a non-aggression pact between Germany and what remained of Czechoslovakia until the territorial claims of Hungary and Poland had been satisfied. Hitler showed Chamberlain a map of Czechoslovakia prepared by the Germans, outlining the new boundaries. It was obvious that Hitler planned to reduce Czechoslovakia to such a small state that it would no longer be a viable nation. Hitler's final statement was that his army was prepared to march into Czechoslovakia at a moment's notice (which was a bluff) but that he would extend his deadline for an agreement of his demands until October 1. If the situation was not resolved by then, Germany would invade Czech territory and take it by force.

Before he left for Germany, Chamberlain had concurred with his cabinet that if Hitler increased his original demands beyond those already stipulated, the Prime Minister would immediately return to Britain to consult the cabinet. Chamberlain chose to ignore this arrangement and remained overnight in Germany to meet Hitler the next day.

The following morning Chamberlain sent Hitler a note asking the Führer if he would agree to an arrangement in which Sudeten German forces would keep the peace in the Sudetenland, supervised by neutral observers, instead of using German forces. Hitler refused to budge from his position, demanding that German forces occupy the Sudetenland.

The two met again late that evening. Hitler gave Chamberlain a memorandum detailing his demands. After some quibbling over the date of withdrawal of Czech forces and the occupation by the German army, Chamberlain left, promising to take up Hitler's demands with his cabinet and the Czech government.

Things went badly for Chamberlain when he returned to Britain. Hitler's new demands met strong opposition in his own cabinet. Then the Czechs flatly refused to accept Hitler's blueprint to carve up their country. In a matter of a few days the Czechs announced a partial mobilization of their army, France recalled reservists to active duty, and Britain ordered a partial mobilization of its army and placed its navy on a war footing. Meanwhile, in Germany, resistance leaders closely monitored fresh troop movements toward the Czech border and watched Germany call up several more divisions to active duty. A new spirit grew within the movement as it saw renewed hope for the coup mirrored in these activities.

On September 24 Hitler returned to Berlin to the great relief of General Witzleben and his co-conspirators. Hitler was now accessible should the coup develop as the menace of war drew nearer. The assault squad was given a plan of the Chancellory by Police vice President count Schulenburg, whose intelligence reported no increase in security measures at Hitler's headquarters.

Two days later, on September 26, the British Foreign Office issued a press statement that put the coup forces on alert for action. The most important part of the statement, from the point of view of the coup leaders, read in part, "if in spite of all efforts made by the British Prime Minister a German attack is made upon Czechoslovakia the immediate result must be that France will be bound to come to her assistance, and Great Britain and Russia will certainly stand by France.[13]

It was the strongest statement yet against Hitler made by any power allied to Czechoslovakia. Surely now the people of Germany would see that Hitler's policies were leading Germany into another two-front war.

On September 27 Sir Horace Wilson met Hitler as Chamberlain's personal representative. Wilson gave Hitler a message from the Prime Minister in which the latter attempted to get Hitler to agree to cancel his invasion threat and continue negotiations to find a peaceful settlement. When Hitler refused to even consider Chamberlain's proposal, Wilson read him a "special message" from Chamberlain that stated clearly that if Germany attacked Czechoslovakia, France would fulfill its treaty obligations and come to Czechoslovakia's aid, and the British government would "feel obliged to support France."

In his reply the following day, Hitler refused to back down from his demand that German troops occupy the Sudetenland until a vote could be taken. Although he clearly rejected Chamberlain's request to modify his demands. Hitler's final sentence left the door open for further efforts by the Prime Minister. The reply appeared to indicate that Hitler might be having second thoughts about the will of the French and British to go to war over Czechoslovakia. If he was having such thoughts, they did not diminish his will for war. To help counter the lack of popular support for a war among the general population, Hitler ordered a "propaganda march" through the central part of Berlin late in the afternoon. It turned out poorly.

Crowds stood in silence as the troops marched and drove past, and even when Hitler appeared on his balcony to review the parade there was an absence of cheers or the raised hands of the Nazi salute. Hitler looked down at the sullen crowds and commented, "I can't make war with such a people."

That evening Hans Oster managed to get a copy of Hitler's reply to Chamberlain, and then next morning he sent it, via Hans Gisevius, to General Witzleben. Witzleben took it to Halder to convince the Chief of Staff of Hitler's determination to go to war. Tears ran down the emotional Halder's face as he read the reply. Halder took the message to Brauchitsch so he would also know that Hitler was no longer bluffing, that he was about to engage Germany in a war it was not prepared to fight. When Halder returned to his office he told Witzleben, who had waited there for him, that the Commander-in-Chief was "outraged and would probably take part" in the coup.

Using the telephone on Halder's desk, Witzleben immediately called Brauchitsch. He told him everything was in place and begged him to give the order for the coup. Brauchitsch said he wanted to defer the order for a coup until he had a chance to confront Hitler directly and demand to know his intentions. On the trip to see Hitler, Brauchitsch was informed that the Führer had issued a stay of the order to begin Operation Green, the code name for the invasion of Czechoslovakia. Relieved, Brauchitsch abandoned his mission and returned to his headquarters. He was grateful that events had removed the urgency for immediate, possibly reckless action against the head of state.

The coup was forestalled because Chamberlain had called his ambassador in Rome to ask Mussolini to act as peacemaker and help bring Hitler to the conference table once more. The Duce immediately sent Hitler a message, via his ambassador in Berlin, Attolico, telling Hitler that fascist Italy would stand behind the Führer whatever he decided to do, but requesting that he, Mussolini, Hitler, Daladier, and Chamberlain meet the next day to try to settle matters. Hitler agreed and set the meeting for the next day in Munich. A deal was in the making.

News of the Munich meeting swept through Berlin. Members of the coup conspiracy gravitated to Hans Oster's home to await developments and monitor the news. General Witzleben told the disheartened group, "You see, gentlemen, for this poor, foolish nation he is again our hotly loved Führer."[14]

At the Munich meeting Hitler renounced his plans to destroy Czechoslovakia. France and Britain allowed him to intervene in Czechoslovakia by occupying the Sudetenland with German troops. The real threat of war was averted. So, too, was the threat to Hitler's life that had been mounted by the coup's assault squad hidden in buildings all around the Chancellory. The assault squad was dispersed and their weapons returned to the Abwehr warehouse.

Everyone who knew of the planned coup recognized that the regular conscript troops would probably refuse to obey orders to arrest Hitler after such a great victory. Nevile Henderson, the Germanophile British ambassador, wrote to Lord Halifax, "by keeping the peace, we have saved Hitler and his regime."[15]

The leaders of the conspiracy met a few days after the Munich conference that gave Hitler all he had wanted without firing a shot. They gloomily burned their plans and maps in General Witzleben's fireplace. They realized, as Hans Gisevius later wrote, "Chamberlain saved Hitler."[16]

6.

A Coup to Save the Peace

Hitler's bloodless victory in Munich disheartened the resistance. Never before had Hitler's popularity been higher than when the Sudetenland was annexed to the Reich. Some of those who took part in the planned coup would never again consider such activities favorably. They felt betrayed by the Allies' spineless capitulation to Hitler's blackmail. Many questioned whether the French and British would ever summon the will to stand up to the Nazis until they themselves were invaded.

Others remained dedicated to the cause of overthrowing Hitler: men like General Witzleben, General Beck, Lieutenant Colonel Oster, Gisevius, Schulenburg, and Major Heinz. Joined by new resistance members, they regrouped to prepare for a renewed opportunity.

The British wildly celebrated Prime Minister Chamberlain's triumphant return to London waving the document that guaranteed "peace in our time." However, the German resistance knew he had not bought peace but had merely forestalled the war. Worse, he had given Hitler time to build his military might so that his next threatened strike would be no bluff. His forces would be unquestionably capable of accomplishing his objectives.

The full import of the Munich debacle did not become entirely clear until after the war. At the Nuremberg trials, Marshal Keitel was asked whether Hitler would have attacked Czechoslovakia had France and Britain taken a stronger stand behind the Czechs. Keitel, who served Hitler faithfully throughout the war answered, "Certainly not. We were not strong enough militarily."[1]

Following the Munich accord, Carl Goerdeler, the former Lord Mayor of Leipzig, wrote to a friend in the United States that Munich "was nothing but capitulation, pure and simple, by Britain and France before bluffing tricksters."[2] Goerdeler, who had resigned his post in Leipzig because the local Nazis demanded the removal of a monument to the Jewish composer Felix Mendelssohn from in front of the city hall, was out of Germany during the time of the Sudetenland crisis. He spent that time recruiting converts to the cause of the resistance or traveling throughout Europe and the United States campaigning for support in the effort to unseat Hitler.

In Britain, Winston Churchill was one of the handful of critics who denounced the Munich agreement. Speaking in the House of Commons, he condemned the accord, calling it "an awful milestone" in British history. He was soon proven correct.

The general euphoria was short lived. By mid-October 1938, Hitler's army and air force began preparations for the military takeover of the remainder of Czechoslovakia. He had not wavered in his determination to destroy this little democracy on his eastern border. Poland, itself soon to fall victim to Hitler's aggression, now led a carrion pack that demanded the wounded and isolated Czechoslovakia hand over the district of Teschen. Hungary joined in as its neighbors tore at Czech territory in a virtual feeding frenzy.

Under pressure from Berlin, whose troops occupied the Sudetenland, Czech president Beneš resigned and left the country. He remained in exile until the end of the war. Thee Czech National assembly appointed Dr. Emil Hacha, a nearly senile sixty-six-year-old man who would easily be cowed by Hitler, to the presidency. The spelling of the country's name was officially changed to "Czecho-Slovakia" in recognition of the new semi-autonomy of its regions that had been forced on it by Nazi agents. All this was part of Hitler's scheme to completely destroy the nation.

The Munich agreement established an international commission to settle all disputes involving Czech territory. This commission decided every dispute in Germany's favor, even sanctioning cancellation of the referendum in the Sudetenland agreed to by Hitler and Chamberlain. The people living in the newly occupied territory had been promised the right to vote on the annexation issue. That promise was cruelly broken and the people were given no option except to become part of Germany.

The Munich agreement spelled the end for Czechoslovakia. Germany was ceded 11,000 square miles of Czech territory without the Czechs having a role in the negotiations. They were simply told by their allies that the agreement had been drawn. Living in the territory given to Germany were 2,500,000 Sudeten Germans and 800,000 Czechs. Czechoslovakia lost all its important fortifications, leaving it defenseless against German aggression. In addition, it lost 66 percent of its coal reserves, 70 percent of its electric power, 70 percent of its iron and steel, and 40 percent of its timber. As William Shirer reported, "A prosperous industrial nation was split up and bankrupted overnight."[3]

The spring of 1939 brought the end of Czecho-Slovakia. On March 14, under extreme pressure from Berlin, the provincial parliament of Slovakia declared its independence and placed itself under the protection of the German Reich. The following day President Hacha was summoned to Berlin and told that German troops were already marching on Prague. If the Czech army did not surrender, the capital city would be leveled by German bombers. The helpless, frightened old man saw no way out for his countrymen, now completely at Hitler's mercy. He ordered the Czech troops to surrender to the Germans, and on March 16 Hitler announced the creation of the Protectorates of Bohemia and Moravia. Czecho-Slovakia ceased to exist.

Other than registering half-hearted protests, Britain and France did nothing about Hitler's violation of the much-heralded Munich accord. Hitler was convinced the Western Allies had no stomach for a military confrontation with Germany.

The German resistance was still determined to remove Hitler; however, they felt virtually powerless without outside support, if even only moral support. Without the threat of military retaliation against German aggression, a coup faced the real possibility of hostility from the general population and even the ranks of the German army itself.

In early spring 1939, Adolf Hitler continued to build on the acquisitions he had acquired. Shortly after Czechos-Slovakia was dissected, German troops went into what was called Memelland, a strip of territory along the East Prussian border that had been annexed to Lithuania by the Versailles treaty. Its capital, Memel, once a great fortress city of the Teutonic Knights, was surrendered to the Reich by Lithuania under threat of a German invasion. On March 23 Hitler occupied the territory, scoring yet another bloodless victory. That same month a trade treaty negotiated between the Reich and Romania effectively brought that country's economy under German control.

On May 22, 1939, Germany and Italy signed the notorious Pact of Steel. Non-aggression agreements with Latvia, Estonia, and Denmark neutralized any resistance to further German expansion from those countries. On August 23 Hitler accomplished his greatest diplomatic coup: The Soviet Union signed a non-aggression pact with the Reich, eliminating the greatest deterrent to Hitler's eastward expansion. Both governments shared a common interest in Poland, which Hitler and Stalin secretly agreed to divide between them.

During the period between the signing of the Munich accord and the invasion of Poland on September 1, 1939, the resistance movement, which had been less an organized movement and more a disjointed series of anti-Nazi or anti-war groups and individuals who had managed against all odds to unite in the 1938 coup, suffered its own dismemberment Military officers were moved to new postings, and government officials, especially those in the Foreign Ministry, were transferred to new locations throughout the Reich. These changes were the result of normal promotions and changes of assignments, not the result of exposure of the activities of the people involved.

At the Foreign Ministry, Weizsäcker and Kordt used their offices to place resistance supporters in German embassies in countries that were traditionally neutral. This afforded them both a foreign listening post and access to neutral or even enemy intelligence agencies with whom the resistance might want to communicate at a later date.

On the domestic front, Hitler, now safe in the assumption that the Allies lacked the will to interfere, unleashed an insidious persecution of the Jews living in Germany in what was the worst pogrom since the Middle Ages–and what ultimately became the worst in the history of mankind. Its goal was the annihilation of the Jews. The campaign began on November 9, 1938. Although anti-Jewish measures were already in place, the Nazis found an opportunity to wrap their pogrom in a national cause in an effort to gain popular support for confiscating Jewish property and oppressing German Jews.

Ironically, that cause centered on the murder of an anti-Nazi German official who at the time of his death was actually under investigation by the Gestapo for his views. On November 7, Herschel Grynszpan, a seventeen-year-old Jewish student living in Paris, upset because his family, which had lived in Hanover, Germany, for twenty years, was deported to Poland by the Nazis, resolved to avenge this treatment by killing the German ambassador in Paris.

Grynszpan arrived at the embassy on the Rue de Lille looking like "a schoolboy, a worried one," as one of the guards described him. He told the guard he had an important message for the official at the embassy who dealt with German secrets. After a brief hesitation the guard took him to the embassy's second floor, where they found a junior staff member opening the morning's mail. The man was a third secretary named Ernst vom Rath, a protégé of Weizsäcker and Kordt, and part of their anti-Nazi circle in the Foreign Ministry.

The guard withdrew, leaving the two together in Rath's office. Moments later Grynszpan took a revolver from his raincoat pocket and fired five times, fatally wounding Rath, who died two days later. Prodded by Propaganda Minister Joseph Goebbels who called Grynszpan "a creeping, cunning, unscrupulous Jew," the Nazis used the murder as an excuse for their hostility toward the Jews.

Hitler made the Jews scapegoats for his failed domestic economic policies, while his successes in foreign affairs fueled his popularity, which soared to an all-time high. Resistance leaders were handcuffed because of Hitler's increased popularity. They feared an overt act to forcibly remove Hitler could ignite a civil war. The specter of civil conflict now hung over the resistance movement's every step. It influenced important decisions by coup planners and caused some to quit the resistance.

Another serious reversal was the unforeseen transfer of the resistance's most important general, Erwin von Witzleben, to command group headquarters 2 in Frankfurt on Main in November 1938. Although the transfer removed Witzleben from control of the troops in Berlin, he was able to convert his new Chief of Staff, Major-General Georg Sodenstern, to the cause. Together the two decided that a coup was the only way to prevent a war more terrible than the world war; but they realized that as long as so many Germans supported Hitler, a coup had little chance of success. They would wait for the opportunity to present itself in the form of a real war that would undermine Hitler's popular appeal. While they waited they worked to expand the number of officers involved, and they began laying plans for making their coup as widespread as possible. They devised strategies to arrest regional Nazi leaders, called Gauleiters, and to control all newspapers and radio transmitters.

Meanwhile, Weizsäcker impressed on Foreign Minister Ribbentrop the importance of having Foreign Ministry "presence" in other government agencies and key military commands. Ribbentrop enthusiastically approved the suggestion, which he believed would permit him to insinuate himself into areas beyond his direct influence. Weizsäcker and Kordt appointed resistance members and supporters as liaison officers in critical posts. These men served a dual role. Ostensibly they were representing the Foreign Ministry, but secretly they acted as intermediaries between the Foreign Ministry resistance circle and the opposition groups inside the agencies to which they were posted. In this way Weizsäcker and Kordt successfully developed a network of trusted operatives throughout the civilian government and in military commands across the Reich. One of the most important of these postings was that of Hasso von Etzdorf as liaison at OKW, the Supreme Command of the Armed Forces, which was under Hitler's personal direction.

Three additional appointments vital to the resistance were Albrecht von Kessel to General Kurt von Hammerstein's command in the west; Ulrich Count von Schwerin to General Witzleben's command, also in the west; and Baron von der Heyden-Rynsch to the Army High Command, OKH. Heyden-Rynsch's position enabled him to devote considerable time at Abwehr headquarters coordinating activities with the dedicated Lieutenant Colonel Hans Oster.

On another front, General Beck and Carl Goerdeler met with Wilhelm Leuschner, a former trade union leader and ex-Social Democrat, to win his support for the coup. They convinced him to join forces with the military resistance against Hitler; and once in the fold, Leuschner accomplished a near impossibility. He brought together in a united effort union leaders of long-held diverse political views who secretly contacted their former members (all such independent unions having been outlawed by the Nazis), urging them to join a strike against the government in support of an anticipated coup. To win this vital support, Beck promised Leuschner the Nazis would be replaced not by a military or reactionary dictatorship but by a representative government. It was a relatively safe promise because except for a scattering of monarchists, most resistance leaders favored a democratic form of government.

While the resistance reorganized, Hitler pursued his designs for conquest. His next objective was former ally Poland. After triumphs in the Rhineland, Austria, Sudetenland, Czechoslovakia, and Memelland, Hitler enjoyed unprecedented popularity at home. He had watched the Allies stand by and do nothing in the face of his earlier aggression, and it was reasonable to expect that despite rumblings from the French and British they would not interfere with his plans for Poland.

Germany's dispute with Poland was based on agreements made as part of the Treaty of Versailles. The German city of Danzig, on the Baltic Sea, was proclaimed an open city under the protection of Poland, and a ninety-mile strip of land connecting Poland with the Baltic Sea was taken from Germany and given to the Poles. This unnatural breach, known as the Polish Corridor, cut directly through Germany, separating the main portion of the country from the province of East Prussia. It was as if an internationally enforced treaty gave Canada a stretch of land sixty-five miles wide running from Canada's border through Vermont and New Hampshire to the Atlantic Ocean, separating the state of Maine from the rest of the United States. Anyone looking at a pre-1939 map of Europe could not fail to see the potential danger that existed in the partition of Germany by territory ceded to Poland.

Hitler demanded of Poland that Danzig be returned to Germany and that Germany be given a secure route through the Corridor, providing a land link between Germany proper and East Prussia. The Poles refused his demands and sent troops toward Danzig in an unwise display of force. To make matters worse, they threatened Hitler with war if he persisted in his demands.

On September 1, 1939, using the fabricated excuse that Polish troops had crossed the frontier and attacked a German radio station, German troops invaded Poland. The dead men in Polish uniforms found at the radio station were actually concentration camp inmates sent there by the SS to stimulate an attack.

The coming of war, followed two days later by declarations of war against Germany by Great Britain and France, generated a flurry of activity among officers and others who felt that Germany was doomed unless Hitler was dead. In one instance, Albrecht von Kessel and Adam von Trott zu Solz, both members of Weizsäcker's Foreign Ministry circle, proposed to Lieutenant General Alexander von Falkenhausen that he invite Hitler to inspect the fortifications on the Bohemian border. Once there, Hitler's schedule would include a tour of a bunker where the general or a close aide would detonate a live grenade. The scheme was a bit bizarre, and Falkenhausen, although a coup sympathizer, did not think the plan was workable. He never sent the invitation.

Hitler did receive another invitation, however. This one was from Colonel General Kurt von Hammerstein-Equord, an independent-minded and tough officer who despised Hitler and the Nazis. Having retired as Commander-in-Chief of the army in 1933, he was recalled during the mobilization for the Polish invasion and appointed commander of Army Detachment A on the Lower Rhine. Although frustrated because his headquarters was in Cologne, far from Hitler, Hammerstein-Equord began plotting ways to kill Hitler as soon as he arrived at his command.

Since it was impossible for him to travel to Berlin without express permission, Hammerstein-Equord decided to invite Hitler to visit him. His persuasion for this visit was that the Allies would hear about Hitler inspecting the western defenses, and this would encourage their belief that Germany's western frontier was well defended. Once he lured Hitler within his reach, he would "render him harmless once and for all." Confidants who knew of his intention to kill Hitler did not doubt that this general, known as the "man of iron nerve," could do it if Hitler accepted his invitation.

Hoping to prevent the Allies from attacking Germany before he had a chance to kill Hitler, Hammerstein-Equord elected to advise them of his plan. He sent his aide, Lieutenant Colonel Egon Sterm von Gwiazdowski, to see Fabian von Schlabrendorff, a trusted member of the resistance, and ask him to deliver the message. Schlabrendorff had won the respect of the British during the Czech crisis when he made several trips to London to stiffen British resolve. Both the allies and the German resistance admired him.

Schlabrendorff received the general's request on the same day that Britain's ultimatum that Hitler retreat from Poland or face war with Britain and France expired. At considerable personal risk he arranged to meet the counselor of the British embassy for lunch at Berlin's Hotel Adlon. Sir George Oglivy Forbes listened with great interest while Schlabrendorff told him of Hammerstein-Equord's plan. Suddenly two SS officers entered the dining room and spoke with the headwaiter, who nodded toward the table where Schlabrendorff and Forbes sat. As they approached there were several tense moments for Schlabrendorff, who was after all having lunch with a representative of a country now at war with Germany. The SS officers paid no attention to their countryman, but instead they spoke briefly to Forbes concerning the details of the embassy's withdrawal of its personnel.

Adolf Hitler was acutely aware of General Hammerstein-Equord's sentiments toward the Nazi Party, and he had no wish to jeopardize his safety by placing himself within the general's reach. He declined to visit Cologne. Shortly afterward, Hammerstein-Equord was transferred to Silesia, and then quickly placed into permanent retirement. Before he died in April 1943, he confided to a friend his disappointment at the generals' placid submission to Hitler's authority, and how most refused to support the movement to overthrow the Nazis. "These fellows," he said, "make me, an old soldier, an anti-militarist."[4] It is unfortunate that in 1938, when the case for action against Hitler became apparent, Hammerstein-Equord had no troops under his command and could not carry out an earlier pledge to kill Hitler if he were given troops.

As Hitler brought Germany closer to war in the late summer of 1939, the resistance was virtually powerless to stop him. Most general officers who supported a coup either commanded troops they felt were unreliable or were stationed too far from the capital to participate effectively. Poland was invaded by both Nazi Germany and the communist Soviet Union, and within a matter of weeks it was conquered and partitioned.

Although both Britain and France declared war on Germany after the invasion of Poland, except for a minor incursion into German territory by a French force that quickly withdrew, the Allies took no direct military action against Germany. Their strongest show of force was a Royal Navy blockade of German ports. This absence of real war, which later became known as the "phony war," gave many Germans hope of escaping another war of the magnitude of the 1914 to 1918 conflict. The absence of actual fighting between the Allies and Germany gave rise to the premise that a compromise could be found to re-establish peace.

All possibility for a peaceful solution vanished on September 27, 1939, when the Führer told the officers commanding the army, air force, and navy that he was determined to "destroy the enemy." He would, he told them, attack France and Great Britain. The neutrality of Belgium and Holland would be swept aside as German forces overran the French in their own country, leaving Great Britain to carry on alone.

As word spread of Hitler's intention to start a shooting war with the Western Allies, the resistance was given a new life and a new cause, to save the peace by preventing a war almost every competent observer knew would ultimately mean the destruction of Germany. Many of the men now proposing to depose the dictator had also been invoked in the aborted coup of September 1938. Again they risked the possibility their actions might result in a civil war between their camp and the masses of new army recruits and the civilian population, most of whom viewed Hitler as a modern Caesar. In addition, what weighed heaviest on General Halder's mind was the fact that Germany was now officially at war with Great Britain and France. He did not want a coup attempt to cause turmoil within Germany that the Allies could exploit by invading the country during the transition from one government to another.

In an effort to neutralize the danger that an Allied invasion might prevent the anti-Nazi forces from consolidating their control of the country, Weizsäcker arranged the appointment of Erich Kordt's brother, Dr. Theo Kordt, to the German embassy in Berne, Switzerland. As a member of the German embassy staff in London a year earlier, Dr. Kordt had tried unsuccessfully to persuade the British government to stand up to Hitler in the Sudetenland crisis. His assignment now was to re-establish a rapport with his British friends and attempt to secure a British pledge that the Allies would not intervene in a coup unfolding in Germany.

It is significant that the men who planned the overthrow and killing of Hitler did so because they were German patriots. While they had no quarrel with many of Hitler's earlier policies, especially reclaiming territory taken from Germany by the treaties following World War I, they did not want to acquire the land by force. Many believed that despite their just cause, force would lead to retaliation against Germany and finally to another war, perhaps another world war.

Before he left London on August 31, the eve of war, Dr. Kordt met secretly with Sir Robert Vansittart, chief Diplomatic Advisor to the Foreign Secretary. The meeting was held at the home of Dr.

Philip Conwell-Evans. The three agreed that the only way to avert war was to overthrow Hitler and establish a non-Nazi government in Germany. Hoping to maintain a link between the German resistance and the British government, they arranged for a secret communication that would permit the Englishmen to know which neutral country Kordt had been assigned. Kordt would send a postcard to either Conwell-Evans, Vansittart, or the latter's secretary, a Miss Dogherty. The card which would be unsigned, would have the postmark of a city in which Kordt would meet Conwell-Evans fourteen days later. The message on the card would be a short verse from Horace.

Unfortunately for the resistance, their British contacts were less than reliable and (perhaps) even less concerned with aiding them to eliminate Hitler. Conwell-Evans was by then employed by the British Secret Service, whose only interest in his contacts with Dr. Kordt was to learn what he could about German war plans. Vansittart spent a great deal of time after the war condemning all Germans for the crimes of the Nazis and was an early advocate of the doctrine of collective guilt. Also after the war, Hans Gisevius wrote that Vansittart might have "prevented terrible evils" if he had taken seriously the efforts of the German resistance.

When Dr. Kordt arrived in Switzerland he sent the prearranged postcard from Interlaken. He and Conwell-Evans missed each other at first but later were able to meet during the last week in October. Conwell-Evans brought with him an extract from a recent speech by Chamberlain in which the Prime Minister said that the British were not fighting the German people but the tyrannical government that ruled their country. He also brought from Vansittart a mandate that the German resistance must establish a government the British could negotiate with in good faith.

Mrs. Kordt took the messages to Berlin and gave them to her brother-in-law, Erich, who relayed them to Hans Oster at the Abwehr. Oster instructed Erich to take them to General Beck's house the following day, which he did. Next they were forwarded to General Halder by way of Major Helmuth Groscurth of the Abwehr, the officer who had supplied the arms that were to be used by the assault squad in the 1938 coup attempt.

Halder later denied ever seeing the documents; however, considering that he was simultaneously preparing for both a war and a coup, his distraction is understandable. In any event, the documents did not carry the weight the German resistance, anxious for British support, placed in them. The critical ingredient, assurance that the Allies would not attack Germany during the coup, was missing; and it would never be supplied because the British and French governments put no stock in the reports of a likely anti-Nazi coup in Germany.

During the next few months Hitler vacillated in implementing his projected invasion of neutral Holland, Belgium, and Luxembourg. His decision to violate their neutrality to provide an easier route to attack France raised opposition from a source that surprised members of the resistance, General Walter von Reichenau.

An early admirer and supporter of Hitler, Reichenau, an intelligent, politically astute, and independent officer, began having second thoughts about the Führer during the Polish campaign when SS units nominally under his command slaughtered several hundred Jewish men, women, and children in the town of Radom. Reichenau ordered a military investigation of the incident and wrote a letter to Hitler complaining about the SS and telling him he no longer wanted such units in his command. Other German generals also complained to Hitler about the actions of SS units attached to their commands. The result of these complaints was that Himmler succeeded in convincing Hitler to remove all SS units from even nominal control of army officers and to place them directly under Himmler's command. Freed of any constraints that the army generals might have had on them, the SS went on a bloody rampage in Poland, killing thousands of Poles, Jews and Christians alike.

Reichenau considered the violation of neutral countries a "criminal" act that was to be avoided. During a meeting with Hitler on October 25 he told the Führer how he felt. Hitler countered with his own opinion that the British, once they were on the continent in sufficient strength, would violate Belgian neutrality to attack Germany. Reichenau replied that he would rather see the British violate a neutral country than have Germany do it. Hitler brushed off his objections, as he did similar objections from

General Fedor von Bock, General Wilhelm von Leeb, and General Gerd von Rundstedt.

When Hitler named November 12 the date for the attack through the Low Countries, Reichenau tried again to dissuade him. He met with Hitler on November 2 and again on November 5, but he failed to change the Führer's mind. The following day Reichenau, long considered a Nazi general by members of the resistance, did something totally unexpected. He contacted Carl Goerdeler, the former Lord Mayor of Leipzig and civilian member of the resistance, and arranged to meet him at the home of one of Goerdeler's associates, Fritz Elsas. Reichenau told the two of Hitler's plans to violate the neutrality of the Low Countries, calling it "crazy." He then suggested that the governments of the three countries and Great Britain be contacted and informed of Hitler's plans. It was his hope that they could take defensive measures that would make it clear to Hitler that the attack would not be a surprise. To this end he suggested that the Dutch make an effort to visibly increase defensive measures around their dikes and canals. The information was passed on by Elsas as the general had suggested.

The next day Hans Oster told his friend, Major Gijsbertus Sas, the Dutch military attaché in Berlin, that Hitler would attack Holland on November 12. During the ensuing months Hitler kept rescheduling the date for the invasion, and as Oster learned the fresh date he told Sas, who passed the information to his government. Unfortunately, Hitler's indecision and constant date switching made Sas look foolish. He lost credibility with his superiors, and when the invasion finally did take place on May 10, 1940, Dutch military authorities who ignored Sas's warnings the previous day were taken by surprise.

By late October 1939, General Halder was surrounded by coup conspirators. His deputy and senior quartermaster of the General Staff, General Karl Heinrich von Stulpnagel, was an active participant in urging Halder to begin planning for a new coup attempt to avoid a shooting war with the Allies. Other officers of colonel and lower rank rallied behind Stulpnagel, including one, Lieutenant Colonel Henning von Tresckow, who would eventually head a future conspiracy to kill Hitler. Hans Oster's representative at OKH—the Army High Command—was Major Helmuth Groscurth, officially the Abwehr liaison. Weizsäcker's contact with the General Staff was the Foreign Ministry liaison, Dr. Hasso von Etzdorf. Both liaisons were responsible for keeping the General Staff aware of diplomatic and political events that affected the military's position but to which the generals might not otherwise be privy. All these resistance forces, whether in the Abwehr, the OKH, or the Foreign Ministry, looked to retired General Ludwig Beck as their leader.

The fall and winter months of 1939 and early 1940 were charged with apprehension for the resistance. Hitler's constant juggling of the date for the attack in the west kept his domestic enemies edgy. As each new date was fixed, the coup leaders reacted with increased tension not unlike the anticipation felt by soldiers who, knowing an attack is about to start, wait tensely for the final order to begin. After each emotional high of preparation there was a letdown in frustration as Hitler once again postponed the attack. Further, many resistance members saw this interval as their last opportunity to elicit from the Allies an agreement to refrain from attacking Germany while a coup was in process. They expected that after the violation of neutral countries and the spilling of French and British blood, the Allies would be in no mood to deal with any Germans, Nazi or not.

The relationship between Halder and his superior, Brauchitsch, so crucial to the success of a coup, suffered during this period. It must be recalled that as Chief of Staff, Halder had no authority to order troop movements. Only the Commander-in-Chief had authority to do that. Another, bolder personality in Halder's place might have surmounted this obstacle, if necessary, by issuing the orders in Brauchitsch's name should he refuse, but Halder did not have that strong determination. During October and November, although Halder constantly kept a loaded pistol in his pocket, he could not call up the courage to use it against Hitler.

At the end of September, Halder and Brauchitsch clashed over the reports of atrocities committed against the Poles by SS and Gestapo groups sent there by Himmler. Halder offered to resign as

Chief of Staff to accept a field command, but Brauchitsch broke down at mention of this and pleaded with Halder, "How am I to contend with this man [Hitler] without your help?"[5] Halder relented and stayed on. Had he left the post it is difficult to conjecture who would have been appointed in his place, but considering Brauchitsch's inability to cope with Hitler it is likely a new Chief of Staff would have been a Nazi or at least a pro-Nazi.

Halder's lack of courage in facing the situation was known to everyone involved. On September 29, Stulpnagel pressed Halder to be prepared to sequester Brauchitsch if necessary and assume command when it came time to issue the coup order. Halder replied that he did not think the field commanders would obey him. Stulpnagel disagreed and volunteered to interview the key commanders, Rundstedt, Bock, and Leeb. Stulpnagel made a tour of their western front commands to determine their attitude.

Rundstedt said he was unable to join a coup because he did not believe enough of his officers would join him. Leeb told Stulpnagel he was ready to act when the order was issued. There is no record of Bock's reply. The key, though, to a successful coup was the man who commanded troops in the Berlin area, not the commanders miles away on the western front. Halder knew that to succeed he would require the cooperation of the commander of the Replacement Army, General Friedrich Fromm.

Halder spoke to Fromm quite openly on October 3 when the latter was on a regular visit to OKH headquarters. He told Fromm he was considering the possibility of arresting Hitler and toppling the current government as a way of obtaining a peaceful settlement to the war before the actual shooting began. Fromm did not respond to the comment, but he later called Brauchitsch and reported the conversation to him.

On October 14 Halder and Brauchitsch met to discuss what position OKH should take concerning the impending attack across the neutral countries of Western Europe. They concluded that they had only three options: They could do nothing and follow orders to attack; they could sit tight and hope that something would happen to change Hitler's mind; or they could engage in a "basic trans-formation," which was a euphemism for a change of government.

Both men rejected the first option, to simply follow Hitler's orders and launch the attack when he instructed them to do so. Brauchitsch rejected the idea of a forced change of government because it was a "negative" response to the situation and would leave the country vulnerable to attack. So both men decided jointly that their best course of action was to await further events. At this critical juncture they decided to do nothing.

Halder apparently recognized that doing nothing was not a real option, because he actually began taking steps leading to the second coup attempt against Hitler in which he was a key figure. Planning for a coup now went on in two locations, one under Oster's guidance at Abwehr headquarters, and the other at OKH headquarters in Zossen, outside of Berlin, where it had recently been moved. Halder placed General Stulpnagel in charge of coup planning at OKH His planning group included Groscurth, who acted as liaison with the group at Abwehr; General Erich Fellgiebel, chief of OKH communications; Hasso von Etzdorf, the Foreign Ministry liaison officer; and Colonel Eduard Wagner of the General Staff. Halder also made use of the only troops over which he had command, those using the army transport service. He discovered that two armored divisions were en route from the east to the western front. Explaining that he wanted to provide them with new equipment, he had their movement delayed and instructed the transport officer, Colonel Rudolf Gercke, to hold them not far from Berlin.

Although Halder gave in to pressure from all quarters to have plans firmly in place should he decide to strike, he was never fully convinced he would go through with it. He constantly wavered between resolve and resignation. Following a visit with the Chief of Staff, Admiral Canaris returned to Abwehr headquarters complaining that Halder was nearing a complete breakdown. He now wanted nothing more to do with the "flabby generals."

The strongest advocates of the coup took Halder's decision to begin making plans as the key to move ahead with all possible speed. The Chief of Staff might be moving forward slowly, reluctantly, and with an unsure step, but the others plunged ahead enthusiastically, hoping their thorough planning would influence the reluctant Halder to order the coup without hesitation when the time came.

Oster revived the September 1938 coup plans and updated them. Groscurth's secretary was kept busy typing lists of people who were to be immediately arrested by Count Helldorff's Berlin police forces once the coup was under way. She also helped prepare public proclamations and orders to the troops for use by Halder.

Once again the question of Hitler's fate was debated. Beck wanted him imprisoned in an insane asylum; Dohnanyi and Canaris favored arresting Hitler and placing him and his closest associates on trial, using information Dohnanyi had collected from Dr. Franz Furtner, the Reich Minister of Justice. Oster and those closest to him continued to believe that Hitler had to be killed to prevent his becoming a rallying point for the Nazis, who would surely try to rescue him. Joining Oster in this belief was Dr. Josef Müller, about whom we will learn more in the next chapter.

The actual plans for the coup were similar to those prepared in 1938, even to the troops that were to be used. To these would be added the two armored divisions Halder was holding. The plan was to strike in the predawn hours with troops surrounding the government buildings in Berlin while police officials arrested every Nazi official they could capture. Hitler would have to be dealt with separatively, since there was no agreement on his fate. General Witzleben, who was to arrest Hitler in the previous year's plan, was now on the western front and unable to take part in the operation, although he remained a strong supporter.

Once the coup succeeded, General Beck was to speak to the country over the captured radio network, and proclamations were to be distributed to the newspapers. He would announce to the German people that the army had assumed control of the government and that he was now chief executive of the armed forces. Martial law and a state of emergency were to be declared, and the Gestapo and the Propaganda Ministry were to be disbanded. Subsequent announcements were to be made about early elections and the opening of peace negotiations. Finally, as a demonstration to the Allies of his sincerity about peace, Beck was to order an end to the blackout that was in effect throughout the country.

The coup planned for 1939 was not as well organized or armed as the coup planned in 1938, but it still had a chance to succeed if Halder could gather the courage to give the command. Unfortunately, Halder was reluctant to do this without Brauchitsch.` Hitler had chosen his men well. The German army was well supplied with strong leaders who could act decisively, but at its apex stood two men who lacked conviction and courage. Brauchitsch was terrified of Hitler the way a small child is cowed by a domineering father, so he was afraid to act against him. Halder seemed incapable of acting decisively to carry out the operation he believed was crucial to the existence of his own country.

Finally, events began to take shape when Hitler announced that his attack on the neutral countries would take place between November 15 and 20. Halder did extract from him a promise that OKH would be given seven days warning to ensure last minute preparations were complete. It was in those seven days that Halder knew the conspirators must act to prevent the war. Preparations moved ahead at full throttle.

About this time, Erich Kordt of the Foreign Ministry decided to take an action that he hoped would free the generals from their oath of allegiance to Hitler. He was one of the few conspirators who had access to the Führer, although it was limited to Hitler's anteroom. He was well known in the Chancellory and could enter the anteroom with impunity. Now his visits became more frequent and his behavior more conspicuous, a tactic calculated to ensure that all the guards got to recognize him as a routine visitor. Oster promised to furnish explosives from the Abwehr supply for Kordt's use. His plan was simple. When Hitler emerged from his inner office and entered the anteroom (as was his practice either to give instructions to an aide or to welcome his next appointment), Kordt would approach him, grab him tightly, and explode the bomb, which would kill both men.

The opportunity never materialized because the Gestapo had assumed control of all explosives in the Reich, including those in the Abwehr arsenal. Gestapo control meant that the distribution of explosives was strictly limited to those who could demonstrate an approved need, which few conspirators could. This answers the many critics who ask, "Why didn't someone blow Hitler up during a meeting, or simply shoot him?" It was almost impossible to enter the Führer's presence without being searched, and carrying a weapon was forbidden. Halder would certainly have been arrested if he was discovered with his pistol in Hitler's presence.

When Hitler received favorable logistical reports of troop and supply movements, he decided to move the date up to November 12. This meant that if the date held, the OKH would be given the final order on November 5. All attempts to dissuade Hitler failed. Field commanders implored Brauchitsch, as Commander-in-Chief, to halt the attack they all believed would end in disaster. Brauchitsch responded to this pressure by requesting a private meeting with Hitler on November 5. Hitler agreed, setting the time for noon, one hour before his promised order to OKH to prepare the attack.

Halder and Brauchitsch drove together to the Chancellory in Berlin. Halder waited in the anteroom while Brauchitsch, gripped with fear, entered Hitler's chamber armed with a briefcase crammed with ominous reports designed to persuade Hitler to cancel the attack.

Once inside, Brauchitsch regained his self-control. He placed his evidence before Hitler, who had little patience for this "cowardly" response from his top military commander. He flew into a rage that Halder said left the Commander-in-Chief "chalk white" and stormed from the room. During the return trip to Zossen, Brauchitsch gave Halder a detailed description of his humiliating twenty minutes with Hitler. Unfortunately, he told Halder about Hitler's expression that his patience was running out on the cowardly "spirit of Zossen" and he would have to put an end to it soon.

This last comment stunned Halder, who was already sensitive about his role in the impending coup. He remembered the June 1934 massacre Hitler had perpetrated on the SA, and he surmised that Hitler had learned of their plans and intended to do the same to the OKH. He envisioned army headquarters surrounded by armed SS groups, the building searched by Gestapo agents, and possibly the members of the General Staff murdered like Röhm and his associates. This fantasy drove Halder to desperate measures, since not enough armed guards were posted at OKH headquarters to withstand an assault by the SS.

Back at Zossen he ordered Stulpnagel to burn all evidence of the planned coup, including proclamations, maps of Berlin and the Chancellory, and troop assignments. Halder called Groscurth into his office and told him, "The forces who had been counting on us are no longer under obligation. You understand what I mean." Groscurth understood immediately and saw there was little chance of reversing Halder's attitude. The man was in a complete panic.

Meanwhile, Hitler issued orders to prepare for the attack and the OKH machinery swung into action. By 4:00 p.m. Brauchitsch appeared to have fully regained his composure. Although he was not officially a part of the coup, the Commander-in-Chief knew something had been afoot. He told Halder he still believed the western offensive would bring disaster, but he could do nothing about it. He would do nothing, he said, "but I also shall do nothing if someone else does something."

Halder recognized Brauchitsch's statement as authority to act freely. Brauchitsch's tacit approval bolstered his confidence. Within an hour he met with Groscurth and told the Abwehr officer he would be ready to act if Admiral Canaris would take the responsibility of killing Hitler.

Groscurth returned to his office and ordered a car to drive him to Abwehr headquarters, where he gave Canaris Halder's proposal. The Admiral exploded in anger and replied that Halder should "shoulder the responsibility in a clear-cut fashion."

The men who had spent tense hours anxiously waiting for the coup to begin heard nothing from Halder. His promised order never came, and they now sat around in small groups at OKH and Abwehr wondering what to do next. Although they were clear about their goals, without a leader they could not order out the troops necessary for the coup.

Hitler began a new series of postponements of the offensive, first to November 19, then November 22, then December 3. His indecision continued until May 1940, when the attack was finally launched. During this time people like Oster, Gisevius, Groscurth,

Canaris, and the other hard-line plotters tried unsuccessfully to persuade Halder to set the coup in motion before the shooting began.

The irresolute behavior of top army leaders, which held to the failure of the two planned coups, the first in 1938 and the second in 1939, convinced most of the conspirators that an elaborately organized coup might not be the best way to topple Hitler. What was required was to present the leading generals with a fait accompli, Hitler's death. From now until 1944, elaborate coup plans took a back seat to efforts by individuals and small groups to assassinate Hitler.

7.

Pope Pius Aids the Resistance

The German resistance continued to struggle in its campaign to win the Allies' support for their cause. Direct appeals to London, which was now the center of influence for both Western Allies, were proving fruitless. If war was to be averted another route had to be found. A new channel of communications would be sought through the Roman Catholic pontiff in the Vatican.

The newly elected Pope, Pius XII, had intimate knowledge of Germany, having served as the Vatican nuncio to Munich in 1917 when he attempted to open peace negotiations between the Allies and the Central Powers. He then served as nuncio in Berlin from 1920 to 1929. As Vatican Secretary of State, Eugenio Cardinal Pacelli spent enormous effort countering Nazi anti-religious practices in Germany. Despite allegations to the contrary, Pius XII was fiercely anti-Nazi. When his intervention was solicited, the knowledge that two officers whom he knew personally, General Beck and Admiral Canaris, were directly involved gave him confidence that the Nazi regime could be removed from power.

The intermediary chosen to represent the resistance in the Vatican had known the Pope for years. Forty-one-year-old Dr. Josef Müller was the product of a Bavarian Catholic farming family. A lawyer and advisor to several ranking church officials and religious orders in Germany, he was highly regarded by church leaders throughout the country. His relationship with the Pope was such that when Germany annexed Austria, Pacelli (later Pius XII) asked Müller to visit each of the Austrian bishops to impress on them the evil that was the Nazi Party.

Using Admiral Canaris's name, Oster asked Müller to come to Berlin for a meeting. When he arrived at Abwehr headquarters, he was surprised to be greeted by Oster and Dohnanyi and to learn that his appointment was with them and not Canaris. Following the usual pleasantries, Oster came directly to the reason for the invitation. He told Müller he knew of his activities in the Catholic Resistance movement and his work for the Catholic Church in Germany, which was struggling for its very existence against Nazi pressure.

Oster then told a shocked Müller that the division of the Abwehr that he commanded, the Central Division, "is also the central directorate of the German military opposition under general Beck."[1] Oster explained that the resistance wanted him to open a channel of communication between the resistance and the government of Great Britain through the Vatican. If Müller agreed, he would be called up for military duty as a reserve officer attached to the Munich office of the Abwehr. He would not be subject to orders from regular Abwehr officers but would be instructed in his duties by General Beck. Membership in the Abwehr would afford Müller a freedom he did not enjoy as a civilian, since he was marked for scrutiny by the security police because of his anti-Nazi activities.

Any reluctance Müller may have felt about joining the military forces under Hitler's command evaporated when Oster told him that the resistance motto was "It is Hitler or us." Soon afterward, Müller was activated as a first lieutenant assigned to the Abwehr office in Munich.

The precise date of Müller's initial visit to the Vatican as emissary of the German resistance is difficult to determine. Resistance files on the entire affair in which Pope Pius XII acted as mediator between the anti-Nazi Germans and the British government fell into the hands of the Gestapo in 1944 and were never seen again. More than likely they were burned along with thousands of other Gestapo documents as the war ground to an end the following year.

Admiral Canaris played no direct role in enlisting Müller in the Abwehr's resistance group, other than helping Oster choose him. Canaris did, however, devise a brilliant cover story to avoid suspicion about employing a known Nazi detractor in military intelligence.

Canaris laid the groundwork for Müller's role beforehand with General Keitel, who as Hitler's chief of the Military High Command was the Admiral's superior, and with Reinhard Heydrich, Himmler's protégé and head of the Sicherheitsdienst (SD) Security Service, whose responsibility it was to uncover "enemies of the state." A master of subterfuge, Canaris played on Keitel's mistrust of the Italians. He told Keitel that the Abwehr intended to use Müller's Vatican connections as a cover for assessing the reliability of Italy's continued commitment to alliance with the Reich. Canaris told Heydrich that Müller's assignment was to establish contact with British intelligence through the Vatican, enabling the Abwehr to be informed of British war plans and intentions. He even asked for Heydrich's cooperation in filtering information to the British, through Müller, to help establish the latter's credibility. Through this clever deceit Canaris insured that if anyone questioned Müller's activities he would see only a loyal German working undercover for the Abwehr against the Allies.

Müller went to Italy in either late September or early October 1939. He took up residence in a modest Rome hotel, the Flora, and at once contacted Monsignor Ludwig Kaas, a German advisor to the Pope, and Monsignor Johannes Schönhöffer, who had been witness at Müller's wedding. Müller also renewed an earlier acquaintance with a Jesuit, Father Robert Leiber, who was Pope Pius XII's oldest and closest advisor and confident.

Müller confided in Father Leiber, telling him of his mission and asking him to speak to the Pope. The German resistance wanted the Pope to appeal to the British government to win the Allies' agreement to withhold military action against Germany during a coup and to establish peace talks after the Nazis were removed from power. When Leiber approached the Pope with this proposal, Pius agreed immediately, because, he said, "The German opposition must be heard in Britain."

This was an exceptional measure for a modern Pope to take. Fifteen years after the war ended, Father Leiber still believed "the Pope went much too far" in his support of the resistance. By acting on behalf of a group planning to overthrow the German government, Pius endangered the Catholic Church and its officials and priests in all Axis-occupied countries. Had Mussolini been aware of the Pope's involvement, he would surely have accused the Pontiff of violating treaty agreements between the Vatican and Italy and would have moved his army against the Holy See.

The arrangements for Müller's future missions were made at the Pope's request. Müller would meet with Father Leiber, who in turn brought Müller's proposals, questions, and responses to the Pontiff. The Pope passed these to the British representative at the Vatican, Sir Francis d'Arcy Osborne, who communicated them to London. British Foreign Minister Halifax had agreed to this arrangement after the Pope vouched for Müller. During this period the Pope never met with Müller in person, to insure if either was questioned about their relationship he could answer honestly that neither one had seen the other since before the war began.

With the Pope's consent, a communications link was established between Beck and Oster in Germany and British Foreign Minister Halifax in London. The link began with Beck, ran through Müller, then to Leiber, then through the Pope, who met personally with Osborne, who reported to Halifax in London. The British had agreed to engage in the discussions on the condition that there would be no German offensive against France while the talks proceeded. This stipulation created several extremely tense situations as the months of October, November, and December crept by and Hitler kept rescheduling his planned offensive. The resistance knew their link to the British could be broken at any time by Hitler, but they were powerless to prevent the offensive.

Each time Müller arrived in Italy he reported to the Rome Abwehr office, from where he called Father Leiber on a special telephone line that was kept free of wire taps. When Leiber answered, Müller said simply, "I am here." Father Leiber's terse response was to state the time he would meet Müller, then he hung up. Their secret meetings took place in Leiber's quarters at the Pontifical University of the Gregoriana where the priest was a professor.

On Müller's regular trips to Rome he also served as a courier for the Church. Catholic bishops throughout Germany and Austria collected evidence of Nazi persecution and forwarded it to Father Johann Neuhausler, who was a political specialist for the Church in Munich. Neuhausler gave the reports to Müller, who took them with him to the Vatican where the information might be broadcast over Radio Vatican if appropriate, or forwarded to French and British Church officials. A collection of these reports was published in 1940 under the title "The Persecution of the Catholic Church in the Third Reich: Facts and Figures."

Müller periodically brought information of even greater importance to the Church. He carried reports passed to Oster's group by Arthur Nebe of the Reich Criminal Police. His position gave Nebe access to reports concerning future action against the Church planned by the Nazi security police, the SD. These included plans for the arrest or interrogations of specific individuals, and reports on the activities of various Church officials who were being closely watched by the Nazis.

During their first meeting Müller told Leiber that General Beck was prepared to come to Rome personally to assure the Pope that he directed the resistance group Müller represented. Pius was impressed with this offer but felt it would needlessly place General Beck in danger, and he advised against it.

Each time he returned to Berlin, Müller carried with him British responses to earlier questions, along with fresh queries and proposals that had been given to the Pope by Osborne. Little is known of these communications since few of the men involved survived the war, and those who did frequently could not recall many details, an affliction not uncommon in aged men. Hidden in the secret wartime files of the British Foreign Office are records that could undoubtedly reveal volumes about these three-party negotiations, but the world will have to wait until the veil of secrecy is lifted from them. There is limited documentary evidence that the negotiations may have been going well when Hitler launched his invasion of France, cutting the link.

To reduce the danger of exposure, Müller's information was not distributed widely within Beck's resistance group. Only selected members were kept informed. Germany was officially at war with Great Britain; any contact with a hostile government, however indirect, was a treasonable offense punishable by death.

One of those who were privy to information about Müller's mission was Major Helmuth Groscurth, the Abwehr representative assigned to the Army General Staff. When Müller's October 18, 1939, report of his most recent visit to Rome reached Groscurth, he wrote in his diary on October 20 that the Pope "was very interested" in acting as mediator for a peace and believed "an honorable peace to be possible." Evidently based on what Pius communicated to Müller through Father Leiber, Groscurth wrote further that the Pope personally guaranteed that "Germany will not be swindled" if a peace could be reached between the Allies and the German resistance. The key sentence of this entry cites the major condition on which the British rested their approval of negotiating directly with the resistance: "With all peace feelers one encounters the categorical demand for the removal of Hitler."[2]

Despite efforts to keep Müller's mission and the Pope's involvement in it secret, a wide circle of church leaders in Rome gradually became aware of it. Two of these were Monsignors Ludwig Kaas and Johannes Schönhöffer, both of whom Müller contacted when he arrived in Rome on his first trip as the resistance representative. Other clerics who came to know of the Pope's role were Monsignor Paul Maria Krieg, chaplain to the Swiss Guard; Abbot General Hubert Hoots, a Belgian who directed the Premonstratensian Order; Reverend Ivo Zeiger, S.J., rector of the Collegium Germanicum; Father Vincent J. McCormick, S.J., rector of the University of the Gregorians; and Father Vladimir Ledochowsky, S.J., Superior General of the Jesuits. Ledochowsky had been vilified in the Nazi press over the observance of his fiftieth anniversary as a priest. The Nazis claimed the celebration was a ruse to win sympathy for his homeland, Poland.

Ledochowsky was alarmed at the potential for danger to the Church if the Nazis discovered the Pope's activities and tried to convince him to stop. Although Pius declined to abdicate his intermediary's role between the resistance and the British, he did heed Ledochowsky's warnings and asked Leiber to change his meeting place with Müller to a less conspicuous locale, a parish house on the outskirts of Rome.

The communications link between the resistance and the British remained open until March 1940, except for a six-week interruption during November 1939 when the Venlo incident described in Chapter 3 occurred. The Pope persuaded Halifax that the resistance had nothing to do with kidnapping two British officers following Georg Elser's abortive assassination attempt against Hitler in Munich, and that it knew nothing about the incident beforehand.

At the Pontiff's urging, negotiations were reopened. On January 11, 1940, Pope Pius warned Osborne that "a grand German offensive" against the west was scheduled to begin by mid-February or possibly sooner. If the German resistance could be assured that Britain would negotiate an honorable peace, specifically not one patterned after the terms imposed on Germany at the end of World War I, they would forcibly replace the Nazis. Once a responsible government was established, Germany would restore Poland and Czechoslovakia as independent nations.

Osborne was uncertain how to respond. He told the Pope that he feared another Venlo incident in which the British could be baited into an arrangement with potential allies who were setting a trap. The Pope assured him that the men involved, especially Beck, Canaris, and Müller, were in no way connected with the Nazi party. When Osborne passed the information on to Halifax, he voiced his misgivings about the Germans who were making this offer. The aftershock from the Venlo incident, in which two British intelligence officers were kidnapped by the Nazis after being lured into a trap by a man claiming to represent a resistance group in the German General Staff, left the British government extremely guarded about any contacts with alleged German resistance groups.

On January 16 the British War Cabinet considered the German offer and concluded that peace negotiations could begin only after the Germans removed the Nazi government. This decision left the resistance in a quandary. The resistance leaders in the military needed to satisfy the field commanders, whose support was essential for success, that the Allies would not exploit the chaos that might temporarily result from a coup inside Germany, and attack. This would require solid assurances from both Britain and France that they would remain detached until a new government was firmly installed and ready to participate in negotiations for an honorable peace. The British, who now informed the French of these contacts, insisted that the resistance act first, without any assurance they would not attack Germany in the midst of the coup, while her defenses were faced inward.

The following month, on February 7, the Pope met again with Osborne. This time reading from four pages of German script, he told Osborne the German resistance intended to replace the Nazis with a decentralized federal form of government that would be democratic in nature. Pius then told the British representative that he had been asked to determine if the union between Germany and Austria could be continued and guaranteed as part of a negotiated peace.

The reply came thirteen days later and revealed the wariness with which the British government viewed the entire affair. It said, in part, "If his Majesty's government were convinced that the intermediaries who approached His Holiness represented principals in Germany who had both the intention and power to perform what they promised," the British and French governments might consider their proposals. It stated further that the British could not seriously discuss these proposals with the French government because they were "emanating from undisclosed sources and so vague in character as those which have been conveyed to you. If any progress is to be made, a definite program must be submitted and authoritatively vouched for. In examining any such program, and in framing their own conditions, what His Majesty's government would look for above all, in addition to reparation of the wrongs done to Germany's smaller neighbors, would be security for the future."[3]

In that reply lies the crux of the problems that led inevitably to the collapse of Allied interest in the German resistance at this stage of the war. The British were not eager for another Venlo incident and kept the resistance at arm's length. This communication has the ring of a bureaucratic bulletin from one government aimed at the bureaucratic fabric of another government. Obviously, British officials failed to understand that the men who were pleading with them through the Pope were living under a totalitarian dictatorship and had neither the freedom nor the opportunity to meet openly to discuss British proposals and to construct their replies in conventional diplomatic language. The German resistance was asking for a simple assurance that the Allies would not attack Germany while a coup was in progress. The British were unwilling to give such assurance unless a "program" for the future had been successfully negotiated. If the British government had insisted on similar requirements from the Yugoslav underground later in the war, perhaps that country would not have been forced to endure nearly one-half century of communist rule.

Several intervening factors affected the British attitude. Numerous private communications channels had been established between various German resistance groups and London, further clouding the issues. One of these secondary avenues was established by Ulrich von Hassell, former German ambassador to Rome and an important advocate of the resistance. As Hitler brought Germany closer to war, concerned anti-Nazi Germans with influential friends abroad tried to use those relationships in desperate efforts to stop him. This crush of appeals for help, concentrated on England, confused some British government officials who were hard put to decide which, if any, were legitimate. British Foreign Office files contain virtually no record of these petitions, possibly to spare the government the embarrassment of having to admit it had bungled an opportunity to prevent the war.

Resistance leaders held great hope that Britain would support their coup and agree not only to take no actions against Germany while the coup was in progress but also negotiate an honorable peace with the new government. Blinded by this hope, members of the resistance frequently read more into British replies than the authors intended, leading ultimately to the drafting of a document called the X-Report.

This document was prepared for presentation to Generals Halder and Brauchitsch in the hope it would prompt them to act against Hitler before the war in the West was launched. It reveals how desperately the resistance leaders wanted to believe that Britain would support their coup.

The X-Report originated with the secret meetings in the Vatican. Usually the Pope met with Father Leiber, giving him verbally the British government's reply to earlier communications. Time permitting, Leiber would in turn brief Müller in the same manner; otherwise he would make notes in his small handwriting, with the understanding that Müller would destroy them immediately after reading them. Müller was always meticulous about observing this procedure except for a brief meeting the two men had on the evening of February 1, 1940.

The meeting was brief because Müller was scheduled for an early morning departure. Father Leiber handed him a single sheet of notes containing the conditions under which the British government would negotiate with a provisional German government if the Nazis were deposed in a coup. Since the paper also contained the Vatican watermark, Müller felt it was too weighty to destroy. He took it back to Germany with him, hoping the Vatican watermark would lend the credibility needed to convince skeptics that his papal contacts with the British, and the British interest in peace following a successful coup, were genuine.

When Müller arrived in Berlin he showed Leiber's handwritten page to Dohnanyi. The two used it as the basis for the X-Report, a chronology of the contacts the Pope mediated with the British government. The report was so named because the central figure in the account, Müller, was identified only as Mr. X. Late that evening, while Dohnanyi dictated, his wife, Christine, typed the finished report. The original document was twelve typed pages; however, several more were added later to include the final trips to Rome.

On March 19, Oster and Dohnanyi joined Beck and Hassell at General Beck's home. They read the X-Report to the two men and asked Beck's advice about what they should do with it. Beck favored having Halder bring it directly to Brauchitsch. It was widely known that the army Commander-in-Chief was upset at reports of SS atrocities against the population in Poland, and also by plans to build an entirely separate army within the SS that would not come under his control but would be led by Himmler. Beck expected that these events, coupled with the consensus among most army leaders that Hitler's impending invasion of the Low Countries would lead to disaster, and the apparent willingness of the British to negotiate with a post-Nazi German government, would finally motivate the Commander-in-chief to act against Hitler.

The job of taking the report to Halder fell to General George Thomas of the army's economic section. Thomas gave the report to Halder, who read the entire document with interest. That same evening he gave it to Brauchitsch, who also read it with great interest but came to a different conclusion than did his Chief of Staff.

The following morning Brauchitsch told Halder angrily that he should never have brought the report to him, that it was pure treason, and that the person who prepared it must be arrested as a traitor, calmly Halder told Brauchitsch, "If you're bent on arresting somebody, you had better arrest me."[4] After the war Brauchitsch is reported to have told Otto John, another member of the resistance,

> Of course, I could have had Hitler arrested and even imprisoned him. Easily! I had enough officers loyal to me who would have carried out even that order if given by me. But that was not the problem. Why should I have initiated action against Hitler—tell me that. It would have been action against the German people. The German people were pro-Hitler.[5]

The efforts by Pope Pius XII to arrange to negotiate the peace sought by everyone except Hitler came to nothing for several reasons. Paramount was Brauchitsch's correct assessment that (1) most Germans continued to support Hitler, and (2) a coup would probably have led to a civil war between the part of the army loyal to the Führer, the SS, and other Nazi groups on one side, and the faction of the army that sought to remove the Nazis from power and even kill Hitler. How long the insurgents could have held out against the forces massed against them if the air force sided with the Nazis, as it likely would have under Göring, is a matter for conjecture.

But all that activity would have been a result of the coup, and it is impossible to predict what portion of the army would have supported the coup, especially if they struck quickly and decisively against Hitler and the other leading Nazis, removing them entirely as rallying points. The coup at this point was doomed in part because the British remained reluctant to deal with any anti-Nazi Germans, partly as a result of the deception played on them in the Venlo incident.

Although the responsibility cannot be placed solely on the British government, a more positive attitude toward the overtures made to them through the Pope might have resulted in a more favorable outcome. As usual with critical points in history, one is left with the question, "What if?" As usual, it is a question that must remain unanswered.

As Hitler scheduled and then rescheduled the invasion of the West, the Pope and several of his emissaries were kept informed of the dates by Müller. This intelligence was passed on to the Belgian and Dutch authorities. Meanwhile, the Pope, Father Leiber, and others in the Vatican who knew of Müller's mission and the Pope's participation waited for the resistance to act against Hitler so the peace negotiations could begin. They continued to wait until the most important condition, no German invasion of the West, could no longer be met.

8.

"The Living Hitler Must Die"

All chance of organizing a coup ended, at least temporarily, on May 19, 1940, when German panzers stormed into Belgium, Holland, Luxembourg, and France with startling success. In a stunning defeat, France signed an armistice on June 22 conceding to Germany the right to occupy half of the country. The Low Countries had capitulated within days of the attack.

Decisive victory boosted Hitler's stature with the German people to even greater levels, while the generals who predicted disaster looked patently foolish. The resistance members now faced the prospect of having no support from troop commanders. Even General, now Field Marshal, Witzleben, a firebrand of anti-Hitlerism, said he had abandoned all hope of a coup because Hitler was far too popular with the people. He said the younger army officers and men would not support a coup because they could see no reason why the man who had restored Germany's national pride and regained the territory taken from her in 1918 should be replaced by force.

With plans for a coup suspended indefinitely, the more virulent anti-Nazis now turned to the remaining alternative, a simple assassination of Hitler. If it succeeded, they hoped the army would act to prevent Goebbels, Himmler, or Göring from taking power. Much like the earlier attempts on Hitler's life by political opponents, assassination plots developed by military officers usually involved a tight circle of conspirators and placed the plotters in grave danger.

At this point in the war, as Hitler began preparations to invade the Soviet Union, virtually every ranking member of the conspiracy against him—including its leaders, General Beck—was reconciled to the inescapable truth that arresting and imprisoning Hitler was no longer a viable option. The Nazi organizations, especially the SS, had grown too large and powerful and would not abdicate their privileges without a struggle, which would result in a civil war. This was especially true if Hitler remained alive and his supporters thought there was a chance they could free him. Except for a small few whose religious beliefs forbade tyrannicide, everyone agreed with Major Wilhelm Heinz, who had commanded the assault squad designated to shoot Hitler in the 1938 coup: "The living Hitler must die."

During the next four years no fewer than twelve bona fide attempts to kill Hitler were made by military officers. Many took their lead from General Hammerstein's 1939 strategy and sought to induce the Führer to visit an army field headquarters.

The first of these assassination intrigues was scheduled soon after the French signed the armistice. Plans were immediately made for a victory parade in Paris, which everyone expected the Führer to review. The parade was set for July 27, and a flood of troops were moved toward the former French capital to take part in the celebration.

In Paris two men planned Hitler's death. They were Lieutenant Fritz-Dietlof Graf von der Schulenburg and Dr. Eugen Gerstenmaier. Schulenburg was a reserve officer who, as vice-president of the Berlin police, had been an active participant in earlier attempted coups in Berlin. He was called to active duty in May 1940. Gerstenmaier was an official of the Evangelical Church who worked in the Information Division of the Foreign Ministry. The two had talked earlier in Berlin of organizing a small officer's cadre to arrest Hitler, but nothing came of it. Now they decided to carry out their mission to unseat the Nazis by killing the Party leader, Adolf Hitler. The coming victory parade in Paris provided the opportunity they needed. Their plan called for shooting Hitler while he stood in the reviewing stand along the parade route.

On July 20 Hitler cancelled the parade. He quietly slipped unannounced into Paris in the early morning hours of July 23 and visited several places of personal interest, including Napoleon's tomb, the Louvre, the Eiffel Tower, and the palace of Justice. Just as discreetly he left the city, his would-be assassins unaware of his brief sojourn there.

Less than a year later, in May 1941, a parade of German troops was again scheduled for Paris. German army and SS divisions were assembled and a reviewing stand for Hitler and other dignitaries was constructed near the Place de la Concorde for the parade on the Champs-Elysées.

A plan to kill Hitler while he reviewed the parade was worked out by staff officers of Field Marshal von Witzleben's headquarters. Witzleben was Commander-in-Chief West, with headquarters outside Paris in St. Germain. The staff members and an operations officer from the Paris commander's staff were to shoot Hitler point-blank. If they failed to kill him, another officer was assigned to throw a bomb at him. The shooters were Captain Graf Schwerin von Schwanenfeld and Major Hans Alexander von Voss, both of Witzleben's staff, and Captain Graf von Waldersee of the Paris staff. Hitler frustrated his enemies once again, declining at the last minute to make the trip to Paris.

A third Paris-based attempt on Hitler's life, of which little is known, allegedly involved Witzleben's replacement as Commander-in-Chief West, Field Marshal Gerd von Rundstedt, SS-Sturmbannführer Hans-Victor von Salviati, and Major Achim Oster. The plotters again invited Hitler to visit Paris in 1942, but the wary Führer refused their invitation.

Most assassination plots relied on Hitler's adherence to a predetermined agenda, but the assassins were invariably thwarted by Hitler's practice of avoiding routine or established schedules in his travels. Hitler's policy was to live his life "irregularly," as he put it.

"Walk, drive and travel at irregular times and unexpectedly" was his personal formula for security against assassins.

War with Russia, which began on June 22, 1941, with a three-pronged German attack across Soviet borders, opened new opportunities to eliminate Hitler. Because many German field marshals and generals considered the invasion a potential disaster rivaling Napoleon's ill-fated 1812 Russian campaign, several of them flirted, although briefly, with the resistance, but some came to stay.

The Soviet campaign was carried out by three army groups, each with its own set of goals and objectives. Army Group North, commanded by Field Marshal Wilhelm von Leeb, crossed from East Prussia into Soviet-occupied Lithuania and drove toward its primary objective, Leningrad. Army Group South, under Field Marshal Gerd von Rundstedt, pushed into Galacia on its way through the Ukraine to seize Kiev. Army Group Center, under Field Marshal Fedor von Bock, swept across northern Poland toward Smolensk, two hundred miles west of Moscow. Army Group Center soon became a hotbed of plots to kill Hitler and overthrow the Nazi government. The architect of these intrigues was a newcomer to the resistance movement, Major General Henning von Tresckow.

Tresckow was a Prussian who had served as a platoon commander during World War I, traveled internationally for a bank following the war, re-entered the army in 1924, and served in various posts, including several years on the General Staff. Concurring with many of his colleagues, Tresckow expected that the war with Russia would be short and disastrous for Germany. Once again German military professionals overestimated the enemy, and the war progressed with resounding successes as all three army groups thrust headlong into Soviet territory.

Many army officers had witnessed the atrocities committed against the Poles in 1939, and some were sufficiently bold to censure the activities of the SS units assigned to exterminate Jews and other non-Aryans. The barbaric behavior by men who commanded these units, and the realization that they were pursuing policies to which the Führer strongly subscribed, caused many field officers to turn against the regime. As the German army advanced across the

Soviet expanse, it was followed closely by the same SS units that continued their merciless slaughter of civilians and war prisoners on an even larger scale. An increasing number of German army officers protested this uncivilized oppression, and some even took individual action against the SS. Repulsed by the heinous crimes committed in Germany's name, officers of every rank gravitated toward the resistance.

Exacerbating the dissatisfaction among officers in the eastern campaign areas toward the regime was Hitler's infamous Commissar Order, issued on June 6, 1941, even before the invasion began. The order required the army to murder immediately all captured Red Army political commissars. It specifically commanded that "on capture they will be immediately separated from other prisoners on the field of battle. After they have been segregated they will be liquidated."[1] This order made German army personnel in the eastern theater feel more like criminals than soldiers.

Growing disgust for the Nazi war crimes enabled Tresckow to expand his resistance base. He used his position as senior operations officer on Field Marshal von Bock's staff to mold the staff into the core of a new resistance movement against Hitler. Among the dissenters who operated at Army Group Center under Tresckow's leadership were Lieutenant Fabian von Schlabrendorff, the man who had informed the British of General Hammerstein's plan to kill Hitler; Lieutenant Colonel Hans Alexander von Voss, who had planned to shoot Hitler in Paris during the planned May 1941 parade; Lieutenant Colonel Georg Schulze-Buttger; Lieutenant Colonel Berndt von Kliest, who maintained communications with the resistance in Berlin; and Colonel Rudolf-Christoph Freiherr von Gersdorff, who would later make a suicide attempt on Hitler's life.

Schlabrendorff, who survived the war and wrote his memoirs of the resistance, traveled to Berlin in October 1941 to examine the possibility of rescuing the coup with resistance leaders there. He met with von Hassell to explore the Allies' attitude toward fostering a change of government, and he was told that the German resistance could expect no help from the Allies but could doubtlessly negotiate a reasonable peace if Hitler was removed.

Tresckow tried to enlist Bock in the resistance with little success, but when the field marshal was replaced in December by Field Marshal Gunther von Kluge, his prospects improved. Although Kluge would not become an active resistance member, Tresckow was able to influence many of the field marshal's decisions through an almost mystical sway he held over him. The problem was that Kluge was an extremely indecisive man who while in Tresckow's presence would take steps the latter requested, but once left to his own devices he would vacillate on a question and sometimes reverse an action or order he had undertaken while under Tresckow's influence.

Tresckow first planned to assassinate Hitler in the late summer of 1941, while the Russian campaign was still going well for the Germans. Bock's troops were only two hundred miles from Moscow, which many of the generals deemed the most important target in the Soviet empire, when Hitler issued an order to divide Army Group Center's panzer and other mobile forces in half, transferring half to Army Group North for its thrust against Leningrad, and half to Army Group South to help von Rundstedt's drive to capture Kiev, capital of Ukraine. Army Group Center would then have basically only infantry troops for its attack on Moscow.

Halder and Brauchitsch at OKH, and Bock at Army Group Center, objected strenuously to Hitler's plan–so strenuously that the Führer decided to visit Army Group Center to personally deliver the order to Bock. Tresckow and Schlabrendorff welcomed this opportunity to kill Hitler and arranged, with a small group of officers, to shoot him when he entered one of their headquarters buildings.

Unfortunately, the conspirators were committed to fighting a war, and their energies were divided between pursuing combat plans and organizing the assassination. Also working against them was Hitler's obsession with the "irregular" in his actions. The visit was scheduled several times only to be cancelled, re-scheduled, then cancelled again.

Finally, in early August a fleet of cars arrived from the Führer Headquarters in East Prussia to await Hitler's arrival. Hitler refused to use cars supplied by the army for fear they might be booby trapped with explosives. When he finally arrived at Bock's headquarters in Borrisow, Tresckow and his fellow conspirators were overwhelmed at the amount of security people that accompanied him and the rigid security measures they imposed. The would-be-assassins barely caught a glimpse of Hitler, much less an opportunity to shoot him.

In an effort to overcome a reluctance by many officers to disavow their oath to Hitler, a convoluted scheme that would permit rebellion without actually breaking the oath was conceived by the resistance leaders in Berlin, including Beck, Hassell, Goerdeler, and Popitz. In December 1941, Hitler had forced Brauchitsch into retirement because he objected too often to Hitler's tactical orders. The Führer himself replaced the ousted general as army Commander-in-Chief, assuming total control of the army, a decision that badly damaged the army's performance during the rest of the war. He later took personal control of the war in the east, ignoring a tradition handed down from the reign of Frederick the Great: that headquarters would issue orders identifying the broad goals of a given campaign or action, leaving the details of exactly how the mission would be accomplished to the commanders in the field. Increasingly, Hitler's orders became so specific and absolute that they crippled the ability of field commanders to function effectively.

The plan devised by the conspirators would capitalize on the contempt with which many field marshals and generals viewed Hitler's conduct of the war. An increasing number became convinced he would lead them to defeat because he simply did not know what he was doing. If the movement could be coordinated, the army commanders would refuse to obey orders from Hitler, not as head of the government to whom they had sworn loyalty, but as commander of the eastern front. The plotters hoped that this distinction would ease the consciences of officers who were unwilling to violate their oath.

In January 1942, Ulrich von Hassell traveled to Brussels and Paris to place the plan before the German army leaders in the West. Both General Alexander von Falkenhausen in Brussels and Field Marshal Witzleben in Paris thought the idea of the eastern field marshals taking such dramatic action was utopian, but both agreed to support any actions that did take place. Witzleben also decided that he could take independent action against Hitler's command some time during the coming summer months, when a new German offensive was scheduled in Russia. In anticipation, he decided to have a badly needed hemorrhoid operation during March so he would not suffer from this debilitating problem during the crucial summer. Unfortunately, Hitler took advantage of Witzleben's temporary absence from command to force his retirement and replace him.

Tresckow continued to work on bringing Kluge into the fold, but he had little success until Schlabrendorff uncovered damaging evidence that enabled Tresckow to blackmail the field marshal into cooperating with the conspirators against Hitler. The evidence was a sixtieth birthday present from Hitler to Kluge in the form of a check for 250,000 marks and a handwritten note from the Führer that said, "A birthday gift, my dear Field Marshal. You may use 125,000 marks to make improvements on your estate."[2] Kluge cashed the check and contacted Albert Speer, who was in charge of all construction, about making the improvements to his estate.

The gift was clearly a bribe, and Kluge should have refused both the check and the building permit if he wanted to remain an honorable man. Tresckow confronted him with this charge and made thinly veiled threats about letting the army know how cheaply Hitler had purchased the field marshal's loyalty. Cowed by Tresckow's rebuff, the field marshal agreed to meet with the very persuasive Goerdeler, who lectured Kluge on the critical need to remove Hitler from power. Tresckow and Goerdeler concluded the meeting convinced they had won Kluge to the cause, but he soon slid back into indecisiveness and continued to waver between loyalty to Hitler and support for Tresckow.

With the plan for organized disobedience in place, resistance chiefs in Berlin waited for an incident that would spark the revolt. They soon found it in the fall of Stalingrad.

Hitler had insisted, against the advice of top military advisors, that Stalingrad be taken by a frontal attack. Suffering heavy losses, General von Paulus's Sixth Army eventually took most of the city by early November. In mid-month the Soviets executed a counter-maneuver, encircling Stalingrad and driving the Germans either into pockets of the city or far enough away to preclude any possibility of helping the troops trapped within. Although the Sixth Army was sufficiently strong to break out of the encirclement, Hitler refused Paulus permission to do so, insisting he remain in the city and hold it to the death.

By year's end everyone who knew the truth about the situation in Stalingrad recognized that an entire army numbering almost three hundred thousand soldiers was doomed. Paulus appealed to Hitler for license to surrender and avoid further losses. Hitler denied the appeal and commanded Paulus to remain firm and not surrender. He then promoted him to field marshal, a ruse calculated to dissuade Paulus from capitulating, because no German field marshal had ever surrendered. Hitler's strategy did not work. On January 31, 1943, Paulus, with Soviet troops banging on the door of the room he used as an office, surrendered to the Red Army.

Before Stalingrad was retaken by the Soviets, General Beck smuggled a letter to Paulus, flown into the city by a Luftwaffe pilot in the resistance. Beck's letter was a request to Paulus for a statement calling on the German people to depose Hitler for his callous disregard for the lives of hundreds of thousands of German soldiers. Field Marshal von Kluge, and Field Marshal von Manstein, commander of Army Group South, both agreed that after Stalingrad fell and the statement by Paulus was made public, they would fly to Hitler's headquarters and demand that he relinquish command of the army in the east and turn it over to them.

Paulus never issued the statement, and his decision to surrender instead of taking his own life so infuriated Manstein that he would have nothing to do with efforts to wrest command from Hitler. The two field marshals did fly to Hitler's headquarters at Rastenburg, but not to unseat Hitler. Manstein reaffirmed his loyalty to Hitler and Kluge went along with him. A thoroughly dejected Beck could only respond, "We are deserted."

Tresckow remained determined to remove the Führer. He organized another, more elaborate, attempt to kill Hitler in March 1943. The war in Russia had turned against Germany, and he was able to attract more officers who realized that the war must end if Germany was to survive, and the surest way to do this was to eliminate Hitler.

Tresckow used his friendship with Lieutenant General Rudolf Schmundt, Hitler's chief Adjutant, to lure Hitler to Army Group Center's headquarters in Smolensk. There he was to meet his death at the hands of a group of officers who had been carefully selected by Tresckow for just such a mission.

Two key principals in Tresckow's conspiracy were brothers, Lieutenant Philipp Freiherr von Boeselager, who became an aide to Field Marshal Kluge in June 1942, and Captain Georg Freiherr von Boeselager, a cavalry officer assigned as tactics advisor with the Romanian forces fighting alongside the German army. During early 1942 Captain Boeselager spent time with his brother at army group center headquarters, where he renewed his acquaintance with the field marshal.

In conversations with Kluge he proposed that the cavalry could be put to better use, particularly to help relieve the critical lack of reserves the army was suffering. Captain Boeselager visualized an elite cavalry force that would function as a crisis brigade, capable of responding swiftly to crucial situations such as a frontline unit in danger of being overrun. It would be created by merging various cavalry units assigned to infantry divisions throughout the army. Recognizing the potential value of such a mobile strike force, Kluge asked Boeselager to discuss the possibility with Tresckow.

Tresckow and Boeselager developed the concept together, ultimately creating the Cavalry Regiment Center. Divided into two battalions, the Regiment consisted of 2,200 men, 650 of whom were Russian Cossacks who had voluntarily joined the Germans to fight the communists. The officers selected for this regiment were predominantly opposed to the Nazis or were men Tresckow believed could be counted on when the time came.

Cavalry Regiment Center's primary mission was a notable success, which helped divert attention from its clandestine purpose. The regiment posed a covert threat, first to destroy Hitler, and then to assist insurgent forces in Berlin to seize control of the government.

In preparation for replacing the Nazi government, Tresckow sent Schlabrendorff to Berlin to confer with the center of resistance there and outline his plan. Schlabrendorff met with General Friedrich Olbricht, permanent aide to the commander of the Home Army, and a man who controlled thousands of Replacement Army troops in cities across Germany. The Replacement Army was composed of garrison troops, units sent home for leave or refitting, and men on sick leave or receiving treatment for injuries. In addition, it became a sort of Home Guard to protect Germany from the possibility that revolts might erupt among the millions of slave laborers employed in German industries.

Olbricht informed General Beck, still the acknowledged head of the resistance, and Hans Oster at the Abwehr. Hans Gisevius was installed in an office at Olbricht's headquarters, just as he had been at Witzleben's Berlin headquarters in 1938, to work on plans for the coup that must follow Hitler's assassination.

Gisevius resurrected the original blueprints for the 1938 coup and began updating them. Initially he had great difficulty identifying the location of new or relocated SS facilities throughout the Reich. This information was vital because the SS would have to be neutralized for the coup to succeed. The Gestapo was the only agency that kept records of SS locations, and the information was highly classified.

Gisevius found a unique solution to this problem. Since government-funded brothels were always opened near SS bases to serve SS personnel, Gisevius was able to obtain (through a friend who had a connection on the Berlin vice squad) a map of all recently opened brothels still in operation. This provided Gisevius the lead he needed to identify most if not all SS bases from which a counter-coup might be launched.

Coordination between the resistance in Army Group Center and the coup headquarters in Berlin was facilitated by Admiral Canaris. The Abwehr chief arranged for a conference of intelligence officers working on the eastern front, to be held at Army Group Center. On March 7, 1943, he flew into Smolensk with Hans Oster, who had since been promoted to Major General, Colonel Erwin von Lahousen, Hans von Dohnanyi, and other members of his staff. The conference was scheduled to cover the true reason for assembling the group, a secret meeting between Schlabrendorff, Dohnanyi, and Tresckow to discuss last-minute preparations and devise a means of confirming Hitler's death without alerting government ministries prematurely. They settled on "Operation Flash" as the code words to communicate the news that Hitler was dead and the coup should begin.

Tresckow was elated when Hitler informed Field Marshal Kluge in late February that he would visit Army Group Center's Smolensk headquarters in early March. The precise date would be given to Kluge later. More than ever Hitler lived in a tight security cocoon, cloaking his every move in secrecy. He suspected everyone, especially army officers, many of whom he was convinced plotted to kill him. In his customary manner he fixed a date for the visit, cancelled, rescheduled, cancelled again, and finally scheduled again for March 13, 1943.

A few weeks before, Tresckow had received word from Oster and Olbricht in Berlin that preparations for the coup were complete and waited only for a signal from Smolensk to begin. Plans were firmly in place for the military to seize all communications and command centers in Berlin, Vienna, Cologne, and Munich.

Goerdeler passed word to his contacts in Sweden, who had access to Churchill, to tell the British Prime Minister that a plot was under way to kill Hitler and put an end to the war. Goerdeler's contacts were the Swedish banking brothers, Jacob and Marcus Wallenberg, who had previously agreed to speak to Churchill on behalf of the German resistance once the Nazis were removed from power.

Meanwhile Tresckow concentrated his efforts on attempting to win Kluge over to the plot, while Boeselager rehearsed his death squad in their assigned roles. Kluge was afraid to participate, giving as his excuse his fear that the German population would not understand the reasoning behind an assassination. He told Tresckow that if successful the coup would appear to many Germans, who did not understand the seriousness of the military situation, as if a group of power-hungry generals had murdered Germany's leader and seized power for their own aggrandizement. Although not irrevocably opposed to the coup, he felt it best to wait until the military situation reached crisis proportions and the need to replace the government became obvious to everyone.

Without Kluge's full support, Tresckow doubted that Boeselager's cavalry regiment could be employed successfully. He and Schlabrendorff hastily developed a backup plan so as not to miss the opportunity to kill Hitler. The alternate plan was to destroy Hitler's plane in midflight. This option had several distinct advantages: Field Marshal Kluge's approval was not necessary, and Hitler's death would not directly involve army officers who could have underlying misgivings because of their oath.

Tresckow's plan required two vital ingredients: (1) a detailed schematic of Hitler's plane, especially the armored compartment where the Führer stayed during flight, and (2) enough sophisticated explosives to do the job. The force of the explosives was critical because Hitler's armored compartment was constructed in such a manner that if his plane was disabled the compartment could be detached from the aircraft and float gently down, using special parachutes that were connected to it. It was therefore vital to destroy the armored section of the plane to succeed.

Tresckow contacted Captain Ludwig Gehre, a member of the conspiracy in Berlin, and asked him to obtain copies of the prints for Hitler's Condor aircraft. Gehre called a close friend and member of the resistance, Otto John, who was employed by Lufthansa, and invited him to his house. Swearing John to secrecy, Gehre outlined the scheme to bomb Hitler's personal aircraft and asked John if he could get plans of the craft. John cautioned Gehre that it would be next to impossible to plant a bomb on the Führer's Focke-Wulf 200 condor. The aircraft was kept under tight security by armed SS guards who searched every person approaching the plane, including the ground crews who serviced and cleaned it. John, however, was able to get drawings of the craft, and these were forwarded to Tresckow in Smolensk.

Next Tresckow and Schlabrendorff needed the explosives with which to do the job. It would seem that senior officers attached to a frontline army headquarters would have easy access to explosives, but this was not the case. All explosive materials in the Third Reich were kept under tight inventory control by the Gestapo. The material for their bomb would have to be acquired in small amounts over a period of time.

Tresckow assigned this task to Colonel Rudolf-Christoph Baron von Gersdorff, the Army Group Center Intelligence Officer. What was required, Tresckow explained to Gersdorff, was explosive material that was compact yet yielded a high energy explosion using noiseless time delay fuses.

Gersdorff told Tresckow that German-made time delay fuses were unworkable because they all emitted an audible hiss. He canvassed several Abwehr supply depots, finding what he needed at an arsenal maintained by the Sabotage Division. Explaining that he was training a cadre to counteract disruptive partisan activity, he asked the officer in charge of the arsenal if he could demonstrate several different types of explosives his teams might use.

Gersdorff settled on "Platic C," a volatile substance the British regularly supplied to partisan bands throughout occupied Europe. Quantities had fallen into the Abwehr's hands when German army units either tracked British parachute drops or recovered them from captured partisans. Plastic C consisted of over 88 percent hexogen, with the remainder an amalgam of materials such as axle grease to prevent the hexogen from crystallizing. An officer who was knowledgeable in the use of Plastic C proudly showed Gersdorff what less than a pound would do, when he detonated it under the turret of a captured Soviet tank. The force of the explosion blew the turret off the tank, hurling it more than twenty yards away.

Gersdorff asked the arsenal commander, Lieutenant Buchholz, for samples of Plastic C, along with various fuses and detonators to demonstrate the explosive for Field Marshal Kluge. After signing the required receipts and receiving thorough instructions on handling the material and the detonators, he was provided a modest quantity. A few more trips to other supply depots gave Gersdorff enough Plastic C to make several test runs, with enough left to sabotage Hitler's plane.

Tresckow, Gersdorff, and Schlabrendorff experimented with the explosive and found its only disadvantage was that at temperatures below zero degrees Centigrade it sometimes failed to explode. Satisfied that Plastic C would do the job, providing the temperature was not too cold, they fashioned a package to look like two bottles of Cointreau, a premium brandy bottled in square decanters. The square shape was easy to duplicate, making the package appear authentic. The package was heavily wrapped and tied tightly with cord to discourage closer inspection.

An ingenious device to detonate the bomb was chosen from Gersdorff's selection. When a small vial of acid in the device was crushed, the acid spilled into a wad of cotton. The acid then ate through a tiny trip wire that released a plunger that drove the detonator into the explosive. Once the capsule was broken, the acid would require thirty minutes until it was absorbed by the cotton and the spring was released.

When the deadly package was ready, Schlabrendorff kept it inside a metal box in his quarters, awaiting Hitler's visit. The conspirators at Army Group Center now had preparations solidly in place for two alternative plans to kill Hitler. No one connected with the plot doubted that if one misfired the other would succeed. As far as the plotters were concerned, when Hitler made his expected visit he was as good as dead.

On March 13, 1943, the sky over Smolensk was a cloudless blue expanse. The operations officer at the small airfield near headquarters heard the steady drone of approaching aircraft and watched the distant specks take sharper form as he called Kluge's duty officer with the news that the Führer's plane was about to land. Tresckow and the field marshal hurried into staff cars for the short ride to the airstrip. Overhead, three Condors approached the runway escorted by a formation of Messerschmidtt-109 fighters. While Kluge and Tresckow went to greet Hitler, Schlabrendorff telephoned Gehre in Berlin to alert him that Operation Flash was about to begin. Gehre immediately informed Olbricht, then Dohnanyi, who promptly told Oster. Oster, in turn, contacted Beck with the news. The resistance waited anxiously for the word to strike.

The Condors landed and taxied off the runway to allow the fighter escort room to land. Hitler stepped from the lead Condor, descended the steps, and greeted Kluge and his staff warmly. He declined Kluge's invitation to drive him to headquarters in his staff car. Hitler, appearing older than most of those present remembered him, and exhibiting a noticeable stoop, proceeded to his personal car, which his chauffeur, Erich Kempka, had driven to Smolensk. The detachment of SS guards that accompanied Kempka was supplemented by a platoon flown in on the second Condor.

Rounding out the entourage were several staff officers; Hitler's personal physician, Dr. Theodor Morell; a stenographer; Hitler's personal chef; and a photographer to record highlights of the visit for posterity. The chef personally prepared all Hitler's meals. Dr. Morell, who like his arch-rival Göring had grown rich and fat off his relationship with the Führer, always tasted Hitler's food in his presence before the Führer ate anything.

On an earlier visit to a frontline headquarters several Soviet tanks had come ominously close to Hitler's plane, prompting the SS to beef up the Führer's security force. His escort for this visit was double the usual complement. Sensing Hitler's preoccupation with security, Army Group Center seized on this opportunity to volunteer a squadron of Cavalry Regiment Center's troops, under command of Major Konig, to augment Hitler's security shield. The officers of this squadron, who had sworn to shoot Hitler, were now perfectly positioned to kill him while he walked from his car to the headquarters building, or when he was returning to his car. An earlier suggestion to shoot Hitler while he ate in the mess was rejected by Kluge because he felt it unseemly to shoot a man while he was eating. Also, there was the risk of hitting one of the officers seated with Hitler, possibly even Kluge, whom the conspirators expected would assume command of the entire front and stabilize the situation until a truce was arranged.

The assassins in Cavalry Regiment Center never received the order to shoot, possibly (as explained later by Major Konig) because Hitler changed his original route and the mounted guard did not have a clear shot at him. It is also not improbable that the SS guards, fingers tight around the triggers of their submachine guns, kept too close a watch on the armed soldiers whom they might have viewed as a potential threat. In any event, no shots were fired.

During lunch Tresckow approached one of Hitler's staff officers, Colonel Heinz Brandt, whom Tresckow saw alight from the Führer's own plane. He asked Brandt if he could take a package of two bottles of Cointreau with him to High Command Headquarters. They were a gift for Colonel Helmuth Stieff, Tresckow explained, and he did not want to risk their being broken if he sent them through the normal mail. Brandt cheerfully agreed.

When lunch was over and Hitler prepared to depart, Lieutenant Schlabrendorff slipped off to his quarters and retrieved the bomb. At the airport he waited until Hitler said his farewells and started to board his plane, followed closely by members of his entourage. Tresckow nodded to Schlabrendorff, who pressed a key against the package, crushing the capsule of acid, then with a broad smile handed the package to Colonel Brandt, who carried it aboard Hitler's plane.

The fighters took off first, circled the field several times, and signaled the all clear. Within minutes all three Condors were airborne, flying a course for Rastenburg in East Prussia.

Tresckow and Schlabrendorff returned to their headquarters where the latter called Gehre in Berlin to tell him that Operation Flash was in its second stage, meaning they were waiting for confirmation of Hitler's death. Tresckow estimated that Hitler's Condor would mysteriously explode somewhere in the vicinity of Minsk, a half-hour's flying time from Smolensk.

For two anxious hours Tresckow and Schlabrendorff waited for news that Hitler's plane had crashed. They expected the first announcement to come from the commander of the fighter planes that escorted Hitler, but no word came. Finally a confirmation was received from Rastenburg that the Führer's plane had landed there safely. Stunned, the two officers could not believe their ears. Schlabrendorff immediately called Gehre and gave him the coded message that Operation Flash had failed. Gehre, sickened by the tension and the disappointment, passed the word to General Olbricht and then Oster and Dohnanyi.

Tresckow and Schlabrendorff were at a loss about what to do next. Obviously, the bomb had not exploded. Had the secret of their lethal package been discovered before it could explode? If so, the Gestapo was surely on the way to arrest them. If the bomb failed to explode because of a defect, the package would have to be retrieved before it was delivered to Colonel Stieff. Either way, the two men could be in grievous trouble.

They had to know what had happened. Finally, Tresckow called Colonel Brandt in Rastenburg and casually asked if he had delivered the package to Stieff. To his great relief, Brandt said he had not had a chance to deliver it yet. Tresckow then explained that Brandt had been given the wrong package, and would he hold on to it until the next day when it would be exchanged for the correct package. Brandt replied that he would be glad to, and the conversation ended.

The following morning Schlabrendorff took a schedule courier flight to Rastenburg bearing a package containing two bottles of Cointreau. When he arrived at Brandt's office, the colonel playfully tossed the package containing the bomb from one hand to the other, joking about dropping the two bottles of expensive brandy he thought it contained. Schlabrendorff, trying to remain calm, exchanged the packages and withdrew as quickly as possible. He had no idea why the bomb had not exploded and he was afraid that Brandt's juggling would cause the explosion right there. Leaving the building, he took a staff car to the railroad station in nearby Korschen, where he boarded a train to Berlin.

On board the train Schlabrendorff locked himself inside the private compartment he had reserved and carefully opened the package. Examining the bomb, he immediately saw what had happened. The capsule had broken under the pressure of his key and the spring to release the detonator, which slammed home causing a blackened mark where it struck, but for some unknown reason the Plastic C had failed to ignite. What probably happened was that Colonel Brandt left the package in the unheated luggage compartment instead of taking it into the heated passenger section with him. The extreme cold caused the explosive material to crystallize immediately–and when the strike hit, nothing happened.

In Berlin Schlabrendorff met with Oster and the other conspirators. He showed them the flawed bomb and how close they had come to killing Hitler.

Later that month another opportunity to kill Hitler would arise. On March 21 the country would observe a national holiday known as Hero's Memorial Day. Traditionally the Führer participated in the ceremonies honoring German soldiers who had died in previous wars. Schlabrendorff was still in Berlin when Tresckow proposed to Gersdorff a way to kill Hitler when he came to the event. As part of the program, Hitler was to inspect an assortment of captured Soviet weapons on display in the Berlin Armory. Because the weapons had been captured largely by Army Group Center, an officer from that army was invited to accompany Hitler on the tour to answer any technical questions he might have. This was an important duty because Hitler was always fascinated by new weapons developments and usually asked tough questions. Gersdorff had been selected for this job.

During their conversation, Gersdorff and Tresckow concluded that the only way to kill Hitler during the tour was through a suicide mission. Gersdorff would have to set off a bomb hidden on his person, then wrap his arms around the Führer tightly until the explosion killed them both. Tresckow was reluctant to ask this of his comrade in the conspiracy, but Gersdorff confessed that since his wife's death a year earlier he really had little to live for, and if through his death he could accomplish the great patriotic good that would come from killing Hitler, he was more than willing to make the sacrifice.

Gersdorff arrived in Berlin two days before the ceremonies and established himself in the Hotel Eden. The following morning Schlabrendorff brought him the bomb package that had been placed on Hitler's plane on March 13. Gersdorff chose from a variety of British fuses. He discarded several instantaneous fuses because he would need time to grab Hitler and hold on to him. He decided to use a ten-minute fuse, which was the shortest timed fuse he had aside from the instantaneous fuses. This would provide sufficient time to set the fuse in action and get close enough to Hitler to grab him in case they were separated. He knew from the schedule, which he had obtained from General Schmundt, Hitler's Chief Adjutant, that the Führer was allotting ten minutes for the weapons tour, so he planned to set the fuse off just before the tour began.

Just after noon on March 21 Hitler arrived for the ceremonies and was greeted by the chiefs of the armed forces and other government and Party dignitaries. Inside the hall he delivered a speech for fourteen minutes while Gersdorff, a bomb hidden in each pocket of his greatcoat, waited patiently by the entrance to the weapons exhibit. When Hitler finished speaking he left the platform and walked toward the exhibit. As Hitler approached, Gersdorff reached into his left pocket, a highly risky gesture when Hitler and his bodyguards were around, and released the fuse. He did not want to press his luck by arming the bomb in his right pocket, and he assumed that when one went off it would ignite the other. He had ten minutes until the explosion.

To everyone's amazement, Hitler ignored Gersdorff and strode into the exhibit hall at an ever quickening pace. Gersdorff rushed to catch up with him, attempting to draw his special attention to certain exhibits in an effort to slow him down, but Hitler continued to ignore him and also paid no attention to others, including Göring, who tried to point out interesting aspects of certain exhibits. Hitler was in and out of the exhibition hall in two minutes, not the ten minutes that had been scheduled.

At the exit Gersdorff was turned back by SS guards, as this was as far as he was supposed to go. The stunned officer watched helplessly as Hitler virtually raced from the hall. Regaining his thoughts amidst the confusion and frustration, he remembered the live bomb in his left pocket. Frantically he looked for some place he could go to deactivate the bomb. He looked at his watch, eight minutes left, and prayed the bomb did not detonate prematurely. Locating a nearby men's room, he quickly went inside and locked himself in a stall. Removing the bomb from his pocket, he pulled off the striker, making the bomb inoperative. Gersdorff collapsed onto the toilet seat and dropped his head into his hands, panting heavily from the tension.

The only positive result of these failed attempts on Hitler's life was that General Olbricht, who had been listening to reports of the ceremonies over the radio and waiting for news of the explosion, uncovered deficiencies in the coup planning that must be corrected before the next attempt. To help with this task, Tresckow asked for and received a sick leave for several months' duration. He spent virtually the entire time working on resistance organizational problems and helping refine the plans for the coup that was used the following year.

So far 1943 had proven to be a year of near misses, but disappointing results, in the attempts by the resistance to assassinate Hitler. The following month, April, proved to be potentially the most disastrous of all and nearly resulted in the complete unraveling of the conspiracy.

Hans Oster's Abwehr conspirators, working under the protection of Admiral Canaris, had served as the nerve center for the whole coup operation. The Abwehr itself was beyond the Gestapo's jurisdiction but not beyond Himmler's aspirations. The SS chief wanted to incorporate the Abwehr into his expanding SS empire. Those working under Himmler in both the SS and the Gestapo knew his ambitions concerning the Abwehr and were constantly looking for ways to discredit Admiral Canaris and his people. The Abwehr resistance power base began to crumble on April 5, 1943.

Ironically, the end came not because the Abwehr officials were engaged in attempting to kill Hitler and replace the Nazi regime but because Canaris, Oster, and Dohnanyi had frequently used their military intelligence service to save Jews from the gas chambers. On several occasions Canaris had spoken to Himmler about some Jews who had been arrested, claiming they were actually Abwehr agents and requesting their release. Once freed, the Jews were usually slipped out of the country and into Switzerland, where they were given Abwehr funds to help compensate for their lost property in Germany.

Admiral Canaris had on several occasions claimed as his agents Jews who could by no stretch of the imagination have been intelligence operatives. Typical of his audacity was the case of twelve elderly Jews who lived in Berlin. When they came under the Gestapo's scrutiny in the summer of 1942, Canaries issued to them Abwehr identifications and provided them with exit permits, claiming they were going abroad to work against the United States.

The chance arrest of a man in Czechoslovakia with $400 in American currency on his person, a serious offense, was reported to the Gestapo. Under questioning the man claimed to be an Abwehr agent and that the money had been given to him by Wilhelm Schmidhuber of the Abwehr's Munich branch. The Gestapo, which had no legal authority to investigate any military agency without prior approval from General Keitel, secretly interrogated Schmidhuber. He broke and named Dohnanyi as the man who handled the illegal funds.

When Himmler received this information, the Reichführer-SS was actually reluctant to move against the Abwehr. He was seriously contemplating using Canaris's contacts with the Allies to explore chances of arranging a truce if his SS organization, which had grown into a state within the state, could remove Hitler and put Himmler in his place. Himmler knew the war was lost and the major obstacle to a peaceful settlement was Hitler. With the Führer out of the picture, the Allies might conceivably accept a new government with Himmler in authority. He referred the case to the military Judge Advocate's office, where it came under the jurisdiction of an ardent pro-Nazi Luftwaffe officer, Manfred Roeder.

Roeder pursued the investigation zealously. He uncovered evidence that Dohnanyi had maintained a secret fund in a Swiss bank to assist Jews the Abwehr had spirited out of Germany. Neither Canaris nor Oster had been accused, but Roeder considered them equally suspect.

Shortly before 10:00 a.m. on the morning of April 5, Roeder, accompanied by a Gestapo officer, Franz Sonderegger, strode into Abwehr headquarters and demanded to speak with Admiral Canaris. He told the Admiral that Dohnanyi was suspected of illegally dealing in foreign currency and other treasonous activities. Schmidhuber, who had been a legitimate exporter occasionally employed by the Abwehr, told the Gestapo, and later Roeder, about Dohnanyi's sending funds out of the country. He also mentioned the Jews he had helped to escape, and he implicated Dohnanyi in clandestine dealings with the Vatican channeled through Josef Müller. Roeder told Canaris that Dohnanyi was to be arrested, and he produced a warrant giving him permission to search Dohnanyi's office.

Canaris was outraged by the intrusion of a Gestapo agent in his headquarters. However, confident that Oster and Dohnanyi would not leave incriminating evidence about, he reluctantly permitted Roeder to proceed.

Canaris, Oster, Dohnanyi, and the Gestapo agent stood by while Roeder searched the safe in Dohnanyi's office. At one point Dohnanyi surreptitiously drew Oster's attention to three sheets of paper that were among the files Roeder had removed from the safe and placed on Dohnanyi desk. Oster picked them up and hastily slipped them inside his jacket. Sonderegger, the Gestapo agent, caught his movement and cried out to Roeder, who whirled around and demanded that Oster surrender the papers.

The papers were extremely incriminating. One contained an organization table for a post-Hitler government. The other documents discussed the existence of military and Christian organizations dedicated to the overthrow of the Hitler government. Dohnanyi was arrested, as were Müller, Dohnanyi's wife Christine, and several others. Luckily for all, they were arrested by the military authorities who relied on normal interrogation methods, not those used by the Gestapo.

An intelligent individual, Dohnanyi, a former Supreme Court Judge, was more than a match for his questioners and never revealed anything the authorities did not already know. Fearing he would be turned over to the SS, Dohnanyi arranged to infect himself with diphtheria, resulting in his transfer to an army hospital. Eventually Dohnanyi, Müller, and Dietrich Bonhoeffer, a protestant pastor and member of Dohnanyi's circle, were incarcerated in an SS concentration camp, but they confessed to nothing more than the authorities already knew and never implicated anyone else in their crimes.

Shortly after Dohnanyi was arrested, the Abwehr headquarters was hit by several bombs during an Allied bombing raid on Berlin. The building and everything in it was destroyed, but too late to help Dohnanyi.

Because of his actions during the search of Dohnanyi's office, Oster was discharged from the Abwehr, placed on the reserve officer list, and subsequently discharged from the army. Within a year Canaris was fired and the Abwehr was absorbed by the SS under a direct order from Adolf Hitler.

In the meantime, resistance fortunes continued to deteriorate. General Beck was discovered to have cancer and had major surgery, which left him incapacitated. While he could no longer actively participate in the resistance, the members still considered him their leader. Under the revised plans drawn by Tresckow, Beck and Goerdeler would assume control of the government until elections could be held.

Since Tresckow no longer served on Kluge's staff, he did not exert the influence over the field marshal he once enjoyed. Other officers, however, including Colonel Stieff, a newcomer to the cause and the man to whom the Cointreau bomb had been addressed, had worked on the field marshal to win his support for a coup. On an autumn trip to Berlin, Kluge was invited to General Olbricht's home where he met with Beck, Tresckow, and Goerdeler. It was here that he finally relented and pledged his support for the resistance. Less than two weeks later, his staff car was involved in an accident and he was hospitalized in traction. A strong pro-Hitler replacement, Field Marshal Ernst Busch, assumed command of Army Group Center.

Late in 1943 Tresckow attempted to get himself assigned as Field Marshal Manstein's Chief of Staff in the hope of convincing Manstein to join the resistance. The field marshal rejected the appointment, telling the army personnel chief that while Tresckow had no peer as a staff officer, he had a negative attitude toward National Socialism. This reproach spelled finis to Tresckow's career and his effectiveness in the resistance. He was transferred to the eastern front, where he could do little except wait to hear that Hitler was dead and the coup had begun.

Before his departure Tresckow engineered three final attempts on Hitler's life. In one, Colonel Stieff secretly gathered a large quantity of explosives to use in an attack on Hitler. Two officers took the explosives to the grounds of Hitler's Rastenburg headquarters in East Prussia, where they buried them under a water tower to wait for the right occasion to use them. Inexplicably, the material exploded for no apparent reason, causing consternation among the SS guards and redoubling of security measures.

With unusual good luck for the resistance one of their member officers was assigned to investigate the incident. Colonel Werner Schrader dragged his inquiry on so long that he never issued a report.

In late November or early December 1943, Hitler was supposed to view a selection of proposed new uniforms for the army. Several alternative samples were made, and he wanted to have the final word on which were to be produced and distributed, especially to the troops fighting in Russia. One of the officers chosen to model the new uniforms was Captain Axel von dem Bussche, a member of Tresckow's inner circle. Bussche dismantled a German hand grenade and fashioned a bomb with a four-second fuse, which he proposed to carry in the pocket of the greatcoat he was going to model. Once in Hitler's presence, he planned to release the timer and grab Hitler so the two of them would be blown up together.

The viewing was postponed repeatedly while Bussche waited impatiently to perform what he expected would be the final act of his life. The sample uniforms were stored in a railroad boxcar parked on a siding in Berlin. One night during the regular allied bombing, the car received a direct hit and was destroyed, along with the uniforms that were to provide the opportunity to place an assassin within reach of the Führer.

In March 1944, Captain Eberhard von Breitenbuch, personal aide to Field Marshal Busch, told Tresckow that he was going to attend a conference at Hitler's Berchtesgaden headquarters where he would shoot Hitler, knowing full well that he himself would probably be shot to death by the SS guards. Tresckow offered to give him explosives, but Breitenbuch said he was an excellent shot and would require only seconds to draw his pistol, aim at Hitler's head, and squeeze off at least one and possibly several shots. He was confident Hitler would be killed.

On the day of the conference, Busch and his aide arrived in the anteroom at Hitler's quarters where they met other field marshals. When the SS major opened the door to the Führer's conference room the conferees entered in ranking order. Breitenbuch, the most junior officer, last. The SS major put his hand out to restrain Breitenbuch and told him that aides were not permitted to attend the meeting. When Busch protested that he required his aide's presence, the major informed the field marshal that it was Hitler's decision and could not be countermanded.

For the next several hours Breitenbuch waited anxiously in the anteroom, brooding over the reason he was excluded from the conference with Hitler. He thought that perhaps someone had learned of his intent to murder the Führer. This seemed to be the most logical explanation, and every time an SS man walked through the room Breitenbuch feared the worst. Around noon the meeting broke up and he followed Busch out of the building, looking nervously around, half expecting to be arrested. No explanation was ever given for his exclusion from the conference, but once again fate stepped in and saved Hitler from an assassin.

With Tresckow's departure to the eastern front, Oster's forced absence from military installations, and Beck's arduous recovery from cancer, a new, young, resourceful officer stepped into the role of leader of the conspiracy, Colonel Claus Count von Stauffenberg. His name would forever be linked with intrigues to kill Adolf Hitler.

9.

Stauffenberg Takes Charge

One needed only to look at Colonel Claus Count von Stauffenberg to know that he had already paid a high price for Hitler's war. A black patch covered the empty socket that had been his left eye. His right hand was missing, as were two fingers of his left hand. Despite these disfigurements, suffered when a U.S. fighter plane attacked his North African panzer column, Stauffenberg remained a handsome and charming officer.

While recovering from the wounds received during what he described as "another of Hitler's lost causes," Stauffenberg learned to write with his left hand, using the thumb and two remaining fingers. He also used those three fingers, together with his teeth, to dress himself, pinning up his right sleeve to keep it from flapping about.

Stauffenberg's contemporaries credited him with a natural ability to inspire and organize people. Descendant from an old family of Swabian aristocrats, his father had been Senior Marshal to the King of Württemberg until the collapse of the monarchy in 1918. The Stauffenbergs were Roman Catholics. This faith instilled in Claus a solid philosophy for life which led him to loathe the Nazis.

In the fall of 1943, after several head operations required by his wounds, Stauffenberg recovered enough to join the active resistance at the strong urging of his uncle, Count Nikolaus von Uxkull. His uncle knew of Stauffenberg's attitude toward Hitler and the Nazis, which was formed indelibly from his experiences in the Russian campaign before he was assigned to Africa. Uxkull confided in his nephew that there were other officers who felt as he did, and that they were organized into a formal resistance group determined to kill Hitler and remove the Nazis from power. He asked his nephew to join them. Stauffenberg wanted time to think it over.

When Stauffenberg was restored to active duty he reported to Colonel General Kurt Zeitzler, who had replaced Halder as Chief of the General Staff in September 1942. The disabled colonel requested assignment to a frontline unit, but Zeitzler, recognizing his enormous potential, felt Stauffenberg's talents deserved to be nurtured. Zeitzler wanted him to broaden his experience so that one day he could command a corps or perhaps even an army. Instead of sending him to the front, Zeitzler appointed Stauffenberg Chief of Staff of the General Army Office under General Friedrich Olbricht.

The next time he saw his uncle, Stauffenberg told him he had decided to join the resistance. He is also reported to have told him that since the generals had failed to unseat Hitler, now it was time the colonels accomplished the task. It was then Count Uxkull felt it safe to tell him that his new superior officer, General Olbricht, was a key figure in the conspiracy against Hitler.

Olbricht summoned Stauffenberg to his Berlin headquarters. During their conversation about Stauffenberg's future, he asked Stauffenberg if he was prepared to join the resistance in its efforts to topple the Nazis. Stauffenberg acknowledged that he was. His first priority, before making a full commitment, was to visit his brother, Berthold, an attorney who served as an advisor on international law to the German Navy High Command. Claus rarely made an important decision without first consulting his elder brother, to whom he was devoted. Berthold agreed completely that

Hitler must be removed, and he supported Claus's decision to join the active resistance.

In September 1943, Stauffenberg helped Olbricht and Tresckow, who was still in Berlin on sick leave, reorganize plans for a renewed coup attempt. They were joined occasionally by General Beck, whose recovery from cancer surgery was taking longer than expected. Pointedly absent from these proceedings was the man who had once been a central figure, Hans Oster. Now under close Gestapo surveillance, Oster had been ordered by Keitel to stay away from military installations. Reluctantly he obeyed, for fear of betraying the identities of the other conspirators.

As a new member of the conspiracy, Claus von Stauffenberg was introduced to a wider circle of people who had been working against Hitler, some for over five years. Tresckow introduced him to Goerdeler, who together with Beck would head a new German government after the coup succeeded. He was then introduced to Fritz-Dietlof Count von der Schulenburg, who introduced him to Dr. Julius Leber, a former Social Democrat Reichstag Deputy who had once been imprisoned by the Nazis for his opposition. His new friends helped Stauffenberg refine his political philosophies, and he quickly became influential in the political circles of the resistance as well as the military circles.

At first there was serious friction between Goerdeler and Stauffenberg. The latter viewed the former Lord Mayor of Leipzig as leading a revolution of "graybeards." He thought Goerdeler too conservative, and apt to lead a post-Nazi Germany back to the days of the Weimar Republic. Stauffenberg objected the accord that had been in place before he joined the resistance, designating Goerdeler Reich Chancellor in the new government. He supported the portion of the plan that named General Beck head of state and Field Marshal Witzleben head of the army, but Goerdeler's role bothered him.

For his part, Goerdeler, the tireless conspirator who traveled endlessly winning converts to the cause of the resistance, thought Stauffenberg too "pig-headed and arrogant." He thought Stauffenberg should confine himself to military matters and had no business involving himself in political plans, which were a civilian responsibility. After several meetings each man came to respect the other's ability and dedication to their cause, and their political differences were subordinated to their shared goal of toppling the Nazi regime.

Tresckow's transfer to the eastern front in October 1943, effectively removed him as the principal motivator behind the plots to assassinate Hitler. He was replaced by Claus Stauffenberg, whom Count Uxkull described as "the finger on the trigger."

The new pattern for the coup that evolved from the original concept of 1938 was "highly sophisticated" as the Gestapo would later admit. It centered around the unlikely use of the Replacement Army, which was a reserve force of walking wounded, trainees, cadets in military schools, workers who could quickly be pulled from their jobs, and men on sick leave. It was not an effective fighting force, but was intended originally to be used to supply replacements to frontline units. The Replacement Army was controlled by General Olbricht's superior, Colonel General Friederich Fromm, an overweight bureaucrat filled with his own importance. Fromm refused to have anything to do with the conspiracy unless the plotters killed Hitler; then, he said, they could count on his support. A typical fence-sitter, Fromm wanted it both ways. He would support the coup or support Hitler, depending on which side appeared to be the winner.

In early 1943 the conspirators, disadvantaged by the fact that not even their leading military officers commanded troop formations, hit on the idea of molding the Replacement Army into a force to support their coup. Olbricht spoke to Hitler about the internal dangers to the Reich presented by the over four million foreign workers and prisoners of war within its borders. Enemy nationals concentrated in such numbers posed a serious threat if they organized a rebellion in any significant strength against the largely inadequate civil police forces. Olbricht proposed to develop a contingency plan using the Replacement Army as a safety valve that could be called on to put down a worker's revolt, or even move against enemy saboteurs who might infiltrate the Reich. Hitler was enthusiastic about the proposal and told him to work out the details. Tresckow and Stauffenberg concentrated on the project throughout the fall of 1943, assisted by a select committee of dedicated officers.

A decision was reached to use Replacement Army reserves, supplemented by troops from the seventeen military districts inside the Reich. Stauffenberg and Olbricht used their authority to influence appointment of members of the resistance to key positions in as many military districts as possible. Their intent was to ensure that when the district forces were needed to support the coup, officers pledged to the resistance effort would be in positions to deliver them. Unfortunately, the flagging fortunes of the German military effort required an increased number of combat replacements, and the frequent rotation of resistance officers was an ongoing, almost daily concern for both men.

The idea of employing these troops to control potential internal emergencies appealed to the High Command; consequently, they gave the Commander-in-Chief of the Replacement Army, Fromm, wide latitude to requisition and deploy troops in case of a domestic disturbance. This should have aided the conspirators, but an impasse existed between Fromm, who refused to cooperate unless the conspirators demonstrated they could succeed, and resistance leaders, who could do little without a commitment of Replacement Army backing. A possible solution to this dilemma was advanced by Olbricht, who decided that when the time was right he would ask Fromm to commit the Replacement Army and the military district forces to the coup. If Fromm refused, Olbricht would arrest him and issue the orders in his name, anticipating that most troop commanders would carry them out.

A set of substitute orders was prepared and updated regularly by Stauffenberg, changing the original response to the signal "Valkyrie," which meant an internal disturbance, to mean "surround and neutralize all SS and Gestapo installations within the Reich, and commandeer all communications facilities, particularly public radio stations." Several officers who were experienced radio announcers were prepared to rush to public broadcast facilities, once the coup began, so that news of the event would be reported in a favorable light.

The script called for them to announce Hitler's murder by a cabal inside the Nazi Party. The traitors, far from the fighting front, would be publicly accused of "stabbing the army in the back" while it struggled for its survival. This ingenious tactic was intended to raise public anger against Hitler's own Party followers. The stunned population would be told that the army was the saviour of the nation and the German people, having arrested or executed the men responsible for killing the Führer. Through this bold subterfuge the conspirators hoped to paralyze the Nazis, especially the SS and the Waffen SS, and throw them into confusion long enough for resistance-led troops to disarm or at least isolate them.

Once Hitler was dead, final success would depend on the ability of resistance members who infiltrated the various military districts to deliver their forces on the side of the coup. This explains why judicious appointments and postings had been Stauffenberg's top priority. Nevertheless, everything hinged on killing Hitler. With the Führer dead, Stauffenberg and Olbricht were convinced that a majority of army officers not yet committed to the conspiracy would rethink their position and quickly join the resistance. To help encourage this, one of the many proclamations drawn up for release during the coup declared that General Beck would head an interim government replacing the Nazi regime, and that Field Marshal Witzleben, who had been put on reserve by Hitler, would take over command of the entire German army. Beck and Witzleben were highly respected by most army officers, and their participation in the coup was expected to win support from troop commanders at all levels.

Consistent with earlier coup plans, neutralizing the SS was a critical issue, since that organization was devoutly loyal to Hitler. Now the Waffen SS became equally important. Grown to parallel the regular army, the Wafen SS had its own panzer and mobilized units, which actually outnumbered the army in some military districts. While a few Waffen SS commanders might throw in their lot with the army if Hitler was dead, many more could be expected to wage a civil war against the army. At the same time, the army would have to maintain its position on all fronts facing the Allies. The speed with which the conspirators moved against these potential opponents was vital to success.

Just as Tresckow before him, Stauffenberg recognized that Hitler's assassination was paramount. With Hitler dead the coup might succeed, but if Hitler was merely arrested or confined, he would be a rallying point for his supporters. Stauffenberg wrestled with his Catholic beliefs, finally concluding that it was a worse sin to permit Hitler's continued destruction of the German people. After conferring with other officers who were candidates for the job of assassin, Stauffenberg decided the surest course of action was to do the "dirty work," as the conspirators called it, himself. When in late spring of 1944 he was appointed Chief of Staff to the Commander-in-Chief of the Replacement army, Stauffenberg soon found the opportunity he needed.

When Stauffenberg became General Fromm's new Chief of Staff on June 1, 1944, an appointment Fromm had requested because of Stauffenberg's organizational skills, he immediately sought ways to try to win Fromm over to the resistance. Fromm nodded agreement when Stauffenberg suggested that a coup was necessary to save Germany from total destruction, especially since an earlier Allied ultimatum demanded nothing short of unconditional surrender. While Fromm appeared to approve of a coup, he steadfastly refused to commit himself, saying only that Stauffenberg should not "forget that fellow Keitel when you make your putsch."[1]

Five days later the Allies swept ashore at Normandy in such overwhelming strength that many German army leaders read the invasion as the prelude to disaster. In the south, the Allies were pushing relentlessly up the Italian peninsula. In the east, the German army steeled for the expected Soviet summer offensive. Intelligence reports made it clear that the Soviet army was now far superior in men and material to the German defenders. With Germany being squeezed on all sides into an increasingly tighter circle, and her cities ablaze and crumbling under continuous Allied bombing, Stauffenberg questioned whether the effort to kill Hitler was still worthwhile, since the end of the war was obviously so near.

Stauffenberg asked Tresckow for guidance. Never one to waver, Tresckow, without hesitation, responded as Stauffenberg doubtlessly expected:

> The assassination must be attempted at all costs. Even if it should not succeed, an attempt to seize power in Berlin must be undertaken. What matters now is not the practical purpose of the coup, but to prove to the world and for the records of history that the men of the resistance movement dared to take the decisive step. Compared to this objective, nothing else is of consequence.[2]

Encouraged by Tresckow's counsel, Stauffenberg forged ahead with his plans. He was pleased to find that as Chief of Staff to Fromm he would have ample opportunity to kill Hitler. As Commander-in-Chief of the Replacement Army, Fromm now regularly appeared at Hitler's military conferences to report on the status of his forces. His Chief of Staff usually accompanied him.

While his infirmities would seem to make Stauffenberg an unlikely assassin, they also made him the least likely to be suspected by Hitler's security people. Also, he had become virtually the only member of the resistance with direct access to the person of the Führer and the resolve to carry out the assassination.

Fate decreed that Stauffenberg was the man. He began preparations for the assassination. Major General Helmuth Stieff had been hoarding a cache of explosives in Rastenberg, and Stauffenberg dispatched two officers who were resistance members to bring them back to Berlin. The explosives used acid-based fuses housed in thin glass tubes about the thickness of a pencil. With both their families moved to the relative safety of the south of Germany, Claus and Berthold Stauffenberg now shared an apartment in a Berlin suburb. Alone in his bedroom each night, Claus practiced with a small pair of pliers squeezing hard enough to break the glass and start the fuse.

On June 7, the day after the Normandy invasion began, Stauffenberg accompanied Fromm on a visit to Hitler's headquarters near Berchtesgaden. The handful of men attending the conference included Himmler and a grossly overweight Göring.

Stauffenberg found the atmosphere at the meeting "rotten and degenerate." He was surprised at what he found had happened to Hitler. He was, Stauffenberg wrote, "a nothing." At fifty-five the Führer appeared years older. He now had a pronounced stoop that exaggerated his grotesque appearance. An ill-fitting uniform hung loosely on his emaciated frame, and his right hand shook uncontrollably. The yellowish complexion and gray hair were contrasted with the burning blue eyes that continued to radiate an intense confidence in his own power.

Despite his revulsion with these "patent psychopaths," Stauffenberg came away from this conference encouraged. He now had direct access to Hitler, and he had entered his presence without being searched. Even his thickly packed pigskin briefcase had stirred no interest. At this conference the briefcase contained nothing but documents, but it would soon carry the explosive intended as the instrument of Hitler's death.

Acting on the latest advice from Tresckow, Stauffenberg flew to Paris on June 23 to visit his old friend, Colonel Eberhard Finckh, Deputy Chief of Staff to the Commander-in-chief, West. Stauffenberg told Finckh of his plans to kill Hitler and the coup that would follow to seize the government and control the army. He asked Finckh to pass this information to General Stulpnagel, the Military Governor, whom Stauffenberg knew would support the coup.

Meanwhile, Tresckow sent Colonel von Boeselager, the cavalry officer who had planned the shooting of Hitler during his visit to Army Group Center, to ask Field Marshal Kluge to support the coup. Kluge had replaced von Rundstedt as Commander-in-Chief, West, when Hitler tired of the old field marshal's "pessimism." As usual Kluge wavered, and Tresckow regretted he had been unable to make the trip himself because he believed he could still hold sway over Kluge. Tresckow sent a message to Kluge suggesting that he allow the Allies to break through the German lines to force the High command to see the futility of the situation. Kluge replied that it was unnecessary to do anything to encourage a breakthrough, since it would happen soon enough anyway.

In Berlin, plans for the coup went forward. It was hoped that the commanders in the West, Kluge and Rommel, who commanded Army Group B, would follow the lead of Beck and Witzleben once Hitler was dead. Rundstedt, Rommel, and even Kluge were resigned that the war was irrevocably lost and that efforts to bring an honorable cessation to the fighting must be redoubled. A new government and emancipated army leadership were imperative if they were to achieve this objective.

The administrative center of the conspiracy was focused in Berlin with strong support from Paris. Despite the difficulty of maintaining secret communications, Stauffenberg and Beck in Berlin were able to establish strong links to Stulpnagel, Military Governor in Paris, and Speidel, Rommel's Chief of Staff.

As the situation on the western front deteriorated, Rommel and Kluge agreed to weigh supporting the coup if Hitler was killed. Neither man would actively participate in the coup planning or execution; they would reserve decision, as did so many other high ranking German officers in pivotal positions.

Stauffenberg had no reservations. To him the situation was clear-cut. He could find no other officer with access to Hitler who was willing to attempt the assassination; consequently, he would do it himself. The other resistance leaders did not favor this decision. Stauffenberg was now the driving force behind the coup, and its success relied heavily on his talents. They feared that his absence from Berlin during the critical hours after the assassination, while he was flying back to the capital, would have an adverse effect on the results.

Stauffenberg readied his briefcase, carefully packing it with two pounds of explosives, and waited for his next opportunity. He felt he was destined to do the job, and he prepared to accomplish it as quickly as possible. He looked forward anxiously to his next trip to Hitler's headquarters.

July 1944 began ominously, with the arrest of several resistance members. Rumors spread that the Gestapo had learned of the coup and was about to seize all the plotters, but no further arrests followed and the work went forward. On July 6, Stauffenberg again went to the Berghof to hear Hitler's order for fifteen newly formed grenadier divisions to be rushed to the eastern front to stop the Soviet advance. Stauffenberg took the briefcase bomb into the conference room but made no attempt to trigger it, for reasons known only to himself. At the meeting's end Hitler assigned him the job of locating the personnel necessary to fill the proposed grenadier divisions.

In early July a decision was reached by the resistance leaders that the explosives Stauffenberg carried to the high level conferences would be used only if both Hitler and Himmler were present. The conspirators, especially Stauffenberg, believed that killing Hitler without also eliminating Himmler would create a dangerous situation. Himmler, a weak-chinned former chicken farmer whose name struck terror into the heart of every German, commanded his own personal army, which he would not hesitate to use against the coup; therefore he must be killed along with Hitler. For the resistance to assassinate Hitler alone, leaving Himmler free to retaliate, would be suicidal. Stauffenberg wanted to add Göring to the list of targets, but he finally agreed with Beck and Olbricht that the Luftwaffe chief was a less dangerous enemy than Himmler. Besides, Göring rarely attended Hitler's conferences personally, and waiting for his presence could only serve to delay the entire operation. Stauffenberg concentrated on his two primary targets.

Himmler was usually represented at Hitler's military briefings by one of his SS generals, but when the Führer decided to put Himmler in command of Stauffenberg's new grenadier divisions, the SS Reichführer's presence was required at the current round of meetings.

Stauffenberg's next chance to put his bomb to use came on Tuesday, July 11. As the growing military crisis threatened the collapse of Germany's eastern front, Hitler called for an update on Stauffenberg's progress in organizing the fifteen new "blocking divisions." Hitler referred to them in this way because he believed they would block the Soviet advance, that they would somehow plug the holes that were expanding daily in the German defenses. On July 8 Soviet troops directed by Marshal Rokossovsky captured Baranovichi, halfway between Minsk and Brest-Litovsk. Three days later the Soviet army reached the outskirts of Vilna in Poland, and the following evening the great new Soviet summer offensive against Army Group North began as the Soviets opened a huge gap in the German lines and quickly rolled over German defenses.

Hitler's attitude before this conference was indicative of his growing panic and vituperative treatment of his lieutenants. Things were going badly on all fronts, and Hitler typically placed the blame squarely on his generals and field marshals who were prudently advocating strategic retreat. Once again he senselessly ordered troops shuffled around like so many pieces on a chess board, ignoring completely the logistics involved. He thought that transporting troops without vehicles and moving vehicles without fuel could be accomplished through the strength of his own will. Refusing to face reality, something no one around him would point out, he assumed Stauffenberg could create crack grenadier divisions from the worn-out veterans and raw recruits in the Replacement Army.

Stauffenberg went over his plans in his mind during the ninety-minute flight from Berlin to the small airfield in Freilassing, just north of Berchtesgaden. Inside his briefcase, under a fresh uniform shirt, was the bomb and timer fuse. He was accompanied by his acting adjutant, Captain Friedrich Karl Klausing. His regular adjutant, Lieutenant Werner von Haeften (who earlier in the year had volunteered for a suicide attempt on Hitler's life) was too ill to travel.

On landing at Freilassing, Stauffenberg instructed the pilot of his Heinkel HE-111 not to wander too far from the plane because he might have to return to Berlin in a hurry; then he and Klausing got into a waiting staff car for the ride into the nearby mountains to Hitler's retreat.

At the Berghof, Stauffenberg, clutching the briefcase with his one hand, told Klausing to stay with the car and be prepared to race down the mountainside to the waiting aircraft if he exited the meeting without his briefcase. Stauffenberg's plan was to set the acid fuse timer, place the briefcase in the conference room, and leave as unobtrusively as possible before the bomb exploded. As the colonel walked up the terraced steps toward the main building, Klausing checked his watch. It was 1:00 p.m.

Inside the building, Stauffenberg left his revolver and hat on the table reserved for this purpose and entered the conference room carrying the briefcase. He set it down carefully under the conference table and listened to the proceedings. Hitler was leaning over the table scowling at the map that showed the position of German and Soviet forces.

"Anything special today?" Hitler asked General Adolf Heusinger, who was representing the ill Chief of Staff, General Zeitzler.

As Heusinger described the deplorable conditions in the east, especially the defenses of East Prussia and the General Government section of Poland, Stauffenberg surveyed the room. His heart sank when he saw that Himmler was not present. Göring was there, but without Himmler Stauffenberg did not want to leave his bomb. He quietly withdrew from the conference room, knowing that the present discussion would continue for at least several more minutes. He started toward a bank of telephones, but first stopped at a nearby washroom where he splashed cold water on his face to ease his tension and rinse off the sweat streaming down his forehead.

Stauffenberg asked the telephone exchange operator to place a call to General Olbricht in Berlin. When the call went through the two conspirators conversed, using predetermined code words. Stauffenberg reported Himmler's absence and the two agreed to abort the assassination, at least until the next conference. Stauffenberg returned to the conference room and waited to give his progress report on the fifteen new divisions that Hitler was convinced would stem the Soviet advance.

At 3:30 p.m. Stauffenberg returned to the waiting car carrying his briefcase. Noting Klausing's surprise at seeing the briefcase again, he explained to him what had happened. Meanwhile General Olbricht contacted the resistance members who had been waiting for the signal to begin the coup. Count Helidorf, whose Berlin police forces were poised to arrest leading Nazis, and the officers of the ninth Infantry Reserve Regiment at Potsdam, who were to lead their troops into the government center in Berlin and isolate it from the rest of the city and country, were told to stand down and await further instructions.

That evening Stauffenberg met with coup leaders in Berlin, including Generals Beck and Olbricht. The conversation focused on what should be done at the next conference if Himmler was not present again. While some saw the need to wait until both Himmler and Hitler could be killed at the same time, others disagreed, saying there was too little time left in which to act before Germany was totally destroyed. They insisted the bomb must be set at the next meeting, whether Himmler was present or not. In the end, no firm decision was reached either way. They would wait to see what happened at the next conference. If Himmler was absent again, Stauffenberg should call Olbricht's office for instructions.

The next attempt was under different circumstances. On July 13, Adolf Hitler moved his headquarters to the Wolf's Lair near Rastenberg in East Prussia. This move surprised some of his staff because advance Red Army units were only sixty miles east of Rastenberg.

Early on the morning of Saturday, July 15, a Junkers Ju-52 transport lifted off through the warm low-lying fog that blanketed and moved northeast toward East Prussia. On board were General Fromm; his Chief of Staff, Colonel Stauffenberg; and the latter's acting adjutant, Captain Klausing. On the floor between Stauffenberg's legs was his briefcase containing the latest reports on his progress in staffing the fifteen blocking divisions and the bomb with which he planned to blow Adolf Hitler to hell.

Stauffenberg approached this conference with no predetermined course of action if Himmler was not present, but the conspirators had taken an unprecedented step that clearly indicated they fully expected this conference to be Hitler's last. Orders were issued for Phase One of Operation Valkyrie.

To insure there would be a minimal lapse of time between Hitler's death and the occupation of Berlin by troops committed by their officers to back the coup, General Olbricht, with Stauffenberg's consent, initiated Phase One at 11:00 a.m. The conference in East Prussia was scheduled for 1:00 p.m., and the explosion was expected to happen soon after. The timing for Phase One to begin allowed troops two hours to move into position before their officers opened the sealed orders they were given. These orders directed that the troops be deployed to isolate all important govern-ment and Party buildings, and to support the criminal police in their efforts to locate and arrest government and Party officials.

Once the command was given to start moving the troops into the city, Olbricht summoned the City Commandant, Lieutenant General Paul von Hase, to his office and told him that Hitler would probably be killed that day, and the city would soon be occupied by troops loyal to the coup. Hase immediately promised allegiance to the coup and placed himself and his own troops at Olbricht's service. Meanwhile, a steady stream of reports was pouring in, con-firming successful troop deployment in key positions on the out-skirts of the city. The officer cadets at the military schools, and an armored infantry battalion, as well as infantry divisions assigned to the Replacement Army, all joined in the exercise.

Fromm (who was ignorant of any of this activity), Stauffenberg, and Klausing (who may have been carrying a second bomb in his briefcase) landed at the secluded airfield in East Prussia at 9:35 a.m. They were driven the short distance to the heavily fortified head-quarters known as "Wolfschanze," or the Wolf's Lair, in time to join other arriving officers for breakfast at the officer's mess. The meal took three-quarters of an hour, after which Fromm and Stauffenberg met with Field Marshal Keitel.

As 1:00 p.m. approached the participants made their way through the compound toward the hut where the conference was to be held. At the door they met Luftwaffe General Karl Bodenschatz and engaged in a brief conversation until Hitler arrived with his naval aide, Rear Admiral Karl Jesko von Puttkamer, and an officer of the SD bodyguard. Hitler greeted the assembled officers with a smile and appeared especially warm toward Stauffenberg, whom he called "My dear Colonel von Stauffenberg."

When the conference assembled, Stauffenberg saw at once that Himmler was not present. He waited until the discussion centered on a message from Rommel concerning the situation in France, a subject that would not require his participation, and quietly excused himself from the room, leaving his briefcase behind. Stauffenberg placed a call to Olbricht's Berlin office, where he knew Olbricht and General Beck waited only for the news of Hitler's death before they moved to take control of the government.

Stauffenberg's call was taken by his close friend, Colonel Albrecht Mertz von Quirnheim. Stauffenberg explained the reason for his call and told Quirnheim to ask Beck and Olbricht for their advice. Mertz von Quirnheim gave the generals Stauffenberg's message and waited for instructions while the colonel held on the line. Both Beck and Olbricht had all along held the position that the assassination should be attempted only if Himmler was present. They now discussed this point again, and after considerable soul searching they decided to cancel the attempt in hope of finding Himmler and Hitler together on another day.

Mertz von Quirnheim relayed this message to Stauffenberg, who was now of two minds on the situation. He asked Quirnheim, "What do you say?" He hesitated a moment, then replied, "Do it."

Stauffenberg returned to the conference room and discovered his briefcase missing. Frantically he searched the room, suspecting that someone had merely moved it out of the way, but it was nowhere to be found. His actions drew a reprimand from Fromm, who asked why he was "bobbing about like a jack-in-the-box." The colonel apologized and explained that his wounds were bothering him.

A few minutes later General Stieff entered the room carrying Stauffenberg's briefcase. Although the two did not discuss Stieff's reason for taking the briefcase from the conference room, it is likely he did so to keep Fromm from looking inside for Stauffenberg's report and discovering the bomb. Stieff was a member of the conspiracy and in fact had hidden the explosives Stauffenberg was carrying until the colonel needed them.

The time had gone. Hitler left the conference and went about his business, leaving Stauffenberg in a cold sweat once again. Remembering that the order for Phase One of Operation Valkyrie had been issued in Berlin and that troops were already on the move, Stauffenberg rushed to the telephone exchange and called Olbricht to tell him what had happened.

General Olbricht immediately cancelled all troop movements being conducted as part of Valkyrie, explaining that the maneuvers had been part of a practice exercise. Unable to reach some units, he drove around the city and its suburbs issuing the cancellation order directly.

The following day, when both Fromm and Keitel were told of the Valkyrie order, Olbricht came in for harsh criticism for taking this step without Fromm's prior knowledge. He was told in no uncertain language that issuing Valkyrie orders was beyond his responsibility. The chastened conspirator knew he would not be able to call out troops for Valkyrie again unless he was fully informed that Hitler was dead. The risk to the entire coup was too great to chance another mishap.

The next few days were dark ones for the resistance. On Sunday, July 16, Stauffenberg received news that General Alexander von Falkenhausen, military commander in Belgium and northern France, and a supporter of the coup, had been dismissed. The following day news arrived that Rommel had been severely injured and hospitalized. Although Rommel was not a member of the resistance, Stauffenberg had hoped he would come over once Hitler was dead, especially since he made no effort to hide his pessimism about Germany's future from Hitler, who now brushed off his one-time favorite as a "coward."

On July 18, Stauffenberg received a report that the Gestapo had been ordered to arrest Goerdeler, a key member of the resistance and the man designated to be Germany's new Chancellor. He warned Goerdeler and told him to go into hiding. Reluctantly, Goerdeler left Berlin for Westphalia.

Tense meetings were held between Stauffenberg, Beck, Olbricht, and other coup conspirators. It was finally decided that they no longer wanted to endure the tension of waiting for news of Himmler's presence at one of Hitler's conferences. Things were getting out of hand. Hitler had to be eliminated at all costs. Stauffenberg was instructed to set his bomb at the next meeting, no matter who was there, as long as Hitler was in the room.

On July 19, General Heusinger was once again at Hitler's conference reporting that the Soviets were breaking through all along the eastern front. He told Hitler that additional troops were needed if the Germans had any hope of halting the Soviet advance, and he asked how many men the Replacement Army could provide for this purpose.

Field Marshal Keitel interrupted with a suggestion that Colonel Stauffenberg attend the following day's conference to provide "facts and figures" about the combat readiness of the fifteen new grenadier divisions he had been ordered to organize.

Hitler rose to his feet, terminating the conference, and said, "Good, send for Stauffenberg tomorrow."

10.

"Valkyrie"

Colonel Stauffenberg worked late into the evening of July 19, 1944, making last-minute updates to the operation tables for the fifteen divisions Adolf Hitler had ordered him to create from the military rubble of the Third Reich. It was not a successful undertaking. With increasing frequency in the past two years, Hitler had prescribed imaginary divisions created out of thin air, largely by reducing existing divisions to half their assigned strength and forming additional units with the overflow.

The German army was rapidly being reduced to little more than a sham force, yet on Hitler's situation maps his army still appeared formidable. To Hitler, a division symbol pinned on a map represented a division, even if heavy losses and transfers had reduce it to regimental strength. Hitler fantasized that his phantom divisions could fight as effectively as fully staffed, well-equipped divisions, ultimately turning the war back in his favor. The military sycophants with whom he surrounded himself dared not contradict Hitler's illusions about rejuvenating his collapsing army with an assortment of men ill-suited for combat.

When Stauffenberg completed his report and left his office, he did not go directly home. Instead, he stopped at the Catholic

Church in Dahlem to pray and reflect on his moral duty. He must have known that the next day the "dirty work" would definitely be done. The decision was now reached that the bomb would be set whether Himmler was present or not. There would be no telephone calls seeking instructions from superiors; he would do it.

Stauffenberg decided that killing Hitler was the lesser of evil. He could kill Hitler, or allow him to live and continue the massacre of the German people. At that moment, alone in the empty church, he quieted his conscience. This courageous young officer who had sacrificed so much for his country sought solace for what he was about to do. One can only imagine his thoughts for the others who would die in the explosion. Some weaklings who were slavishly loyal to the dictator and shared his rule should probably share his death. However, there would surely be others: officers duty-bound to attend the conference who were blameless, and who perhaps despised Hitler as much as Stauffenberg. There was no denying that innocent men would die, but because of the physical impediments from his wounds, the colonel distrusted his ability to attempt to assassinate Hitler with a pistol. The sole remaining option was the bomb.

Word had gone out to some of the leaders of the coup that the next day would be Hitler's last. In the late morning Field Marshal Witzleben, who was designated to take over as Commander-in-Chief of the army, arrived in Berlin and met secretly with Colonel General Erich Hoepner, who had agreed to assume the post of Minister of War in the new government. Also arriving in Berlin during the day, or already in the city and making preparations for the coup, were Lieutenant General Paul von Hase, Commandant of the City; Captain Ulrich Wilhelm Count Schwerin von Schwanenfeld, who was to be the new State Secretary; Police President Wolf Count von Helldorf, who would remain in that post in the new German government; and dozens of other officers who had prominent roles in the coup that would hopefully bring down the Nazi regime when confirmation was received that Stauffenberg's bomb had killed Hitler.

When Stauffenberg arrived at the apartment he shared with his brother, his exhilaration was apparent. Berthold asked him what was happening to cause his excitement, and Claus told him that Hitler wanted him at the Wolf's Lair the next day. "Tomorrow it will be done," he said.

The Stauffenberg brothers, discussed the upcoming opportunity long into the night. Claus recounted the previous military conferences when he had carried the deadly bomb, and he vowed this time he would succeed. The two finally retired and listened, as they did every night, to the enemy bombers that rained death and destruction down on Berlin. Amid the sounds of numerous explosions Claus fell into a fitful sleep.

Secure in his Wolf's Lair headquarters deep in the East Prussia forest at Rastenburg, Hitler was awake until past 2:00 in the morning. Typically, his practice was to engage in animated conversation with aides until well past midnight and sleep until late in the morning, which is why the "morning military conference" seldom began before 2:00 p.m. On this night the Führer sat up regaling two of his secretaries, Christa Schroder and Johanna Wolf, with stories of his early successes.

When he finally dismissed the two women, Hitler swallowed the nightly sleeping potion his personal physician and food taster, Dr. Morell, prescribed. He changed into his nightshirt and gave his field-gray nondescript uniform to his valet, Heinz Linge, and settled into bed. He left instructions that he should be awakened at 9:00 a.m., an unheard of hour for the Führer; however, he was expecting Mussolini in the afternoon and his "morning military conference" was actually scheduled for late morning.

Daybreak on July 20, 1944, carried with it a promise of oppressive heat. A few minutes before 6:00 a.m. Claus von Stauffenberg labored from his bed with the practiced motion that compensated for his imbalance from having only one usable arm. He washed, shaved, and dressed skillfully despite his enormous handicap. He wore a freshly pressed staff officer's uniform. Ready to depart for what he expected would be a momentous day for Germany, Stauffenberg stopped for a moment, studying the briefcase beside his bed. His driver, Corporal Karl Schweizer, had delivered it the previous afternoon, after driving to Potsdam to pick it up from one of General Olbricht's staff officers, Lieutenant

Colonel Fritz von der Lancken. Lancken had volunteered to act as custodian of the briefcase, which now contained a second reserve bomb, between Stauffenberg's trips to Hitler's conferences. Stauffenberg placed his "blocking divisions" reports in the briefcase and relocked it.

Claus and Berthold were picked up minutes later by Corporal Schweizer. They sped through deserted streets to the home of Claus's aide, Lieutenant Werner von Haeften, who was waiting at the curb, along with his brother, Navy Lieutenant Bernd von Haeften. The four officers rode in silence while Corporal Schweizer chauffeured them to the airport at Rangsdorf where a Junkers JU-52 transport was readied for takeoff. Stauffenberg had arranged with General Eduard Wagner, Deputy Chief of Staff of the Army, to provide a much faster Heinkel H-111 dive bomber for the return trip to Berlin, when speed would be far more important.

At the Rangsdorf field Major General Helmuth Stieff and his aide, Major Röll, joined the Stauffenberg party. After bidding their respective brothers good luck and farewell, Berthold and Bernd watched the Junkers lift off for the 350-mile flight to Rastenburg.

Because he had been called to Rastenburg on such short notice. Stauffenberg left behind him in Berlin some loose ends that would cause serious problems for the coup. Not all members of the conspiracy who should have known about the trip had been informed. Two men who had key responsibilities, Lieutenant General Otto Hitzfeld, Commandant of the Infantry School at Doeberitz, the member of the coup charged with seizing the Broadcast House facilities, thereby giving the resistance control of the public radio network, and his aide, colonel Wolfgang Müller, were both away from their posts at the critical time of the coup. Neither man knew Stauffenberg was making another attempt to kill Hitler that day.

Adding to these communications problems, General Olbricht was stymied by Fromm's directive forbidding him to issue orders for the preparation of Valkyrie. The previous assassination attempt had been cancelled after the troops were ordered out of their barracks, resulting in Olbricht's reprimand by Fromm and Keitel. This time he would be forced to wait until word of Hitler's death reached him.

There was yet another serious problem created by the fact that Fromm was not going to Rastenburg but was remaining in Berlin, where he would be able to countermand orders from Olbricht to begin the movement of troops in preparation for Valkyrie. These complications cost valuable hours when timing was most crucial.

The circumstances were further exacerbated because Stauffenberg, who was now the leading stimulus behind the coup, would be out of communications with the conspirators in Berlin during the fundamentally critical two hours following the start of Valkyrie. General Beck had voiced his concern about this lapse when he reminded Stauffenberg that he was the only one who could coordinate all the elements of the coup.

The Junkers landed at the airfield that had been hewn from the forest surrounding Rastenburg at a few minutes past 10:00 a.m. When Stauffenberg's party stepped down from the plane they were met by a staff car sent from Wolf's Lair to pick them up. The day before one of Fromm's aides, Captain Heinz-Ludwig Bartram, had called the Operations Officer at Wolf's Lair, Captain Heinz Pieper, and asked him to look after Stauffenberg when he arrived, Pieper had sent the car.

When Stieff, Röll, Stauffenberg, and Haeften deplaned, the latter two carried identical briefcases. We can surmise from later events that each briefcase held one of the matching explosives that constituted the complete bomb package. This was undoubtedly a measure designed to preclude losing the entire bomb if one briefcase was somehow misplaced.

The four-mile drive to Hitler's headquarters was negotiated in almost total silence. When they arrived the party separated, with Haeften accompanying Stieff and Röll on an errand, and Stauffenberg joining Pieper and a group of medical officers for breakfast which was served at a table under a large oak tree outside of Mess Hall 2.

A few minutes before 11:00 a.m., Stauffenberg attended his first meeting of the day, with General Walter Buhle, chief of OKW's Army Staff, and several other officers. They discussed Stauffenberg's report. Following this meeting Haeften rejoined Stauffenberg and the two went to Field Marshal Keitel's office, where

Stauffenberg briefed the OKW Chief on the formation of the new divisions, which consisted largely of underage, overage, and wounded soldiers commanded by young, inexperienced officers. During the meeting, Hitler's valet called to remind Keitel that the Führer's conference had been rescheduled for 12:30 p.m.

Outside Keitel's office Haeften nervously paced the hall with his briefcase in death grip. When the meeting broke up, Keitel urged everyone to hurry so they would not be late for the Führer's conference. Stauffenberg, who required several minutes to set his bomb, asked one of Keitel's aides where he could go to change his shirt, indicating that his wounds required him to do so. The officer pointed in the direction of an empty room at the end of a hall. Haeften followed Stauffenberg to the room.

Inside the room the men opened their briefcases and began rearranging the contents. Stauffenberg apparently decided to place both bombs in his briefcase along with his report, but Keitel's inadvertent interruption prevented him from completing the transfer. Keitel, who was waiting for Stauffenberg outside the building, became increasingly impatient with the delay. One of his aides dispatched a sergeant-major named Vogel to hurry Stauffenberg along. Vogel opened the door to the room just as the two officers were preparing to stuff both bombs inside Stauffenberg's briefcase. When Vogel gave Stauffenberg the message to hurry, the colonel angrily replied that he was moving as quickly as he could. Vogel stubbornly remained in the doorway waiting, so the second bomb was not put into Stauffenberg's case. Using his pair of pliars, adjusted to fit his three fingers, Stauffenberg crushed the glass capsule activating the fuse. The bomb was now set to explode in ten minutes.

Stauffenberg walked quickly toward Hitler's conference building, talking with General Buhle. Twice officers accompanying them offered to carry Stauffenberg's briefcase, but each time he politely declined. As they drew nearer to the building, Stauffenberg did allow Major Ernst John von Freyend of the OKW General Staff to carry his briefcase inside. Stauffenberg asked Freyend to find him a place close to Hitler because his hearing was poor owing to the head wounds he had received when he lost his arm and eye.

Freyend, wanting to accommodate this much-decorated war hero, obliged by moving the naval representative at the conference, Rear Admiral Voss, to another place at the conference table. He put Stauffenberg's briefcase on the floor next to Lieutenant General Heusinger, who was in the middle of reporting on the status of the eastern front defenses.

When he entered the room, Stauffenberg must have realized the bomb he was carrying might not be sufficient for the job. Instead of a solid concrete structure in which these conferences were usually held, this building was constructed of wood and contained several large windows that were open to allow a summer breeze in. Stauffenberg had expected a solidly built conference chamber that would contain the blast and increase the force of the explosion, but now it was obvious that the wood walls and windows of the room being used would allow at least a portion of the blast to escape the room, reducing the damage it would inflict to those inside.

A massive oak table on which several military maps were spread occupied a large portion of the 18-by-40-foot room. Close to either end of the table were thick oak supports practically the width of the tabletop. Over two dozen men stood in place around the table, with Hitler himself standing near the center, his back to the door and facing the open windows.

Meanwhile, Haeften, the second bomb still in his briefcase, went off to locate the vehicle he and Stauffenberg would need for the return trip to the airport. The car he expected to be waiting for Stauffenberg was gone, apparently returned to the motor pool. Although this was probably routine, it sent Haeften into a state of alarm as he imagined the two of them trapped in the compound after the bomb exploded. Haeften rushed to the communications center where he found General Erich Fellgiebel, head of Army Signals, chatting with the camp's Army Signal Officer, Lieutenant Colonel Ludolf Sander. Fellgiebel, a member of the conspiracy, was responsible for alerting the Berlin coup leaders that Hitler had been killed, thus setting the coup in motion.

Haeften asked Fellgiebel to get him a car quickly, as time was rapidly running short until the bomb was set to explode. Fellgiebel, himself a visitor to Wolf's Lair, had no official authority, so he asked Sander if he could find Haeften a car, which he did.

Inside Hitler's conference room Heusinger, who had been told by his friend, General Tresckow, that an attempt on Hitler's life would soon be made, was detailing Germany's precarious predicament on the eastern front. Massive Soviet columns were moving forward, but German intelligence could not pinpoint their positions. Ground reconnaissance units had lost sight of them several days earlier, and the Luftwaffe had been unable to break through the screen of Soviet fighters that controlled the skies over the front. German field commanders had no idea where the Soviets would attack.

Stauffenberg, satisfied that his briefcase was placed under the table as close to Hitler as he could get it, and possibly fearing that the unseasonably high temperature could accelerate the chemical reaction and detonate the bomb prematurely, quietly informed Keitel, "Herr Field Marshal, I have to make an urgent call to Berlin." Keitel nodded his permission and Stauffenberg unobtrusively left the meeting. Stauffenberg's departure attracted no particular interest, since officers were constantly entering and leaving the conference room for a variety of reasons.

Having left the room, Stauffenberg, struggling to retain an outward calm, walked out of the building, forgetting completely his cap and gunbelt on the table in the hall. He quickly paced off the 200 yards to the communications center to tell Fellgiebel the bomb had been set.

Meanwhile in Berlin, General Beck, wearing his uniform for the first time since his resignation took effect in 1938, sat patiently in General Olbricht's office at the War Ministry building in the Bendlerstrasse. The two were waiting for Fellgiebel's call confirming that Hitler was dead. The wait was much longer than they expected.

Inside the conference room, General Heusinger continued his assessments of the situation on the eastern front. His aide, Colonel Brandt, moved closer to the table and into the place Stauffenberg had just vacated. Stauffenberg's briefcase interfered with his footing. He tried to move it with his foot, but it fell over on its side. Reaching down, he moved the case away from him, propping it against the outside of the table support, away from where Hitler stood.

Stauffenberg, Fellgiebel, Haeften, and Sand were just leaving the communications center when the explosion shattered the peaceful countryside. It was 12:42 p.m. The three visitors were stunned by the explosion, but Sand considered it a routine occurrence, explaining that such explosions were not uncommon since the animals in the nearby forest regularly set off the mines that were part of the heavy security fortifications surrounding the compound.

General Heusinger was summing up the situation in East Prussia. Just as he said, "If the Army Group does not withdraw from Lake Peipus, a catastrophe will…" a violent blast hurled everyone to the floor, setting fire to hair and uniforms. Over the bedlam several officers could hear the ever-faithful Keitel, unhurt by the blast, calling out, "Where is the Führer? Where is the Führer?" General Heusinger, who was momentarily knocked unconscious, came to and found himself on his back next to Hitler, who was also unconscious. Heusinger crawled to the door and managed to drag himself painfully into the hall, where several officers and men helped him exit the building. His uniform, face, body, and legs were burned, and both ear drums had been broken. His right arm and hand bled profusely from numerous splinters that had been launched into the air when the table was ripped apart by the bomb.

Keitel groped his way through the thick smoke and dust, past wounded men crying out for help, until he found the Führer just regaining consciousness. The Field Marshal helped Hitler to his feet; the latter's pants had been shredded. Hitler looked at Keitel with a dazed expression, then collapsed into his arms. He was carried to his quarters, where a doctor dressed his wounds, which turned out to be superficial.

Others in the room were not so lucky. Hitler's stenographer, Heinrich Berger, had both legs blown off and died a few hours later. General Schmundt, Hitler's adjutant, lost a leg and died in a hospital on October 1. Two days after the blast General Korten, Chief of Staff for the Luftwaffe, and Colonel Brandt died of their wounds. Everyone's uniform was burned or tattered, and most received wounds that required a stay of several days in the hospital at Rastenburg.

Investigators later concluded that had the explosion occurred inside the bunker-like structure usually used for these conferences, everyone in the room would have been killed, many of the bodies unrecognizable from the blast and fire. When it was learned that Stauffenberg and Haeften had a second bomb identical to the first, most investigators agreed that no one could have survived if both bombs had exploded simultaneously. Once again, Hitler had cheated death. Had Sergeant Major Vogel not interrupted Stauffenberg and Haeften, they might have stuffed both bombs into Stauffenberg's briefcase and set both fuses to explode at the same time, but once again luck betrayed them.

In the first few minutes following the explosion there was great confusion about what had actually happened. Some thought an enemy aircraft had dropped a bomb directly on the conference building. Hitler thought one of the foreign construction workers at the compound had thrown a hand grenade through an open window. The brief confusion continued just long enough for Stauffenberg and Haeften to escape.

The instant the bomb exploded, Stauffenberg and Haeften got into their waiting car and ordered the driver to take them to the airport. As they left the complex, Stauffenberg caught a glimpse of the conference building. It looked as if a 75-mm artillery shell had scored a direct hit on the building. Men were converging on the site from every corner of the compound, and several ambulances were rushing in. Stauffenberg was persuaded that no one could have survived the blast. He said a quiet prayer that the victims had died quickly with a minimum of suffering.

The powerful eight-cylinder Mercedes swept past silent woods as Stauffenberg, sitting in the front passenger seat, urged the driver, Lieutenant Kretz, to higher speeds. As the car approached Guard Post 1, Stauffenberg saw the gate was lowered blocking the way. Although no one had ordered the exits sealed, the young lieutenant in charge of the Post had taken it on himself to close the gate hearing the explosion.

Stauffenberg's aristocratic charm, together with his combat medals, armless shirt sleeve, and eye patch, induced the impressionable young officer to let him pass. The car sped through and hurried on to the next checkpoint, where things did not go as smoothly.

The second checkpoint was controlled by a cynical sergeant major named Kolbe. Before the fugitive car reached his station Kolbe had been alerted to permit no one to go through without clearance from the Camp Commandant. Stauffenberg tried the charm that had worked earlier, then he played on sympathy, pointing to his wounds. When these ploys failed, he imperiously demanded obedience from his noncommissioned subordinate. Kolbe remained unmoved. Finally Stauffenberg demanded that Kolbe call the Commandant's office. The call was taken by Captain Leonhard von Mollendorff, who, while not yet aware of what had caused the explosion, had no reason to connect it in any way with Stauffenberg. He advised Kolbe to allow the colonel to pass.

When the car was well past this guard post, the driver happened to glance in his rear view mirror just when Haeften threw a package into the woods. On his return to the compound, Kretz was questioned about Stauffenberg's activities. He told the SS about the package, which when retrieved was found to contain the second bomb, its fuse capsule still intact.

At the airfield Stauffenberg and Haeften quickly boarded the waiting H-111 dive bomber and ordered the pilot to take off immediately.

At Wolf's Lair General Fellgiebel delayed sending the message to Berlin that Hitler was dead until he could verify it himself. Following the explosion he joined the crush rushing to help the dying and wounded. At about 1:15 p.m., as Stauffenberg's plane was taking off, Hitler emerged from his quarters in a fresh uniform, looking, as one aide said, "lively, with an almost cheerful expression of a man who had been expecting something terrible to happen, and now luckily survived it."[1]

Fellgiebel was stunned. Hitler was still alive. The Führer immediately ordered all communications with the outside sealed. No word of the assassination attempt was to be leaked until the SS determined who was responsible. Fellgiebel was at a loss as to what to do. He could not call Berlin with the information that Hitler was still alive and virtually unscathed by the explosion. Even if he managed to get through, the phones were probably monitored by the SS. He could not simply relay news that Hitler himself had expressly forbidden. He could do nothing but await developments. The only other ranking officer present who knew of Stauffenberg's bomb, General Stieff, also decided to sit tight and wait. Both were powerless to warn fellow conspirators in Berlin that the assassination had failed.

In Berlin General Olbricht and Beck waited for news of Hitler's death long past the time they had expected to hear it. Olbricht asked Lieutenant General Thiele to call Wolf's Lair and find out what was happening. First attempts failed because Hitler's Luftwaffe adjutant, Colonel Nicolaus von Below, had shut down all communications pending Hitler's further orders even before Hitler reappeared from his quarters. The only calls processed during this time were to Himmler and Göring, summoning them to Rastenburg immediately. Finally, sometime after 3:00 p.m., Thiele got through to someone he thought was Fellgiebel, but probably was not, and learned of the explosion. Although the guarded respondent indicated that several officers had been injured, he made no mention of Hitler. Thiele reported this to Olbricht and Beck.

Knowing that an explosion had taken place prompted Olbricht and Beck to swing into action, even though they had no confirmation Hitler had been killed. Both men assumed that Hitler was dead, but if not, the fact that Stauffenberg's bomb had exploded left them no choice. If Hitler survived the blast and they did nothing, the Gestapo investigation was certain to unearth their complicity anyway, so better to move ahead and attempt the coup

At Wolf's Lair men were beginning to piece together what had happened. Everyone in the conference was accounted for except Colonel Stauffenberg, who it was quickly learned had sped away immediately following the explosion. When it was found that Stauffenberg's H-111 was airborne, a hurried call was placed to Luftwaffe headquarters in Berlin with orders to scramble a fighter squadron to shoot down a westbound H-111 bearing the identification number of Stauffenberg's plane. The fighters never took off. It is believed that the order was suppressed by Major Friedrich Georgi, General Olbricht's son-in-law on the air staff, who suspected it had something to do with his father-in-law's coup. Luck had finally favored the coup.

General Fellgiebel took steps to extend the communications blackout ordered by Below. His goal was to prevent all communications, even those of the Nazi leaders, in or out of Wolf's Lair, especially since the assassination had failed. He felt that the coup could still succeed if Hitler and his chief lieutenants remained isolated in the compound. This was an almost impossible task, considering the numerous communications channels in use. The army's communications center was one of two major communications installations at Wolf's Lair, and there were several small ones belonging to various government agencies. On his initiative several repeater stations transmitting radio communications were shut down until early evening, but even this measure did not completely isolate the Führer's headquarters. The portion of the coup plan that called for isolating Wolf's Lair was not unlike many other elements of the plan, insufficiently detailed and leaving too much to chance. The task assigned to Fellgiebel, the total shutdown of all means of communications, was as near an impossible task as could be imagined.

A great amount of differing opinion exists concerning how and when the conspirators in Berlin were informed that Hitler was still alive, but it is definitely known that they were notified at least once and possibly twice, by 3:00 p.m. that afternoon. Some reports indicate that Fellgiebel may have been able to reach Thiele by telephone. He is purported to have told him, "something fearful has happened, the Führer's alive." Unfortunately his enigmatic message left Thiele, Olbricht, and Beck with serious doubts. They did not know whether Stauffenberg's bomb had been discovered and he had been arrested, in which case they would all be in grave danger; or if he had committed suicide, in which case they were in no immediate danger and therefore should not begin the coup. This indecision was based on their knowledge that there were many field commanders who could be counted on for support only if Hitler was dead, but who would take no part in the coup as long as he lived. It was not until after 3:00 p.m. that they began to understand what had happened, and they responded with the decision to begin the coup. At least two invaluable and irreplaceable hours had been lost, during which communications between Wolf's Lair and Hitler's supporters, while not impossible, were extremely difficult for the Nazis to accomplish.

If Stauffenberg could have delegated an alternate to plant the bomb while he stayed in Berlin, the coup would have gotten off to a better start; but during this time of indecision the one man who would have been decisive, and who had the respect of all the plotters, was out of touch on the return flight from East Prussia. On the other hand, had this coup been as well organized as the 1938 attempt, it might have succeeded despite Hitler's survival of the Wolf Lair's explosion.

Meanwhile, some basic assumptions were emerging at Wolf's Lair. Once it was determined that the bomb had probably been set by Stauffenberg, the assassination attempt was thought to be the act of a single individual. It did not apparently occur to anyone that the bombing might have been part of a conspiracy. In fact, Hitler himself was the likely author of the single assassin theory. Not until nearly 4:30 p.m. when Hitler lifted his communications blackout and word was received that Operation Valkyrie was in progress, did anyone suspect that a coup attempt was related to the bombing. Until now nothing was done to safeguard the Nazi regime against a coup because none was suspected. Now Himmler entered the investigation, calling on his Berlin Gestapo headquarters to find out what had happened and who was involved. Meanwhile, considerable time had passed, and neither side had actually made any significant headway.

The root of much of the indecision by the conspirators was poor contingency planning. The plotters were clear about what to do if Stauffenberg's bomb had killed Hitler. If the attempt was once again aborted, they would simply go about their business and do nothing. But now they were put in a situation for which they had not prepared. The bomb had exploded, yet Hitler was alive. Without Stauffenberg's electric personality and fire leading them, precious hours were lost. They were the most important hours of the coup, hours in which the head of the government was not even aware a coup was in progress.

Stauffenberg's close friend, Colonel Albrecht Mertz von Quirnheim, Olbricht's deputy, exhorted the general to act. Finally, as 4:00 p.m. approached, the Valkyrie orders were released to the military schools in the military districts. Olbricht then called Hase, the city Commandant, to inform him that the coup was to begin. Hase dispatched the Grossdeutschland Guard Battalion to take up positions around several government buildings.

Berlin Police President Count Helldorf waited anxiously in his office with Gisevius for the authorization to begin arresting government and Party officials. Helldorf used a clever ploy, inviting several Party leaders to attend a meeting in his headquarters, expecting this would simplify the job of finding and arresting them. The meeting was planned for 3:00 p.m., but the Nazis departed before a frustrated Helldorf, who had been told the assassination would take place today, received instructions from Olbricht. At 4:00 p.m. Olbricht called to tell Helldorf to ready his police force to begin operations in half an hour.

Olbricht then went to see Colonel General Fromm and explained that Hitler had been killed and the army, using Fromm's own Replacement Army, was seizing the government. Fromm was incredulous and decided to call Field Marshal Keitel for confirmation. His call went directly through to the OKW chief, and Fromm told him that Berlin was alive with wild rumors that Hitler had been assassinated, was it true?

"Nonsense!" Keitel responded. "There was an attempted assassination, but it failed. The Führer is alive and received only superficial injuries. By the way, where is that Chief of Staff of yours, Colonel von Stauffenberg?"[2]

Fromm responded that he had not returned to Berlin.

That settled it. Fromm, who until now had been noncommittal about participating in the coup, reached a firm decision. While Hitler was still alive he would have no part in the coup. A few minutes later, Stauffenberg arrived and declared categorically that Hitler was dead. Fromm remained adamant. He was promptly arrested and Colonel General Erich Hoepner, a long-time member of the resistance, assumed command of the Replacement Army.

Soon the prepared message announcing Hitler's death, the army's seizure of the government, and the arrest of SS security forces in Berlin was dispatched to the communications room at the Bendlerstrasse headquarters, which now served as the coup operations center. The message was assigned a high priority and a top secret security classification. This was a mistake, since both delayed distribution of the page-long message signed by Field Marshal von Witzleben, as the new Commander-in-Chief. It was more than four hours before the message was disseminate to all military commands. Had it been sent without the security requirement, which actually was unnecessary, it would have reached all commands via the communications "round-robin" system in a matter of minutes. Because of the security classification the message had to be hand-typed to each command separately, turning the job into a laborious and time-consuming affair.

Field Marshal Witzleben arrived and met with Stauffenberg and Beck. He was appalled at the lack of concrete planning, the lost time, and the absence of sufficient troop strength to control Berlin. This last he considered a minimum requirement for a successful coup. In a fit of temper he stormed from the office, proclaiming that he was going home. He did return to his home briefly, but then he went on to army headquarters at Zossen.

Five hundred and forty-eight miles away in the capital of occupied France, the resistance had better chances of actually succeeding because many of the officers who supported an ouster of the Nazi regime commanded troops they believed would follow their orders, even if those orders meant combating forces loyal to Hitler, such as the SS and the Gestapo. Although various garrison forces were billeted in the area, there were also large numbers of combat troops who hated both Nazi organizations.

The key man in Paris was Colonel Eberhard Finckh, Quarter-master and Deputy Chief of Staff, German Army West, serving under the perpetually indecisive Field Marshal Kluge. Finckh was deeply involved in the resistance and kept the secret orders to be issued after Hitler's death safely locked inside his office safe. On the morning of July 20 he had received a message from General Eduard Wagner, Army Deputy Chief of Staff, that Stauffenberg's third attempt on Hitler's life would be made that afternoon. Finckh cancelled all plans for the day and remained either in his office or nearby throughout the morning and afternoon, waiting for word the assassination had taken place. Like so many others in the resistance, Finckh prayed this time the assassination would be a success.

Other important figures who knew Stauffenberg would try again to take Hitler's life were General Stulpnagel, Military Governor of France, and most of the officers on his staff; the City Commandant of Paris, Lieutenant General Hans von Boineburg-Lengsfeld; and his Chief of Staff, Colonel Carl von Unger.

Finckh had been transferred to France because of a unique ability he effectively demonstrated on the eastern front: to locate supplies, material, and fuel for beleaguered German troops when others thought there was none, after two weeks he had come to realize that when the Allies established their beachhead in Normandy, it was the beginning of the end for Germany. They could not be thrown back into the sea, as the Führer insisted the army must do.

The code word Finckh had been given for the third try at Hitler's life this month was "Exercise," meaning that the assassination would be attempted today. Now he waited anxiously for "Exercise finished," which would mean that the assassination had succeeded. When he received the first code word he immediately called Lieutenant Colonel Caeser von Hofacker, another member of the resistance and an officer on Stulpnagel's personal staff, who in turn informed Stulpnagel.

While the resistance members throughout the western area of operations waited for word of Hitler's death, they must have all wondered what Field Marshal Kluge was going to do. Kluge, who knew nothing of the assassination attempt, would be a key figure in the coup's success, if he responded as the resistance hoped he would.

During the first week of July, the man who had been Commander-in-Chief, West, since March 1942, Field Marshal von Rundstedt, had been dismissed by Hitler because he suffered from "defeatism" concerning Germany's chances of throwing the Allies back into the sea, as Hitler had ordered him to do. When Kluge arrived in France to replace Rundstedt, he was infected with the contagious optimism that Hitler instilled in him when he was appointed. His first official act was to confront his celebrated subordinates, Field Marshal Rommel, Commander of Army Group B in Normandy. Hitler told Kluge that he suspected even Rommel was now courting defeatism. Kluge told Rommel in no uncertain terms that he had better change his views. Their discussion became so heated that their staff members left the room. Rommel told Kluge that the war was lost and that if he did not believe it he should tour the front and speak with seasoned frontline commanders. Kluge agreed to do so.

On July 12 Kluge returned from his tour of the front in full agreement with Rommel's assessment that the Allies would crack the German defenses and the entire front would crumble in less than a month. Once this happened, the Allies' overwhelming superiority in men and materiel would enable their forces to plunge headlong into Germany itself. Essentially, the war was lost and it was time to come to terms with the Western Allies, if that was possible considering the Allies' frequently avowed policy that Germany must surrender unconditionally.

Rommel had already established radio channels with the U.S. forces and had on two occasions, on July 2 and July 9, arranged the exchange of badly wounded prisoners. On learning of this, Hitler was furious. He raved against Rommel, whose tenure as a field commander was now near an end. Before Hitler could dismiss him, Rommel's staff car was attacked by British fighters on July 17. He was seriously injured and required hospitalization. Hitler immediately removed him from command of Army Group B and replaced him with Kluge, whom he expected to be more aggressive. Kluge was left in charge of a massive army without the help or support of a peer officer on whom he could depend for honesty and guidance.

Reports indicate that both Rommel and Kluge knew there was an assassination plot in the works, and that both men agreed to support General Beck's interim government once the Führer was dead. They made it clear that if there was no assassination they would not become involved in the coup. It is incredible that these two men, with hundreds of thousands of combat troops at their command, and who were both resolved that Germany was headed toward a crushing defeat, feared Hitler so much that they refused to do anything to stop the carnage unless he was dead.

Late in the afternoon of July 20, probably around 4:00 p.m., Colonel Finckh received a phone call with the code words "Exercised finished." He was stunned and sat at his desk for what seemed an eternity, contemplating what the Fuhrer's death would signify for Germany and adjusting himself to the realization that the long-awaited event had finally been accomplished after two disappointing failures.

Finckh immediately set off to inform the Chief-of-Staff, West, General Gunther Blumentritt. He made the twenty-five-minute drive from his office near the center of Paris to Army West Headquarters in St. Germain-en-Laye in a state of high excitement and apprehension. With Hitler dead, would the Allies agree to a ceasefire and negotiate a peace? Would the SS and Gestapo engage in a civil war against the army and try to regain control of the country from Beck's government? These questions were also in the minds of army and civilian coup supporters throughout Germany and the occupied countries.

Blumentritt greeted Finckh warmly when the colonel entered his office and closed the door behind him. The only other person in the room was Blumentritt's aide, Captain Beckenbach. Finckh wasted no time telling Blumentritt that he had just received word that there had been a Gestapo putsch in Berlin that had resulted in Hitler's death. Despite Hitler's death, the coup had failed and the army was in control of the government. Field Marshal von Witzleben had come out of retirement to take over as Commander-in-chief of the army, and General Beck was temporarily serving as head of the new government. This was the version the conspirators decided would best serve their interests in winning to their side general officers who might waver if told the coup and the assassination had been conducted by army officers. It also provided the foundation for the orders to arrest all SS and Gestapo personnel that followed.

Finckh's report was greeted with a stunned silence. Then the amiable and efficient Blumentritt said he hoped the new government could end the fighting in France that he, along with so many others, knew was destroying the German army.

"Finckh," Blumentritt asked, "where did you get this news?"

Finckh was caught off guard by this question, but he quickly recovered. "The Military Governor, Herr General."[3]

The Chief of Staff had no reason to doubt Finckh's manufactured reply, or the report of Hitler's assassination and the Gestapo coup that had evidently come from General Stulpnagel. Blumentritt explained to Finckh that Field Marshal Kluge had moved to Army Group B headquarters the night before to assume command of Rommel's army. He turned to Captain Beckenbach and told him to call Army Group B's headquarters at La Roche-Guyon immediately. Before Beckenbach made contact, Finckh said farewell and departed for his drive back to Paris.

When the captain got through to La Roche-Guyon, the call was taken by General Dr. Hans Spiedel, Chief of Staff of Army Group B and the man who had tried to enlist Rommel in the resistance. Spiedel explained to Blumentritt that Kluge was away at the front since before 9:00 that morning, meeting with frontline commanders to better assess the situation and to try to find a way to stop the disintegration of the German defenses.

Afraid the Gestapo might be listening in, Bumentritt mumbled into the phone, 'Things are happening in Berlin.' He then whispered the word "dead," hoping Spiedel would understand. He did, and it prompted him to begin asking questions, wanting details of what had occurred. Blumentritt cut Siedel short, telling him he would drive to La Roche-Guyon himself to brief the field marshal.

About the time Finckh returned to Paris, Stauffenberg called the Military Governor office and spoke to his cousin, Lieutenant Colonel Caeser von Hofacker. Stauffenberg told him the Führer was dead and to proceed with the prepared plans. Stulpnagel called his staff to a meeting in his headquarters at the Hotel Majestic in Paris and informed them of the assassination and the coup. A few minutes later, shortly after 5:00 p.m., the City Commandant, Lieutenant General Hans von Boineburg-Lengsfeld, arrived with his Chief of Staff, both of whom knew of the planned attempt on Hitler's life. Stulpnagel ordered Boineburg-Lengsfeld to proceed with the arrest of all SS and SD officers in Paris. Boineburg-Lengsfeld was prepared to shoot any SS officer who resisted. Stulpnagel's staff had drawn a map of the city for him identifying all SS and SD living quarters. The arrests were to begin shortly after 11:00 p.m., when the city curfew took effect and the targeted personnel were expected to be in their quarters.

Boineburg-Lengsfeld immediately called to the First Regiment of the 325 Security Division, which was under his direct command, and gave orders that the Regiment prepare to move out.

When Blumentritt arrived at La Roche-Guyon, he found that Spiedel had already briefed Kluge about the assassination of Hitler and the Gestapo coup, but he also had to tell him that there had just been a radio broadcast claiming that Hitler had not been assassinated, merely slightly injured. Now things began to go wrong. The failure of the conspirators to either take control of or put out of commission all means of communications with Wolf's Lair, a task made nearly impossible due to the fact that there were so many radio and telephone links operated by every civilian and military agency that normally required contact with Hitler's headquarters, was eventually to be their undoing.

The conflicting reports of Hitler's alleged death gave Kluge exactly what he needed to do nothing except wait to see what happened. When General Beck called Kluge from Berlin a few minutes after 6:00 p.m. to request that he support the provisional government, Beck told him, "Kluge, the fate of Germany is at stake." Kluge refused to commit himself, saying he wanted to think it over and would call Beck back shortly.

Still struggling with the question of where to place his loyalty, Kluge tried to call the Wolf's Lair but could not get through. Instead he called Major-General Stieff at Mauerwald, the army camp not far from Wolf's Lair. Stieff, who was a member of the resistance, knew the game was up and saw no point in lying to Kluge. He told the field marshal that there had been an attempt on

Hitler's life but that it had failed. Hitler was well and had met that afternoon with Mussolini at Wolf's Lair.

Kluge then called the headquarters of the Replacement Army on the Bendlerstrasse in Berlin. He asked to speak to Fromm, but Stauffenberg came on the line instead and said that Fromm had been removed from command and had been replaced by Colonel General Hoepner. Hoepner explained to Kluge that the claims of Hitler's survival were simply a smokescreen initiated by the SS, and that orders to all army commands were at that moment being sent by teleprinter.

During the next few hours a communications battle was waged between Wolf's Lair and Stauffenberg at the Bendlerstrasse. From Wolf's Lair came regular reports that Hitler was alive and well. Using the telephone and teleprinters at his command, Stauffenberg countered with denials and issued fresh orders for the arrest of all SS and SD members throughout the Reich and the occupied territories. All this activity confused Kluge, who, although not directly involved in the coup, was a pivotal factor for its success because of the number of troops he commanded and because he could quickly contact the Allies and request a cease-fire. For a while Kluge leaned toward the conspirators, temporarily convinced the radio broadcasts claiming Hitler had survived the assassination were attempts by Hitler's followers to gain control of the government before the nation knew for sure the Führer was dead. Still hedging his bet, he did nothing to implicate himself in case the reports were true.

Following another round of telephone calls, Kluge swung the other way and called the whole affair "a bungled assassination attempt." He had Stulpnagel and Hofacker, whom he quickly learned had already placed in motion the forces that would arrest the SS leaders in Paris, summoned to his headquarters for a meeting at 8:00 p.m.

While the army leaders were playing out these intrigues and counter-intrigues, the skies over western Europe were choked with Allied bombers and fighters, and the Allied armies in Normandy pressed forward on all fronts. These were not ideal conditions for Kluge to think clearly about what side he should support or what action he should take. A man of proven courage in the face of enemy forces, he was terrified of the reprisals Hitler would extract should the report of his death be wrong.

Meanwhile, the extraordinary orders to arrest Gestapo and SS leaders were radioed throughout German-controlled Europe. Some commanders called Berlin for confirmation of the teleprinter orders. The orders were verified not by Fromm, whom they all had called, but by his Chief of Staff, Lieutenant Colonel von Stauffenberg. In Vienna, Prague, Bohemia, Moravia, and other locales, German troops were rounding up and arresting high ranking members of the SS, Gestapo, and the security police forces.

When Stulpnagel and Hofacker arrived in La Roche-Guyon they met with Kluge and his staff. Kluge told them he believed Hitler was still alive, and under the circumstances he would not act against the Nazi government. Stulpnagel said he had already initiated operations in Paris to round up and arrest SS and Gestapo people. Kluge had Blumentritt call Stulpnagel's office and order the arrests cancelled, but Stulpnagel's chief of Staff told him the troops had already been dispatched throughout the city and could not be recalled. Kluge told Stulpnagel to return to Paris and personally retract the orders, then remove himself from the office of Military Governor.

As Stulpnagel and Kluge parted company for the last time, the arrests in Paris were under way. Lieutenant General Boineburg-Lengsfeld personally directed the first Regiment, aided by Major General Walther Brehmer, who wore the Nazi's highest award, the blood Order. At 10:30 p.m. whistles blew throughout the city and the troops began to move. Within minutes all SS and SD residence quarters were occupied by the army with only one shot fired, and that was accidental.

By midnight, twelve hundred SS and SD men had been taken into custody and trucked to two army prisons. Brehmer personally arrested SS-Gruppenführer Carl-Albrecht Oberg, the senior SS officer in Paris. The senior SD officer, SS Standartenführer Dr. Helmut Knochen, was more difficult to locate, but then he was discovered in a night club. He was given an urgent message to return to his headquarters, where he too was arrested. Along with the other senior officers of the SS and SA, these two were held in custody at the Hotel Continental.

The courtyard at the First Regiment barracks was filled with men piling sandbags against one wall. The conspirators planned on wasting no time. Summary court-martial were to be convened quickly so the leading SS and SD figures could be speedily tried and executed in the courtyard.

The coup was fairing much better in Paris than in Berlin. Valuable time lost waiting for Stauffenberg had cost dearly and could never be regained. In the confusion during those hours no one had thought of posting troops to protect the conspirators' command post in the Replacement Army's headquarters within the War Ministry on the Bendlerstrasse, or to secure other important buildings in the government quarter. Finally, General von Hase, the city Commandant, had ordered the Grossdeutschland Battalion to surround and seal all entrances and exits to a list of government buildings, including several housing the SS. The battalion was commanded by a young officer, Major Otto Remer, who had a distinguished combat record but whose loyalties had not been determined.

Other units, including a panzer regiment and several infantry regiments, were delayed in responding to the coup because their commanders had not been informed of the latest attempt on Hitler's life. Several were away from their headquarters and it took some time to reach them.

Major Remer followed orders; he surrounded the buildings he had been assigned and set up roadblocks around the government quarter. So far these were the only troops at the disposal of the coup. The police were held in readiness by Count Helldorf, who waited for instructions that never came.

A liaison officer between Remer's battalion and the Propaganda ministry became suspicious of the orders and slipped off to see the Propaganda Minister, Joseph Goebbels, in his apartment on the Hermann-Göringstrasse. When informed of the army's activities and the rumor that Hitler was dead, a shocked Goebbels agreed that Remer should be brought to him.

After some soul searching about his responsibility as an officer, Remer decided to answer Goebbels's summons. Following a brief discussion during which Goebbels ascertained Remer's loyalty to the Führer, he called Wolf's Lair. His call went through with no trouble, demonstrating once again the fatal error on the part of the conspirators of failing to close down even civilian communications within Berlin.

At Wolf's Lair copies of all transmissions from the Bendlerstrasse to military district and field commanders were received routinely through the communications network. In this manner Hitler and his aides were fully aware that a coup was in progress and that the assassination attempt was part of it, not the work of a lone assassin. The telephone lines from East Prussia were kept humming with messages to every military command they could reach with denials of Hitler's death, and with instructions to refuse to obey orders from the commander of the Replacement Army. Hitler assumed that Fromm had masterminded the coup not knowing the luckless general was locked in an office at his own headquarters.

Goebbels explained the situation in Berlin, as he now knew it, to Hitler, and handed the phone to Remer. This single brief telephone conversation was the turning point in Berlin, and it spelled ultimate disaster for the coup. Hitler told Remer that a failed attempt had been made on his life. He placed Remer in charge of all troops in Berlin and instructed him to arrest anyone involved in the coup, and to shoot all who resisted him.

This was an intoxicating moment for the young major. Hitler had made him his personal military representative in Berlin, responsible to the Führer only. If Remer had been part of the resistance, perhaps it might have had a better chance at success. Remer immediately recalled his own troops and took control of all other units the coup leaders had ordered into the city. He then surrounded the Replacement Army headquarters on the Bendlerstrasse, signifying to anyone who cared to look that the coup against the Nazi government had failed.

11.

Aftermath of Failure

Shortly before Major Remer's newly organized force sealed off the Bendlerstrasse, Hans Gisevius left in response to a summons from Helldorf, the Police President. He found Helldorf, along with Arthur Nebe, Director of the Reich Criminal Police, in a depressed mood. On his way to Helldorf's office, Gisevius observed well-armed troops moving about briskly and establishing control positions. From the windows at the Bendlerstrasse Olbricht also watched this flurry of activity. Both men assumed the troops were responding to the Valkyrie mobilization. Until Remer's telephone conversation with Hitler this was true. Now Gisevius learned differently. Helldorf told him that Major Remer of the Grossdeutschland Battalion had been authorized by Hitler to arrest everyone participating in the coup and was at that moment surrounding the Replacement Army Operations Center at the Bendlerstrasse. Even worse, Himmler was en route to Berlin to take command of all troop formations in the city and to deal with the traitors.

Although Gisevius realized before leaving the Bendlerstrasse that the coup was not going well, he was shocked. Helldorf had already known the coup was lost. When Gisevius suggested that to take some of his policemen to the airport to shoot Himmler when he arrived, Helldorf retorted that no policemen could accomplish what the field marshals and generals had failed to do. No, Helldorf said, it was over and everyone had better find a way to disassociate himself from the men leading the coup. Nebe agreed with Helldorf's assessment that "now only impudence can help us. We will deny everything. We'll pretend that nothing happened."[1]

Helldorf and Nebe each had a cover story to cloak their participation in what they now knew was a failed coup. Helldorf advised Gisevius, who should have been at his post as vice-consul in Switzerland instead of at the center of a coup, to disappear. Gisevius decided to return to the Bendlerstrasse and asked Helldorf for a car. Helldorf tried to dissuade him from this suicidal decision, but Gisevius was adamant, saying it was a matter of personal honor that he return to Beck's side to face the end with his comrades.

Helldorf scoffed at Gisevius's notion of personal honor. "Don't kid yourself, Gisevius. For years the generals have shit all over us. They promised us everything; they've kept not one of their promises. What happened today was right in line with the rest—more of their shit."[2]

Helldorf and Nebe wished Gisevius luck and departed. Gisevius located a police car outside the building and ordered the driver to take him to the Bendlerstrasse. The car was turned away at several points by Remer's troops, who would permit no entry to the streets surrounding the War ministry, where the Replacement Army headquarters was located. Even a priority pass signed by Stauffenberg would not persuade them. Finally the police driver, probably grasping the personal danger of the situation more fully than he did when Gisevius got into his car, asked him to get out. Fortunately for Gisevius, they were on their way to the radio station on the outskirts of the city when the driver put him out, and he was able to make his way to the sanctuary of a friend's home.

When Remer's troops first arrived, some officers in the Bendlerstrasse assumed they were coup supporters sent to protect them—until they realized the guns were trained on the building not away from it. The end had finally come, and even Stauffenberg understood the coup was lost. He placed a call through to Paris to afford the conspirators there a chance to save themselves before they too were trapped.

Olbricht armed a small group of trusted staff officers with submachine guns and stationed them in defensive positions at the half dozen entrances to the building, supplementing the handful of Olbricht's own soldiers who had remained loyal. The coup leaders were steeling for a final stand against the forces of Adolf Hitler.

Incredibly, there were officers still in the building who remained loyal to the Führer and had not understood until now that the coup was not initiated by the SS, as they had been led to believe, but was actually being conducted by army officers, and that the center of the coup was here in the same building with them. Why these men had not been put under guard, or at least sent away so they could not interfere with the coup, is a puzzling question. Having learned the truth, they now acted to help put down the revolt.

At 10:30 p.m. the army soldiers stationed around the building by Major Remer were replaced by a unit of the SS. Whether the presence of the dreaded SS or the realization of the truth about the coup prompted them to act is unclear, but the Hitler loyalists in the building, joined by others whose support of the coup had been lukewarm at best, located a cache of small arms locked in a storeroom and moved against the coup leaders.

The armed band grew bolder as it roamed the building searching for coup supporters. The man in charge was Lieutenant Colonel Franz Herber, a supply officer. The group pushed its way into General Olbricht's office and demanded to know the truth about the coup. Olbricht, aware that all was lost and bidding for time, told them to ask Colonel General Fromm. In the confusion that ensued, with both sides now armed, numerous shots were fired. The first to be wounded was Stauffenberg, who was shot in the shoulder. In another confrontation Captain Klausing, who had been Stauffenberg's aide on his first two attempts to plant a bomb at Hitler's meetings on July 11 and July 14, exchanged shots with Herber in a hall, but neither man was hit. The shooting lasted only a short time, until most of the coup supporters were apprehended and the leaders detained in Fromm's office.

An officer was sent to Fromm's apartment, where he had remained under guard. The officer released him and, after explaining what had happened, escorted Fromm to his office. There he found Stauffenberg, Olbricht, Hoepner, and Beck, looking extremely old and tired.

"Well, gentlemen," he told them, "now I am going to do to you what you wanted to do to me this afternoon."[3]

Fromm told them they were all guilty of treason and would immediately face a court-martial. Beck told Fromm that he was carrying his personal pistol and would like to use it himself. Fromm agreed. Beck, his hand trembling, held the weapon to his head and fired. The bullet creased the top of his head and he fell back in his chair, still alive and conscious. Fromm ordered two officers to take the pistol away from him, but Beck wrestled free and fired again. He fell to the floor, unconscious, but still alive.

Two officers dragged the former Chief of Staff into another room, where a noncommissioned officer finished the job.

Fromm then asked the men under arrest in his office if they wished to write any messages to loved ones, because they had a few minutes left while a firing squad was preparing. He determined to eliminate the conspirators quickly, fearing that if they were questioned by the Gestapo they would implicate him in their conspiracy as an act of revenge for not supporting them. He knew such an accusation would be reason enough for Hitler to execute him.

General Olbricht asked for a pen and some paper, and he wrote a brief note to his wife. Hoepner asked to speak to Fromm alone. The two went into another room where Hoepner evidently pleaded with Fromm to allow him to face a trial rather than be shot. Fromm, probably because of their long friendship, acquiesced and decided to send him to the military prison at Moabit and let Hitler deal with him. The others would be dispatched quickly, before anyone arrived from Hitler's headquarters to arrest them so the Gestapo could interrogate them.

"In the name of the Führer," Fromm said to them, "a court-martial called by myself has condemned four men to death: Colonel of the General Staff Mertz von Quirnheim, General of Infantry Olbricht, this Colonel and his Lieutenant, whose names I will not mention."[4] The names he refused to allow to touch his lips were, of course, Stauffenberg and Haeften, members of his own staff.

The four were taken to the courtyard where a firing squad was waiting. Several cars and trucks had been drawn in a semi-circle with their lights focused on the row of sandbags where the condemned men stood silently. Seconds before the shots were fired, Stauffenberg shouted, "Long live holy Germany!" In a final act of loyalty, Haeften threw himself in front of Stauffenberg, who was merely wounded by the first round. A second volley was needed to finish him. The soul of the conspiracy against Hitler died at 12:30 a.m., July 21, 1944.

Minutes later Fromm entered the courtyard and delivered a rousing speech to the assembled troops. He then left for Goebbels's residence, where he intended to reaffirm his loyalty to Hitler's Nazi regime.

A few hours later the bodies of General Beck, Colonel Stauffenberg, General Olbricht, Colonel Mertz von Quirnheim, and Lieutenant Haeften were taken in the back of an army truck to the cemetery at the Matthaus churchyard where they were buried by torchlight. The following day SS men dug up the bodies, photographed them, and had them cremated. The ashes of these brave men were scattered to the wind at Himmler's orders.

When Fromm arrived at Goebbels's residence he found that General Hase, the Berlin City Commandant, had preceded him to ask the Propaganda Minister if he knew what was happening. Hase attempted to hide his complicity by feigning ignorance of the coup. He did not succeed and was now under arrest in Goebbels's music room.

Goebbels was in no mood to indulge Fromm, whom he suspected of being the ringleader of the coup. The Propaganda Minister praised Stauffenberg as a man of iron, saying it was a shame he was on the wrong side and surrounded by weaklings. He made it clear he considered Fromm one of the latter. Fromm would be arrested the following day.

After Fromm left the Bendlerstrasse, a second group of conspirators was assembled in the courtyard for execution. These included Claus's brother Berthold von Stauffenberg, Lieutenant Peter

Yorck von Wartenburg, and the only civilian found in the building, Eugene Gerstenmaier. Although he was a member of the resistance and part of the small group that had plotted to kill Hitler in Paris in 1940, Gerstenmaier had only just arrived in Berlin when he heard the news of the coup and rushed over to see how he could help. If he had not entered the building he might never have been linked to the coup.

Before the second round of executions could be carried out, they were stopped by SS Obergruppenführer Ernst Kaltenbrunner, who was acting as Himmler's personal representative, and SS Sturmbannführer Otto Skorzeny, Himmler's choice to command the Replacement Army. They wanted prisoners who could be interrogated, not corpses.

Before he left his headquarters for what would be the last time, Fromm telegraphed orders to all commands that a coup attempt by "irresponsible generals" had been ruthlessly crushed and the leaders shot. All communications issued in the names of Witzleben, Olbricht, Hoepner, and Beck were to be ignored. He added one self-serving line probably intended to buttress his position with Hitler. "I have again assumed command after my temporary arrest by force of arms."[5]

Now everyone everywhere knew the coup had collapsed, including Major General Tresckow and Lieutenant Schlabrendorff, two important figures in the resistance currently occupied with their duties on the eastern front. Sometime during the afternoon Colonel Mertz von Quirnheim had called Schlabrendorff at his Army Group Center post to tell him Hitler was dead and that he and Tresckow should immediately come to Berlin to help organize the coup.

Tresckow and Schlabrendorff were in the process of arranging transportation when a radio bulletin announced that an attempt on Hitler's life had failed. Tresckow decided they should remain where they were until they could determine the truth of the matter. Like so many others who were involved in the conspiracy, their first inclination was that the news bulletin was a lie to conceal the Führer's death from the populace, but they would wait for further confirmation.

Then the communiqués began arriving from Wolf's Lair with instructions to disregard all orders from the Bendlerstrasse calling for the arrest of SS officers. A promise that Hitler himself would speak to the nation late that evening followed. Shortly after Fromm's dispatch about the executions was transmitted. Hitler delivered his promised address. Schlabrendorff rushed to Tresckow's quarters and woke him with the news that the coup had failed and their friends were probably all dead. Tresckow, badly shaken by these calamitous developments, told his aide he was going to shoot himself. He knew the Gestapo would be ruthless in its interrogations and would inevitably discover his earlier attempts to kill Hitler and his part in planning the coup. "They will try to extract the names of others from me. To prevent this, I shall take my own life."[6]

The following morning Tresckow bid Schlabrendorff farewell and urged him to try to find some way to survive. He drove to the Twenty-eighth Rifle Division and engaged in a brief conversation with a Major Kuhn. He then strode purposefully into the no man's land separating the German and Soviet forces. After firing several shots from his pistol, perhaps hoping to draw enemy fire, he detonated a rifle grenade. When his body was recovered, Schlabrendorff was appalled to find the grenade had decapitated his old friend.

At the same time Stauffenberg and the others were murdered, the arrest of SS and SD forces in Paris had just gotten under way. Stauffenberg's desperate call to Paris as the coup collapsed around him was received by Colonel von Linstow, Stulpnagel's Chief of Staff. Linstow immediately rushed to Suite 703 in the Hotel Raphael, where Stulpnagel's staff awaited their commander's return from meeting with Kluge at La Roche-Guyon.

Stunned by Stauffenberg's report of the defeat, Linstow staggered into the room. The half-dozen officers at first thought Linstow, who was known to have a serious heart condition, was suffering a heart attack from the tension, but he quickly found a seat on a nearby sofa and explained, "It's all over in Berlin," he gasped, "Stauffenberg just called. He gave the news himself and told me that his assassins were at the door."[7]

One of those present, Lieutenant Colonel Friedrich von Teuchert, told him that all was not lost. "Even if the coup in Berlin has failed, we must still succeed in Paris. Our organization here is solid."[8]

In any case, things had gone too far, what with almost the entire SS and Gestapo organizations in the city either under arrest or soon to be. Besides, they were waiting for Stulpnagel, who was driving back from meeting with Kluge; perhaps he brought good news from the field marshal. With the commander of all troops in the West on their side, they might not need the coup to succeed in Berlin; they could conduct it from Paris and petition the Allies for a truce. Linstow could not bring himself to tell them about the call from Blumentritt cancelling the arrests.

When Stulpnagel arrived, he told them that Kluge said he would think over his support for the coup and give his answer in the morning. It is unclear why Stulpnagel chose to withhold the truth from the other members of the conspiracy. Perhaps he thought it was too late to change things anyway, since the arrests were in progress, or perhaps he may have thought he could pull things together, even sway Kluge over to his side, if he seized military control of the Paris area and arrested all Nazi officials. In any event, the Paris phase of the coup went forward at full throttle.

The arrests, completed by midnight, were an unqualified success. Despite the earlier reports of Hitler's assassination, neither the SS nor the Gestapo appeared concerned about security. No extra guards were stationed at city buildings occupied by the Nazi organizations, and those on normal guard duty offered no resistance when the heavily armed soldiers who shouted, "Hands up!" burst into offices and living quarters. The arrests were concluded with such incredible ease and swiftness that they proved a serious embarrassment to SS and Gestapo chiefs in Paris.

After midnight the situation began to unravel. At 12:30 Admiral Theodor Krancke, Commander-in-Chief, Naval Group West, called Field Marshal Kluge to protest the Paris arrests. He had already spoken with his superior, Grand Admiral Donitz, who told him Hitler was alive and to disregard all orders from Berlin except Himmler's.

Krancke's response was to place the one thousand marines under his command on alert. Kluge's curt response admonished the admiral that everything was being taken care of. "There's no cause for alarm," Kluge told him. Not satisfied with this, Krancke ordered his marines to prepare for combat. He called Kluge again to demand further details about how he intended to reverse the arrests in Paris. The field marshal did not accept his call, and Krancke was told he was in a meeting. This did not sit well with Krancke, who was by nature suspicious of army generals. He felt none were as loyal to Hitler as he admirals.

The turning point came at exactly 1:00 a.m., July 21, when Hitler broadcast a speech that was carried throughout occupied Europe. In his harsh, flat voice the Führer announced the unsuccessful attempt on his life: "Men and women of Germany, I do not know how many times there have been plans and attempts to assassinate me. If I speak to you today it is, first of all, in order that you should hear my voice and know that I am unhurt and well, secondly that you should know of a crime unparalleled in German history."

Hitler went on to identify Stauffenberg as the intended assassin of the Führer and high-level German military leaders. He called the conspirators a "small clique of ambitious, unscrupulous, and at the same time criminal and stupid officers." He compared them with the anonymous cowards who had stabbed the German army in the back in 1918. To emphasize that the plotters had not infected the army with their poison, he assured his listeners that "this circle of usurpers is very small and has nothing in common with the German Wehrmact." They were, he went on, "a tiny gang of criminal elements that will be ruthlessly exterminated."

Hitler than described the measures he had taken to excise what he called "this tiny clique of traitors." Himmler was made Commander-in-Chief of the Replacement Army and charged with punishing the conspirators. "This time we are going to settle accounts with them in a manner to which we National Socialists are accustomed."[9] These were chilling words for the conspirators in control of Paris. They knew exactly what Hitler had in store for them. Death would be a slow, torturous agony for the men who had plotted Hitler's death and the destruction of the Nazi government.

Hitler's broadcast was followed by brief speeches from Admiral Donitz and Field Marshal Göring. Each man echoed the Führer's sentiments and delivered a vehement diatribe against the men who had tried to kill Hitler.

Hitler's tirade prompted Admiral Krancke to act immediately. He ordered his Chief of Staff, Admiral Karl Hoffmann, to call Lieutenant Colonel Kurt von Kraewel of the First Regiment and inform him that the arrests had been a mistake. He must halt them at once and release all SS and Gestapo prisoners. Kraewel replied that he would consult his superior, Lieutenant General Boineburg-Lengsfeld, the City Commandant, for confirmation. Hoffman then spoke to Blumentritt, who told him he had been ordered to remove Stulpnagel from his military Governor's duties and free the prisoners.

Admiral Krancke, still distrustful of the generals, called the Paris City Commandant's Chief of Staff, Colonel Karl von Unger, threatening that if the prisoners were not released immediately he would dispatch his marines to do the job. The prospect raised the specter of a battle in the streets of Paris between German soldiers and German marines. Unger, a member of the resistance, explained patiently that he could not countermand orders from his superior simply because an admiral ordered him to do so.

Krancke next called Stulpnagel's Chief of Staff, Colonel Linstow, also a member of the resistance. The admiral, by this time his blood in a boil, was given the same brush off. But the game was up. Stulpnagel realized that with everyone aware that Hitler was definitely alive, and without Kluge's support, the revolt was lost. Officers who were not part of the resistance but had followed orders out of conscience would begin to falter when they considered the fate of those who had arrested the SS. Finally, at 2:00 a.m. Stulpnagel ordered the more than twelve hundred prisoners released. He also had the firing squad station that had been erected in the First Regiment's barracks courtyard quietly dismantled.

Colonel Linstow telephoned Admiral Krancke's headquarters and informed him that the SS, SD, and Gestapo prisoners were no longer in custody. This forestalled the possibility of open warfare in the streets. Krancke relaxed the alert but kept his marines and sailors on standby just in case the "reactionary army officers" reneged on their commitment.

Lieutenant General Boineburg-Lengsfeld at first tried to dissuade Stulpnagel from terminating the Paris revolt, but eventually even he had to face the truth that they had failed. Ironically, when the SS prisoners were removed from their cells and told they could leave, many refused, expecting to be shot as they left and listed on official records as "shot while attempting escape." These men often used this same ploy as a cover for murdering prisoners in their custody.

The prisoner release caused a gloom to settle over the men who had arrested them. Although only a few officers knew they were actually revolting against the German government, most of the First Regiment officers and men despised the SS and Gestapo for being the cruel barbarians they were and took extreme pleasure in arresting them. Now for some unfathomable reason they were ordered to release them. This was a development they simply did not comprehend.

Boineburg-Lengsfeld himself drove to the Hotel Continental, where the highest ranking SS and SD officers were held, most of them under army guard in the grand ballroom. When he entered, monocle firmly in place, he smiled, delivered a Hitler salute, and called out, "Good evening, gentlemen," to the confused men standing and sitting around the room.

SS Gruppenführer Oberg, the senior SS official in Paris, and Dr. Knochen, an SS Standartenführer and senior SD officer, were held in a separate suite. The two had wiled away the hours drinking cognac, wondering what fate awaited them. Boineburg-Lengsfeld entered the room briskly, gave them the same compulsory salute, and announced that they were now free to go.

When Oberg demanded to know why he and the others had been detained, Boineburg-Lengsfeld replied that the Military Governor had requested that Oberg accompany him to the Hotel Raphael, where he would receive an explanation. Stulpnagel had requested Oberg's presence in the hope they could come to some understanding about the arrests and what had caused them. He was helped in this by the timely arrival of the German ambassador, Otto Abetz.

Oberg entered the dining room, where Stulpnagel and the other army officers were gathered, in a white rage. The military Governor rose to greet the man he had ordered arrested, and the two glared at each other for a moment. Then Ambassador Abetz set about trying to alleviate the rancor. He told them both that what happens in Berlin is one thing, "here what matters is that the Normandy battle is raging, here we Germans must show a united front."[10]

Abetz explained to Oberg that Stulpnagel had ordered his arrest because he had received word from Berlin that a coup against Hitler had taken place by the SS and the Gestapo. Although that information later proved to be false, the military Governor had acted as any military commander would under the circumstances. While he spoke, bottles of champagne and brandy were brought to their table and glasses handed around.

When Oberg asked how the loyalty of the SS and the SD could be questioned, Stulpnagel handed him copies of the teleprinter messages ordering the arrests. Abetz then offered that Oberg could not accuse the general of disloyalty either, for he had merely followed orders from Berlin. No mention was made of the fact that Stulpnagel and many of the army officers present had actually taken part in an attempted coup against the Nazis after erroneously learning one of their fellow conspirators had killed Hitler.

As the tension in the room, which was quickly filling with both army and recently released SS officers, gradually eased, Abetz conceded that a plausible explanation for what had happened in Paris would be beneficial for all concerned. It would certainly help the army explain why its troops had arrested Hitler's minions and would alleviate the embarrassment to Oberg and the others at the ease with which their vaunted forces had been disarmed and imprisoned.

About this time Kluge's Chief of Staff, Blumentritt, arrived from Saint Germain. Along the way he had picked up Knochen, who had been released with Oberg. Knochen, also smarting from the embarrassment of the arrests, suggested a "formula" that would resolve the situation: For the consumption of the French public, which enjoyed a momentary euphoria when word of the arrests had spread, and the ranks of the army and the SS, it would be announced that the entire affair had been a training exercise to insure the army could deal with any threat of a revolt within the city.

Blumentritt, although not involved in the coup, was at heart a supporter of its aims. He made every effort to shield as many of his comrades who were involved as possible. The one person it might be impossible to protect was Stulpnagel. Blumentritt had been instructed to remove the Military Governor from his post and temporarily assume his duties until another could be appointed. He told Stulpnagel of this and advised that he return to his quarters to await further word from Field Marshal Kluge. The formula on which everyone agreed was worked out in detail so that the truth might also be kept from Hitler and Himmler. As far as anyone was to know, the overnight activities of the army and the SS and SD were part of a joint exercise. The soldiers were not told of this until the following day. They were told they had not been informed it was an exercise beforehand because the army and SS leaders wanted it to be as realistic as possible.

It was a good, if hastily conceived, plan. It might have worked if it had not been for Kluge. Afraid that he might be implicated in the coup, Kluge called Wolf's Lair and explained in detail exactly what Stulpnagel had done. He made it clear he had had no information beforehand and had not approved of any of the Military Governor's actions, especially the SS arrests.

Based on Kluge's information, field Marshal Keitel sent word to St. Germain that Stulpnagel was to report to Berlin immediately.

Meanwhile the party at the Raphael (for it had indeed turned into a party of comrades, both army and the SS) continued until the next morning. During all this Stulpnagel, who realized early on that he was a doomed man, remained calm and in control. He continued to stress that his officers had simply obeyed his instructions, as military rules required. Stulpnagel hoped to keep as many of his followers as possible from suffering the same fate he knew awaited him, and in this he was successful, aided by others including Blumentritt.

When the party broke up Stulpnagel returned to his office at the Hotel Majestic, between 8:00 and 8:30 a.m. on July 21. Less than thirty minutes later orders arrived that he should immediately take a plane and return to Berlin. It was his death warrant. Stulpnagel knew it and took it calmly, thanking his secretary, Countess Podewils, for her loyal service. Shortly before noon he called army headquarters in Berlin and left word for Keitel that he would report at 9:00 a.m. on July 21, a Saturday. He had decided to drive instead of fly as ordered. Stulpnagel bid farewell to Linstow and the other members of his staff who had gathered for what they knew was their final parting. In a tear-filled scene the general left Paris with only a driver and guard sitting in the front seat of the car.

Once out of the Paris area Stulpnagel gave his driver, Sergeant Major Schauf, instructions for a roundabout drive that took them past battlefields of the Great War in which the general, then a young captain, had seen so many of his comrades die. A half mile outside the village of Vacherauville, Stulpnagel told Schauf to stop. He got out of the car, said he wanted to walk alone for a while, and told them to drive on to the next village, Champs, and wait until he caught up with them there.

Reluctantly, Schauf and Corporal Fisher, Stulpnagel's orderly who served as guard, drove on. Concerned about the possibility of partisans in the area, they stopped the car at the next bend in the road and waited. Suddenly the quiet of the countryside was shattered by what sounded like two shots. They turned the car around and rushed back to the place where they had left the general. A frantic search of the area turned up nothing until they discovered Stulpnagel floating in a nearby canal, surrounded by blood-filled water. One eye had been blown completely out of his head, leaving a gaping, bloody hole. Near his right temple was a bullet entry hole. Thinking this was the work of partisans, the two dragged Stulpnagel out of the water and bandaged him as best they could, using their field dressings. He was unable to talk, with only a rattling sound coming from his throat. Schauf raced the car at top speed to Verdun, where he knew there was a German military hospital, trying to save the general's life. Neither Schauf nor Fischer had known of the events the evening before in Paris, and neither would have even guessed that Stulpnagel had attempted to take his own life.

At Verdun, Schauf called the military Governor's office in Paris and reported what had happened. The news swept through the city. Stulpnagel's aide, Lieutenant Fritz Baumgart, and an intelligence officer named Humm, took the fastest staff car available and raced to Verdun. At the hospital the senior medical officer told Stulpnagel could neither see nor speak, but that he was recovering as well as could be expected from the emergency operation that had been performed. Soon agents of the Gestapo were at the hospital to question the general who had ordered their arrest. With his voice regained he answered their questions but steadfastly refused to give them the names of others involved in the conspiracy.

Just as quickly as the coup in Berlin had unraveled, so did the entire network of conspirators. Himmler turned the SD and the Gestapo loose in a bloodlust vengeance against anyone who was even remotely suspected of complicity in the assassination and the coup. When it was fully over, between six hundred and one thousand Germans had lost their lives. Some were executed just days before the war ended in a Nazi purge of all enemies.

Many of these men and women might have survived had it not been for the German penchant for keeping meticulous records of everything, even the conspiracies to kill Hitler. At the behest of both Beck and Oster, the Abwehr center of the conspiracy had kept copies of every memorandum, coup plan, lists of people to be arrested, and most incredible of all, names of virtually everyone involved in the conspiracies since the first coup of 1938. It is probable that they hoped to give the world an accurate description of how these Germans opposed Hitler, but when this cache was discovered in a security zone safe on September 22, 1944, it spelled death for hundreds of people who otherwise might never have been suspected.

This record of the assassination plans altered the probe of the July 20 bombing. Originally the Gestapo worked under the impression that the attempt on Hitler's life was provoked by army officers who were unhappy with the course of the war, but now they knew that the planning had been going on for six years by officers and civilians who were anti-Nazi, and they now knew there had been several other attempts on Hitler's life. As a result, hundreds of new names were added to those slated to appear before the infamous People's Court for quick trial and execution.

Looking back at the years of planning and effort that had gone into various attempts to unseat Hitler, we are forced to ask how it was possible none ever succeeded. Could Hitler have been so lucky as to walk away from such men who plotted his death? Was Providence really on his side, as he so often claimed? Neither of these is accurate. In truth the answer is simple. The men who plotted the destruction of the Nazi government were simply not revolutionaries. They were not assassins. Many of them were too deeply religious to act in a manner required to bring down a bloodthirsty tyrannical government. Such an act requires men who can become as bloodthirsty as their opponents.

The final act, the bombing and coup of July 20, 1944, proved to be a failure because it was poorly planned, perhaps partly due to the uncertain date of Hitler's death. By then Beck had grown old and tired and still suffered from Cancer and the results of his operation; Tresckow was too far removed to hold a commanding role; Oster was being closely watched by the Gestapo and therefore could play no role; too much decision-making responsibility was placed on Olbricht, who was a loyal member of the group but incapable of making the swift decisions the situation required; Stulpnagel was in Paris where he conducted his own mini-coup, as we have seen, and perhaps things might have gone differently if he was in Berlin. In the end the entire burden of command rested on Stauffenberg, the impetuous young colonel who expected all army officers to join in the coup once Hitler's death was announced. He expected too much of men who feared Hitler and had spent too many years nourishing themselves at the Nazi's table. Had someone of his abilities to quickly organize things been in charge at the Bendlerstrasse, perhaps the right troops would have been used and the police forces would have been called out instead of spending the entire day waiting for orders that never arrived. What was missing was an individual who could make sure all the pieces were in place when they were needed.

Then, of course, there was the problem of Hitler's death. If Stauffenberg's bomb had worked, perhaps the colonel's expectations might have been realized. But it hadn't, and in the end that was all that mattered.

12.

"A Gang of Criminals"

In the Introduction to this book we noted that there were many more individuals who fought the Nazis in whatever way was open to them than could be included in this book. Just as we limited those mentioned throughout the book to persons who were deeply involved in the attempts to assassinate Hitler and replace his government, we must limit this discussion of their fates to the same individuals. There were thousands of others who paid the ultimate price for their opposition, but unfortunately for future generations the names of many of them will never be known.

Hitler's rage was directed at anyone who might possibly have ever spoken against him, not just the assassins and plotters. The Nazis also ruthlessly applied their "kith and kin" method of dealing with opponents. This meant that every member of a traitor's family, including those by marriage, was to be hunted down and exterminated. When it came to the Stauffenbergs, Hitler himself ordered that the entire family be "made harmless." On August 3, 1944, Himmler, now the undisputed master of Germany with all police, SS, and Home Army forces under his direct control, said the entire Stauffenberg family "will be exterminated down to its last member."

Tens of thousands of family members, even remote cousins, were arrested. Some paid for their relations with their lives. Small children and infants were torn from their mothers' arms and sent to camps from which they were to be provided new identities and given to SS families to raise as loyal Nazis, ignorant of who their parents were.

Many of the plotters were put on trial in what the Nazis called the People's Court, usually under the presidency of an obscene Nazi fanatic named Roland Freisler, who regularly screamed and cursed the defendants while the government's movie cameras rolled. For the most part the defendants conducted themselves with such dignity that most of the film shot could not be used for propaganda purposes, as Goebbels originally intended. Although all means of execution were used, hanging was favored. The method of hanging that was used generally insured that the victim would suffer a slow, painful death.

Following is what is known of the individual fate of some of those who dared to attempt to rid the world of Adolf Hitler.

General Ludwig Beck: In 1938 Beck resigned his post as Chief of Staff of the German army in protest against Hitler's plans to invade Czechoslovakia. Beck had hoped other general officers would follow his lead, but none did. He retired soon afterward. Following his retirement he became the leader of the military groups that plotted a series of coups against Hitler. On the evening of July 20, 1944, faced with the failure of the final attempt to assassinate Hitler, Beck shot himself twice in the head. A third and final shot was administered at the order of General Fromm. Beck was sixty-four years old when he died.

Lieutenant Colonel Robert Bernardis: An Austrian, he handled communications at the Bendlerstrasse during the July 20 coup. He had been active in the resistance for several years. He was arrested when the building fell to the SS and was among the first prisoners to be tried. He was hanged on the afternoon of August 8, 1944.

Lieutenant General Hans von Boineburg-Lengsfeld: Because of the understanding reached with SS-Gruppenführer Oberg, many of the officers involved in the coup in Paris were able to escape death. Boineburg-Lengsfeld was removed as City Commandant and placed on reserve. A short time later he was assigned to the staff of the new Military Governor.

Captain Eberhard von Breitenbuch: Although numerous members of the resistance who had been arrested and tortured knew of Breitenbuch's attempt to shoot Hitler at a military conference on May 11, 1944, his role was never exposed to the Gestapo.

Captain Axel von dem Bussche-Streithorst: Under Stauffenberg's guidance, Bussche constructed a bomb he could conceal under a uniform he was scheduled to model for Hitler. When the shipment of uniforms was destroyed in an air raid, the captain was transferred to the eastern front, where he lost a leg in battle. He carried the bomb in a small wooden box through a series of military hospitals for several months until he was finally able to dispose of it. His wounds precluded his further participation in the resistance.

Admiral Wilhelm Canaris: A master at covering his tracks, the fifty-seven-year-old Canaris was finally undone by the massive evidence the Gestapo accumulated concerning the coup activities of his subordinates. On February 11, 1944, Canaris was relieved of his Abwehr command because of a series of mishaps that exposed the admiral's organization as a far less masterful spy network than he claimed. Arrested by the SS on July 23, 1944, and held in various prisons and camps, resisting all attempts to use torture to obtain a confession, he was tried on Sunday, April 8, 1945, at the Flossenburg concentration camp and automatically found guilty. At 6:00 a.m. the following morning he was stripped of his clothing and taken to a gallows just outside the building, where he "died a staunch and manly death."

Dr. Hans von Dohnanyi: At age forty-two an important member of the resistance group under Hans Oster at the Abwehr, he was arrested on April 5, 1943, for, among other offenses, helping Jews escape from Germany. Dohnanyi was held in custody until he was executed on April 9, 1944, at Sachsenhausen concentration camp by means never disclosed.

General Alexander Falkenhausen: The former Military Governor of Belgium was arrested on July 29, 1944. On April 7, 1945, along with a group of other prisoners, he was moved from Flossenburg concentration camp to the Dachau camp, from which he was released by U.S. forces. He died in 1966 at the age of eighty-eight.

General Erich Fellgiebel: An active member of the resistance since 1939, the fifty-eight-year-old Fellgiebel was charged with the responsibility of alerting Berlin coup leaders that Hitler was dead following the explosion of Stauffenberg's bomb. He was among the first conspirators to be arrested when the Nazis realized the Wolf's Lair bombing was part of a larger conspiracy. He was severely beaten and tortured for weeks afterward. Following a trial at which he told Judge Freisler that he had better hurry along with the hangings, otherwise he, Freisler, might hang first, Fellgiebel was hanged on September 4, 1944.

Colonel Eberhard Finckh: One of the few members of the conspiracy who could not be saved by the efforts of Oberg and Blumentritt, this "genius in the field of supply" was executed by hanging on August 31, 1944.

Colonel Wessel von Freytag-Loringhoven: head of the Army Affairs Section of the Army High Command, Freytag-Loringhoven was an active member of the resistance who was responsible for, among other things, maintaining the safety of the explosives that were used on July 20. He committed suicide on July 23, 1944.

Major General Rudolph Gersdorff: The Gestapo never learned about Gersdorff's attempt to kill Hitler in a suicide bombing during the Führer's inspection of captured enemy equipment on March 21,

1943. Hitler's swift tour of the exhibition hall thwarted the attempt before Gersdorff's bomb could explode.

Dr. Eugen Gerstenmaier. The only civilian arrested by the SS when it assumed control of the Bendlerstrasse. Gerstenmaier narrowly escaped execution by firing squad on the evening of July 20. When he was brought to trial the prosecutor demanded the death sentence, but to Gerstenmaier's own astonishment he received a sentence of only ten years of hard labor.

Dr. Hans Gisevius. A driving force behind the coup attempts from 1938 until the failure of the July 20, 1944, bombing, Gisevius, age forty, was slated to be State Secretary in the government meant to replace the Nazis in 1944. Following the collapse of the July coup Gisevius went into hiding, and on January 23, 1945, he used his old Gestapo badge to bully his way across the border to safety in Switzerland. In 1947 his memoirs were published under the title *To the Bitter End.* The book was dedicated to the memory of Hans Oster. He died in West Germany on February 23, 1974.

Dr. Carl Friedrich Goerdeler. The former Mayor of Leipzig was an active participant in the coup plans starting in 1938, and he was to serve as Chancellor in the post-Nazi government. After weeks of hiding and narrowly eluding the Gestapo, he was finally arrested on August 12, 1944, and executed on February 2, 1945, at age sixty-one.

Lieutenant Colonel Helmuth Groscurth: An Abwehr officer who advocated killing Hitler starting with the 1938 coup attempt, Groscurth was arrested and sent to a concentration camp where he died of unknown causes.

Lieutenant Werner von Haeften: Stauffenberg's thirty-six-year-old aide, and the man who accompanied him on the fateful trip to Wolf's Lair on July 20, was executed by a firing squad on orders of General Fromm immediately on his own release from arrest. Haeften's older brother, Hans-Bernd, age thirty-nine, was also a member of the resistance, although he was opposed to assassination on moral grounds. At his trial he told the court, "My conception of the Führer's role in world history is that he is a great perpetrator of evil."[1] He was executed on August 15, 1944.

Lieutenant Albrecht von Hagen: He worked tirelessly to procure explosives for the use of the various assassins who attempted to blow up Hitler from 1942 through 1944. He was hanged on August 8, 1944, at Plötzensee prison.

Colonel General Fritz Halder: Nominally in charge of the 1938 coup attempt, Halder was dismissed from his post of Army Chief of Staff in September 1942. Arrested shortly after the July 1944 coup collapsed, Halder was incarcerated in a concentration camp until April 28, 1945, when U.S. forces liberated the camp. He died in 1972 at the age of eighty-eight.

Lieutenant General Paul von Hase: A participant in earlier coups, Hase was commander of the Berlin garrison and directly responsible for ordering troops to surround government buildings, a job at which he failed when he relied on the unquestioning obedience of a young officer who was not a party to the conspiracy. During the evening of July 20, while the coup was still in progress, he responded to a summons from Propaganda Minister Goebbels that resulted in his arrest. He was executed on August 8, 1944.

Ulrich von Hassell: A former German ambassador to Italy, Hassell was intimately involved in the conspiracy from its beginnings. He was to serve as Foreign Minister in the post-Nazi government. Arrested on July 28 in his office, where he sat patiently waiting, he was executed on September 8, 1944. In an unusual act for a conspirator, Hassell kept an extensive diary. It was published in 1947 with the English title *The Von Hassell Diaries 1938-1944*.

Lieutenant Colonel Friedrich Heinz: The man who led the assault squad sent to kill Hitler during the 1938 coup remained an active member of the resistance to the end. On July 20, 1944, he was commander of the army's Berlin Patrol Service and made an attempt to arrest Goebbels but failed because the regular army troops sent to help him switched their allegiances. Arrested by the Gestapo, he was briefly released and took advantage of the error to escape. He made his way to Italy and safety.

Wolf Heinrich von Helldorf: The Berlin Police President was a part of the conspiracy against Hitler from 1938 on. Although the coup leaders failed to make use of them, Helldorf kept his police forces on alert throughout July 20, waiting to support the coup's army troops. He was arrested on July 24 and executed on August 15, 1944.

Colonel General Erich Hoepner: He was a member of the resistance since 1938, when he was prepared to use his armored division to prevent SS units in Munich from marching on Berlin should the planned coup succeed. He was dismissed by Hitler in 1941 when he withdrew his panzer group from a threatened encirclement by Soviet forces. On July 20 he replaced Fromm as commander of the Replacement Army, until the coup collapsed. He was executed on august 8, 1944.

Lieutenant colonel Caesar von Hofacker: A member of General Stulpnagel's staff in Paris, he had intimate knowledge of the attempt on Hitler's life and the planned coup. He was arrested on July 25. When questioned by the SS he readily admitted to everything he had done and everything he planned to do, but he steadfastly refused to implicate anyone else. With his strength and courage Hofacker saved the lives of many of his accomplices in Paris. The forty-eight-year-old officer was executed on December 20, 1944.

Otto John: John was an Abwehr agent who was posted to a position as legal adviser to Lufthansa Airline. This job provided him cover for missions abroad in which he attempted to open communications links between the Berlin conspirators and Washington, and then later with General Eisenhower after the latter was appointed Supreme Commander. When he arrived at the Bendlerstrasse on

July 20, he was shocked to find the coup leaders disorganized. When the situation appeared to be improving he went home, having nothing to do until the coup was over. On July 24, he slipped aboard a Lufthansa flight to Madrid and freedom. His brother, Hans, was killed by the SS on April 23, 1945.

Captain Friedrich Karl Klausing: Klausing had accompanied Stauffenberg on the latter's first two attempts to plant a bomb at Hitler's conference. During the confusing final minutes of the coup he was able to escape from the Bendlerstrasse, but he was later arrested and executed on August 8, 1944.

Colonel Hans Otfreid von Linstow: Stulpnagel's Chief of Staff was arrested on July 27 when the agreement with the local SS could no longer prevent Himmler from demanding the arrests. He was executed on August 30, 1944.

Colonel Albrecht von Mertz von Quirnheim: A close associate of Stauffenberg, Mertz von Quirnheim was a driving force within the Bendlerstrasse on July 20, pushing the reluctant General Olbricht to issue the orders to get the coup started. He was shot alongside Stauffenberg on July 20, 1944.

Josef Müller: The Munich lawyer who opened a communications link with the British government through Pope Pius XII was arrested in April 1943 and kept chained in a lighted cell on a starvation diet. He was released by U.S. forces on May 4, 1945.

Arthur Nebe: The director of the Reich Criminal Police was a member of the resistance from the time of the planning of the 1938 coup. For a time following the July 20 coup he did not come under suspicion but was actually assigned responsibilities in the investigation of the conspiracy. When Helldorf, the Berlin Police President, was arrested, Nebe decided it was time to go. He faked his suicide and went into hiding, but he was found on January 16, 1945, and was executed shortly thereafter.

General Friedrich Olbricht: Destined to be the Minister of War in the new government, Olbricht was the center of the coup in Berlin but hesitated to call the troops out because he had previously done so and was reprimanded for it. His hesitation cost the coup several important hours and contributed to its failure. He was executed on July 20, 1944, by firing squad.

Major General Hans Oster: A firebrand among conspirators, he was arrested on July 21, 1944, and executed at Flossenburg concentration camp on April 9, 1945, four months before his fifty-seventh birthday.

Lieutenant Fabian von Schlabrendorff: General Tresckow's trusted aide and participant in the resistance was arrested on August 17, 1944, and imprisoned in the Gestapo cellars in the Prinz Albrechtstrasse and treated to a prolonged period of severe torture. As his trial was about to begin, a U.S. plane scored a direct hit on the People's court, resulting in the death of Judge Freisler. At the next trial, on March 16, 1945, he gave details of his torture. Since this was illegal and the Gestapo refused to defend itself, the new court released him. He was immediately arrested by the Gestapo and shipped to a concentration camp, from which he was rescued by U.S. forces. His memoirs, *The Secret War Against Hitler,* were published in 1965.

Count Fritz-Dietlof von der Schulenburg: The Vice-President of the Berlin Police was an active participant in the attempted coups since 1938 and an advocate of assassinating Hitler. He was to be a member of the cabinet in the new German government. Schulenburg was arrested in the Bendlerstrasse when the July 20 coup failed. He told the Nazi court, "I expect to hang for this, but I do not regret my action."[2] He was executed on August 8, 1944.

Captain Ulrich Wilhelm Schwerin von Schwanenfeld: An adjutant to Witzleben, he was active in the military side of all coup plans and was to serve in the post-Nazi cabinet. Arrested at the Bendlerstrasse on July 20, he was executed on August 8, 1944. He was forty-two years old.

Lieutenant Commander Berthold von Stauffenberg: Claus's brother and ardent supporter, he was arrested at the Bendlerstrasse. He was executed on August 8, 1944.

Colonel Claus von Stauffenberg: At age thirty-seven Stauffenberg became leader of the conspiracy to kill Hitler and remove the Nazi government. On July 20, 1944, his bomb failed to take the Führer's life but did set in motion the final attempt to stage a military coup. He was shot shortly after the coup collapsed on the evening of July 20, 1944.

Major General Helmuth Stieff: Responsible for procuring and storing the explosives used by Stauffenberg, he was arrested soon after the bomb exploded on July 20 and was executed on August 8, 1944.

General Karl Heinrich von Stulpnagel: Following his suicide attempt, Stulpnagel was arrested while still hospitalized. He was executed on August 30, 1944.

Major General Henning von Tresckow: When Tresckow's body was recovered he was reported as killed in action and buried at his family's estate. When the Gestapo learned he was part of the plot to kill Hitler, his body was exhumed and abused while his family was forced to watch. The body was used in a macabre attempt to force a confession from Schlabrendorff, but when this failed it was burned.

General Eduard Wagner: A military planner involved in all coup attempts, Wagner knew he would soon be arrested because of his close ties to Witzleben and because he had provided Stauffenberg with the aircraft he used to escape from Wolf's Lair after planting the bomb. On July 23, 1944, he took his own life with a bullet to his head.

Field Marshal Erwin von Wizleben: A central figure in the resistance since 1938, Wizleben was forced into retirement by Hitler. One of the oldest and most respected opponents of the Führer, he was to become Commander-in-Chief of the German army after the coup. The Nazis did everything they could to humiliate him during his trial, including forcing him to wear clothing several sizes too large and providing him neither suspenders nor a belt. Each time he stood he was forced to grasp the oversized pants to keep them from falling. Throughout the trial he was fearless in responding to accusations from Freisler, the judge. At one point he told Feisler, "You can hand us over to the executioner, but in three month's time this outraged and suffering people will call you to account and drag you alive through the mud of the streets."[3] He was executed on August 8, 1944.

Peter Yorck von Wartenburg: A forty-three-year old lawyer active in opposition circles, he was employed at the Bendlerstrasse, when he became a participant in the coup planning and execution. Arrested when the SS took control of the building, he was tried with Witzleben and executed on the same day, August 8, 1944. In a last letter to his wife, he wrote, "I believe I have gone some way to atone for the guilt which is our heritage."[4]

There were two other deaths that must be noted here. They were men who had the opportunity to support the coup and whose support might have spelled success, but they both refused and even turned on the conspirators in an attempt to save themselves.

Field Marshal Gunther Hans von Kluge: After the July 20 bombing and the coup in Paris, Kluge came under suspicion by Hitler. Although he did not suspect Kluge was part of the conspiracy, Hitler did believe the field marshal knew about it in advance and did nothing to prevent it. On August 17, 1944, Kluge was removed from command and instructed to return to Berlin. In a scene reminiscent of General Stulpnagel's suicide attempt, Kluge had his car stop near the World War I battlefield of Verdun for lunch. When he finished his meal Kluge bit into a cyanide capsule and died instantly.

Colonel General Friedrich Fromm: Fromm was suspected of complicity in the coup from the beginning, and it was true he knew in advance that Hitler was to be killed, but he refused to take part until he was sure of the Führer's death. Arrested almost immediately after the coup failed, he was put on trial for cowardice when his complicity could not be proved. His trial took place in March 1945, and he was condemned to death. Just before he was hung he again pledged his loyalty to Adolf Hitler.

Bibliography

Barnett, Correlli, ed. *Hitler's Generals*. New York: Grove Weidenfeld 1989.

Breitman, Richard. *The Architect of Genocide*. New York: Knopf, 1991.

Brett-Smith, Richard. *Hitler's Generals*. San Rafael, CA: Presidio Press, 1977.

Casey, William. *The Secret War Against Hitler*. Washington, DC: Regnery Gateway, 1988.

Churchill, Winston S. *Memoirs of the Second World War*. New York: Houghton Mifflin, 1948-1954.

Colvin, Ian. *Master Spy*. New York: McGraw Hill, 1952.

Cooper, Matthew. *The German Army 1933-1945*. Chelsea, MI: Scarborough House, 1990.

Deutsch, Harold C. *The Conspiracy Against Hitler in the Twilight War*. Minneapolis: University of Minnesota Press, 1968.

FitzGibbon, Constantine. *20 July*. New York: Norton, 1956.

Forman, James. *Code Name Valkyrie*. New York: S.G. Phillips, 1973.

Galante, Pierre. *Hitler Lives*. London: Sidgewick & Jackson, 1982.

Gilbert, Martin. *The Second World War*. New York: Holt, 1989.

Gisevius, Hans Bernd. *To the Bitter End*. Translated by Richard and Clara Winston. Boston: Houghton Mifflin, 1947.

Goerlitz, Walter. *History of the German General Staff*. Boulder, CO: Westview Press, 1985.

Graml, Hermann, et al. *The German Resistance to Hitler*. Los Angeles: University of California Press, 1970.

Hassell, Ulrich von. *The von Hassell Diaries*. Garden City, NY: Doubleday, 1947.

Henderson, Sir Nevile. *Failure of a Mission*. New York: Putnam, 1940.

Herwarth, Hans von. *Against Two Evils*. New York: Rawson, Wade, 1981.

Hoffmann, Peter. *The History of the German Resistance 1933-1945*. Cambridge, MA: MIT Press, 1977.

Hoffman, Peter. *Hitler's Personal Security*. Cambridge, MA: MIT Press, 1979

Hoffman, Peter. *German Resistance to Hitler*. Cambridge, MA: Harvard University Press, 1988.

Hohne, Heinz. *Canaris: Hitler's Master Spy*. Translated by J. Maxwell Brownjohn. Garden city, NY: Doubleday, 1979.

Irving, David. *The Trail of the Fox*. New York: Avon Books, 1978.

Irving, David. *Hitler's War.* New York: Avon Books 1990.

Jacobsen, Hans-Adolf, ed. *July 20, 1944.* Bonn: Press and Information Office of the Federal Government, 1969.

John, Otto. *Twice Through the Lines.* Translated by Richard Barry. New York, Harper & Row, 1972.

Kramarz, Joachim. *Stauffenberg.* Translated by R. H. Barry. New York: Macmillan, 1967.

Leber, Annedore. *Conscience in Revolt.* Translated by Rosemary O'Neill. Westport, CT: Associated Booksellers, 1957.

Manvell, Roger, and Heinrich Fraenkel. *The Men Who Tried to Kill Hitler.* New York: Coward-McCann, 1965.

Manvell, Roger, and Heinrich Fraenkel. *Himmler.* New York: Paperback Library, 1968.

Manvell, Roger, and Heinrich Fraenkel. *The Canaris Conspiracy.* London: Heinemann, 1969.

Mason, Herbert Molloy, Jr. *To Kill the Devil.* New York: Norton, 1978.

Mosley, Leonard. *On Borrowed Time.* New York: Random House, 1969.

Müller, Klaus-Jurgen. *The Army, Politics and Society in Germany, 1933-45.* Manchester, England: Manchester University Press, 1987.

Payne, Robert. *The Life and Death of Adolf Hitler.* New York: Praeger, 1973.

Prittie, Terence. *Germans Against Hitler.* Boston: Little Brown, 1964.

Ritter, Gerhard. *The German Resistance.* Translated by R. T. Clark. New York: Frederick A. Praeger, 1958.

Roon, Ger van. *German Resistance to Hitler.* Translated by Peter Ludlow. London: Von Nostrand Reinhold Co., 1971.

Rothfels, Hans. *The German Opposition to Hitler.* Translated by Lawrence Wilson. Chicago: Henry Regnery Co., 1962.

Schlabrendorff, Fabian von. *The Secret War Against Hitler.* Translated by Hilda Simon. New York: Pitman Publishing, 1965.

Schlabrendorff, Fabian von, and Gero v. S. Gaevernitz. *Revolt Against Hitler.* London: Eyre & Spottiswoode, 1948.

Schramm, Wilhelm von. *Conspiracy Among Generals.* Translated by R. T. Clark. New York: Scribner's Sons, 1956.

Schachtman, Tom. *The Phony War 1939-1940.* New York: Harper & Row, 1982.

Shirer, William L. *The Rise and Fall of the Third Reich.* New York: Simon & Schuster, 1960.

Snyder, Louis L. *Louis L. Snyder's Historical Guide to World War II.* Wesport, CT: Greenwood Press, 1982.

Snyder, Louis L. *Encyclopedia of the Third Reich.* New York: Paragon House, 1989.

Snyder, Louis L. *Hitler's German Enemies.* New York: Hippocrene Books, 1990.

Taylor, Telford. *Munich: The Price of Peace.* Garden City, NY: Doubleday, 1979.

Toland, John. *Adolf Hitler.* New York: Ballantine Books, 1977.

Wheeler-Bennett, John W. *The Nemesis of Power.* New York: Macmillan, 1964.

Notes

Epigraphs

1. Roger Manvell and Heinrich Fraenkel, *The Men Who Tried to Kill Hitler* (New York: Coward-McCann, 1965), p. 165.
2. Constantine FitzGibbon, *20 July* (New York: Norton, 1956), p. 216.
3. Wilhelm von Schramm, *Conspiracy Among Generals*, translated by R. T. Clark (New York: Scribner's Sons, 1956), p. 113.
4. Peter Hoffman, *The History of the German Resistance 1933–1945* (Cambridge, MA: MIT Press, 1977), p. 526.
5. William Casey, *The Secret War Against Hitler* (Washington, DC: Regnery Gateway, 1988), p. 120.

Chapter 1 - A Question of Loyalty

1. Matthew Cooper, *The German Army 1933–1945* (Chelsea, MI: Scarborough House, 1990), p. 6.
2. Ibid.
3. David Irving, *The Trail of the Fox* (New York: Avon Books, 1978), p. 533.

Chapter 2 - The Early Assassins

1. John Toland, *Adolf Hitler* (New York: Ballantine Books, 1977), p. 809.

Chapter 4 - The Resistance Is Born

1. Peter Hoffman, *The History of the German Resistance 1933–1945* (Cambridge, MA: MIT Press, 1977), p. 75.
2. Harold C. Deutsch, *The Conspiracy Against Hitler in the Twilight War* (Minneapolis: University of Minnesota Press, 1968), p. 34.
3. Ibid.

Chapter 5 - Chamberlain and the September Coup

1. Roger Manvell and Heinrich Fraenkel, *The Canaris Conspiracy* (London: Heinemann, 1969), p. 35.
2. Ibid., p. 36.
3. Leonard Mosley, *On Borrowed Time* (New York: Random House, 1969), p. 32.
4. Sir Neville Henderson, *Failure of a Mission* (New York: Putnam, 1940), p. 32.
5. Manvell and Fraenkel, *The Canaris Conspiracy*, p. 39.
6. Fabian von Schlabrendorff, *The Secret War Against Hitler*, translated by Hilda Simon (New York: Pitman Publishing, 1965), p. 91.
7. Hans Bernd Gisevius, *To the Bitter End*, translated by Richard and Clara Winston (Boston: Houghton Mifflin, 1947), p. 289.

8. Peter Hoffmann, *The History of the German Resistance 1933-1945* (Cambridge, MA: MIT Press, 1977), p. 91.
9. Telford Taylor, *Munich: The Price of Peace* (Garden City, NY: Doubleday, 1979), p. 771.
10. Ibid., p. 742.
11. Ibid., p. 782.
12. Ibid., p. 806.
13. Winston S. Churchill, *Memoirs of the Second World War* (Boston: Houghton Mifflin, 1948), p. 136.
14. Harold C. Deutsch, *The Conspiracy Against Hitler in the Twilight War* (Minneapolis: University of Minnesota Press, 1968), p. 41.
15. Peter Hoffmann, *German Resistance to Hitler* (Cambridge, MA: Harvard University Press, 1988), p. 88.
16. Hans Bernd Gisevius, *To the Bitter End*, translated by Richard and Clara Winston (Boston: Houghton Mifflin, 1947), p. 326.

Chapter 6 - A Coup to Save the Peace

1. Peter Hoffmann, *The History of the German Resistance 1933–1945* (Cambridge, MA: MIT Press, 1977), p. 427.
2. Hans Bernd Gisevius, *To the Bitter End*, translated by Richard and Clara Winston (Boston: Houghton Mifflin, 1947), p. 328.
3. William L. Shirer, *The Rise and Fall of the Third Reich* (New York: Simon & Schuster, 1960), p. 422.
4. Hoffman, *German Resistance*, p. 113.
5. Harold C. Deutsch, *The Conspiracy Against Hitler in the Twilight War* (Minneapolis: University of Minnesota Press, 1968), p. 192.

Chapter 7 - Pope Pius Aids the Resistance

1. Harold C. Deutsch, *The Conspiracy Against Hitler in the Twilight War* (Minneapolis: University of Minnesota Press, 1968), p. 116.
2. Ibid., p. 120.
3. Peter Hoffmann, *The History of the German Resistance 1933-1945* (Cambridge, MA: MIT Press, 1977), p. 159.
4. Ibid., p. 167.
5. Otto John, *Twice Through the Lines*, translated by Richard Barry (New York: Harper & Row, 1972), p. 63.

Chapter 8 - "The Living Hitler Must Die"

1. Peter Hoffman, *The History of the German Resistance 1933-1945* (Cambridge, MA: MIT Press, 1977), p. 267.
2. Fabian von Schlabrendorff and Gero v. S. Gaevernitz, *Revolt Against Hitler* (London: Eyre & Spottiswoods, 1948), p. 66.

Chapter 9 - Stauffenberg Takes Charge

1. Herbert Molloy Mason, Jr., *To Kill the Devil* (New York: Norton, 1978), p. 171.

2. Fabian von Schlabrendorff, *The Secret War Against Hitler*, translated by Hilda Simon (New York: Pitman Publishing, 1965), p. 27.

Chapter 10 - "Valkyrie"

1. Herbert Molloy, Jr., *To Kill the Devil* (New York: Norton, 1978), p. 189.
2. Ibid., p. 192.
3. Wilhelm von Schramm, *Conspiracy Among Generals*, translated by R. T. Clark (New York: Scribner's Sons, 1956), p. 27.

Chapter 11 - Aftermath of Failure

1. Fabian von Schlabrendorff, *The Secret War Against Hitler*, translated by Hilda Simon (New York: Pitman Publishing, 1965), p. 565.
2. Ibid., p. 566
3. Herbert Molloy Mason, Jr., *To Kill the Devil* (New York: Norton, 1978), p. 213.
4. Peter Hoffman, *The History of the German Resistance 1933-1945* (Cambridge, MA: MIT Press, 1977), p. 507.
5. Roger Manvell and Heinrich Fraenkel, *The Men Who Tried to Kill Hitler* (New York: Coward-McCann, 1965), p. 154.
6. Schlabrendorff, *Secret War*, p. 294
7. Wilhelm von Schramm, *Conspiracy Among Generals*, translated by R.T. Clark (New York: Scribner's Sons, 1956), p. 72.
8. Ibid.
9. Robert Payne, *The Life and Death of Adolf Hitler* (New York: Praeger, 1973), p. 515.
10. Schramm, *Conspiracy*, p. 105.

Chapter 12 - "A Gang of Criminals"

1. Peter Hoffmann, *The History of the German Resistance 1933-1945* (Cambridge, MA: MIT Press, 1977), p. 526.
2. Ibid.
3. Ibid.
4. Ibid.

Index